Secular Missionaries

A VOLUME IN THE SERIES

Culture, Politics, and the Cold War

EDITED BY

Christian G. Appy

Secular Missionaries

Americans and African Development in the 1960s

Larry Grubbs

UNIVERSITY OF MASSACHUSETTS PRESS

Amherst and Boston

Copyright © 2009 by University of Massachusetts Press
All rights reserved
Printed in the United States of America

LC 2009044160
ISBN 978-1-55849-734-4

Designed by Sally Nichols
Set in Joanna MT
Printed and bound by Thomson-Shore, Inc.

Library of Congress Cataloging-in-Publication Data

Grubbs, Larry.
　Secular missionaries : Americans and African development in the 1960s / Larry Grubbs.
　　p. cm.
　Includes bibliographical references and index.
　ISBN 978-1-55849-734-4 (cloth : alk. paper)
　1. Africa—Relations—United States. 2. United States—Relations—Africa. 3. United
States—Foreign relations—1953–1961. 4. United States—Foreign relations—1963–
1969. 5. Africa—Foreign public opinion, American. 6. Public opinion—United States.
I. Title.
　DT38.7.G78 2009
　338.91'730609046–dc22

                                                                    2009044160

British Library Cataloguing in Publication data are available.

Contents

Acknowledgments

Kendrick A. Clements made this book possible through his steady and constant support, clear guidance, and consummate professionalism. As my advisor during graduate school and as a friend thereafter, he has helped me in countless ways. His faith sustained me when I had lost mine.

Adam Mack's friendship and intellectual collaboration have been vital. His critical perspective never fails to complicate, yet strengthen, my ideas.

Ronald R. Atkinson, Patrick J. Maney and Jerel A. Rosati read my dissertation—an early version of this book—and provided helpful commentary. Ron, in particular, played a key role in inspiring my interest in Africa and gave me a vital introduction to Africanist historiography and African perspectives.

At the University of Georgia, where I worked as a postdoctoral fellow, I received guidance from Timothy Cleaveland. I also owe a debt to the efforts of the library staff, who retrieved many useful sources. My postdoctoral colleagues Ian Lekus and Andrew Falk gave encouragement and read drafts, while Kevin McCarthy's friendship enriched an otherwise frenetic period of writing, teaching, and job-hunting.

Several people provided helpful comments on the portions of this book that I presented at conferences. I thank Emily Rosenberg, Kevin Gaines, Cary Fraser, Hakim Tijani, David Engerman, and Christopher T. Fischer. Chris's comments, in particular, and his ongoing support for my project, were invaluable. Christine Skwiot, Abou Bamba, and Mary Rolinson offered encouragement as I finished the writing shortly after joining them at Georgia State University.

Grants from the John F. Kennedy Library Foundation, the Lyndon B. Johnson Library Foundation, and the Society for Historians of American Foreign Relations supported my research.

My editors at the University of Massachusetts Press, Clark Dougan, Chris Appy, Carol Betsch, and Kay Scheuer, have been terrific. Chris's interest in my project and his comments on the writing, as well as those of an anonymous reviewer, helped me clarify its focus.

My largest debts are to Vanessa Grubbs, whose patience over a number of years allowed me to complete graduate school, endure the vicissitudes of our search for academic employment, and finish the book. Her gentle prodding to complete the book prevented it from getting lost in the shuffle, and her companionship has meant everything. This book is dedicated to her.

Secular Missionaries

Introduction

"Mixing Nigerian Cocktails"

Describing the 1964 World's Fair in New York City, *Time* reported, "The African Pavilion is the swingingest—and the noisiest—place at the fair. . . . For $1 you can walk past monkeys, giraffes, and native objects d'art into a gravel clearing surrounded by African huts flying the flags of 24 small nations," where the visitor could observe "red-robed Royal Burundi drummers, [Babatunde] Olatunji and his passion drums, and gaily garbed Watusi warrior dancers." Thus, one could "have your eyes opened to a dozen nations you never knew existed, and a year or so ago you were right."[1] After sampling these classic Western exhibitions of African culture (and the innovative sounds of Olatunji, the Nigerian father of African music in the United States), visitors entered the pavilion's restaurant. There, reported the *New York Times*, eight bartenders from Harlem—self-described "real mixologists"—did a brisk business "mixing Nigerian cocktails in their colorful African garb." Given that Nigerians generally prefer taking their liquor straight (and that palm wine and stout were more popular than spirits) the "real mixologists" probably poured drinks Nigerian in name only. That did not matter. American cultural constructions of Africa required no precise knowledge, only impressions, aspirations, and fears. The concoctions were, after all, for American consumption. The Fair, like its colonial-era predecessors, displayed Africa as exotic spectacle. If no longer represented as primitive or savage, as they had been a half century earlier, Africans still figured as passionate, emotional, and emphatically different.[2]

I

Representations of African otherness extended far beyond such sites of recreation. This book explores the making of "Africa" as an object of American academic, popular, and policymaking attention. Declaring the 1960s a "Decade of Development," the United Nations and U.S. President John F. Kennedy expressed optimism and a sense of mission at the very moment when Africans won their freedom from European colonialism. "Africa" burst into American consciousness for the first time; signifying an important world region, an object of assistance, a subject of scholarly and middlebrow writing and Cold War policymaking.[3] *Secular Missionaries* is a cultural history of U.S. promotion of development and nation building during Africa's first decade of independence, a period with renewed salience for contemporary American interest in Africa.[4]

Though moved by Cold War concerns and the restless expansion of American global power, the United States "discovered" Africa because Africans thrust it into the limelight. After years of resistance and creative adaptation to European colonialism, educated African leaders mounted nationalist political movements during the middle of the century. By the late 1950s a European scramble out of Africa had begun.[5] When, in 1957, the British colony known as the Gold Coast became an independent Ghana, it inaugurated a wave of African decolonization. Nineteen-sixty became the "Year of Africa." Of the more than four dozen countries in Africa, most became independent in that year or shortly thereafter, and with freedom from British, French, or Belgian rule, they demonstrated their arrival in world politics by sending representatives to the UN. Though Europeans had but grudgingly conceded African independence, and the Dwight D. Eisenhower administration in the United States had more than a few reservations about the sudden shakeup of world affairs, Africa basked in the glow of enthusiastic world opinion. Its nationalist leaders, Ghana's Kwame Nkrumah first and foremost among them, strode confidently forward with a mandate to free of all Africa and replace the era of colonial exploitation with one of African self-improvement and progress. The Decade of Development, they insisted, must include Africa.

Decolonization stalled, however, in key parts of Africa, threatening the development of the entire continent. In the vast Central African colony of the Congo, Belgium's remarkable economic achievements based on mining failed to translate into meaningful preparation for African self-rule. The Year of Africa was thus marred by the chaos ensuing from the Congo's sudden independence. The "Congo Crisis" of the early 1960s deeply involved the UN, many African states including Ghana, the Belgians, the United States, and the Soviet Union. A Cold War battleground, the Congo would not be truly independent for years, and when the international crisis ended, the country lapsed into three decades of cruelly imposed stability under the American-backed dictatorship of Mobutu Sese Seku. Broad-based economic development and the achievement of a unified national identity would have to wait indefinitely.

South of the Zambezi River, decolonization would have a longer wait, as it collided with the hard rock of colonialism, the white settler states. Portugal, the least prosperous European colonial power, applied increasing doses of repression and schemes of economic modernization in a vain but protracted bid to retain Angola, Mozambique, and its small West African territory, Guinea-Bissau. Britain's colony of Rhodesia, named for the man who symbolized white power in Africa, remained under the control of brutally racist settlers. Declaring independence in 1965 in defiance of world opinion, the white ruling class plunged the country into years of armed struggle rather than compromise with the rising African nationalist movement. Meanwhile apartheid—the most systematic and violent racist system in the postwar world—reached its apogee. To the growing fury of Africans within and beyond the Republic of South Africa, Afrikaner Nationalists reveled in an economic boom that was the envy of the continent while nearly crushing dissent. The fate of black liberation in Southern Africa forced the United States into as awkward a diplomatic position as possible at a time when the Third World had become a key arena of the Cold War.

Responding to Africans' impact on world politics, Cold Warriors in the United States belatedly organized American knowledge of Africa. Lacking the colonial archive of experience classifying and governing Africans, yet fearful that blacks could not be trusted to run newly independent nations and keep Communism at bay, Americans sought an "Africa policy." In 1958 the Department of State added an African Bureau. The final two years of the Eisenhower presidency witnessed National Security Council meetings with real, if necessarily disjointed, discussion of African decolonization and its impact on American security. With the election of Kennedy, Africa found a place in the New Frontier envisioned by the ambitious new president. As a likely target of Soviet subversion and internal turmoil, Africa had a manifest claim on Washington's attention. An admirer of the optimistic Cold War zeal of the middlebrow novel *The Ugly American* (1958), and a self-styled critic of colonialism, Kennedy saw Africa—like much of Latin America, Asia, and the Middle East—as fertile ground for American projects to promote nation building and economic development. Confident in American technology, capital and know-how, Americans had already launched the Marshall Plan in Europe and technical assistance around the world. Americans would lead the charge against "underdevelopment," a global commitment as sweeping as (and ultimately, more elusive than) winning the Cold War. That quest, anticipated in expansive statements of American exceptionalism like Henry R. Luce's "American Century" (1941) and poetic statements of policy such as President Harry S. Truman's Point Four Address (1949), acquired added force with the rise of modernization theory. Close collaboration between academics, major foundations, and Washington and the popularization of the leading ideas of modernization in such works as *The Ugly American* created a powerful discourse of development. Only in the last decade have scholars across several disciplines dissected the origins, meanings, and consequences of development.[6] This book demonstrates the importance of Africa's place in the development imaginary.[7]

Secular Missionaries is a history of representations of "developing" or "underdeveloped" Africa and the conceptual and practical problems that bedeviled American aid to Africa. Not a comprehensive account of all aspects of U.S.–African relations, it aims to open new intellectual space for scholarship on the relationship. It insists that culture and economics must not remain marginal to historians and political scientists more familiar with traditional explanations for American behavior in Africa, such as geopolitics and national security strategy. Like many other studies in cultural history and American Studies, therefore, this book seeks not to close a debate with an authoritative account of what has caused Africa's woes and America's erratic, often distracted Africa policies. Rather, the intention is to incite more of a sense of how fraught this international relationship has been with ideas, images, values, hopes, fears, and fantasies, which comprise the cultural and epistemological context of development. Though certain African nations are seldom discussed, it is not because I discount their importance. Not all of the current fifty-three African countries bulked large in American ideas or policy. When I discuss those that did, such as Nigeria and Ethiopia, my interest is in connecting the American encounter with these nations to the overall United States enterprise of imagining, developing, and disciplining Africa.

One other caveat seems necessary. The focus of this volume is America and sub-Saharan Africa. Again, it might be helpful to illustrate my intention by invoking a similar disclaimer by a recent author. In his fascinating study of American representations of the Maghreb, *Morocco Bound*, Brian T. Edwards is compelled to offer a geographical explanation. In writing of America and the Maghreb "as a distinct entity," he assures us, "I am neither being controversial nor am I minimizing regional antagonisms or the movements across the Sahara (and the Mediterranean) that have long marked the region." He focuses on Morocco, Algeria, Tunisia, and the Sahara because those were the "places that have been of major American interest" in North Africa.[8] In the same fashion, I wish to emphasize that this book in no way seeks to uphold the myth of an absolute distinction between sub-Saharan Africa as a region and the rest of the continent. Historically, there have always been crucial cultural, political, and economic ties across the desert, such as the medieval gold-for-salt trade and Islam. True, Americans often speak misleadingly of Africa south of the Sahara as "Black Africa" or "Tropical Africa," in spite of the region's tremendous racial and ecological diversity. African American conceptions of Africa, however, have frequently disregarded the alleged geographic and cultural barrier of the Sahara while invoking as an inspiration the achievements of ancient Egypt, or the fiery nationalism of Gamal Abdel Nasser.[9]

My focus south of the desert is not, therefore, intended to reinforce white efforts to reify the importance of the Sahara. Rather, it reflects how Americans—especially Washington—came to construct "Africa" as a sub-Saharan region. Although some American writing and policymaking treated the continent as a whole—as when discussing Pan-Africanism—the assumption that race lay near the heart of the essence of Africa always privileged the sub-Saharan definition. William G. Martin and Michael O. West, in Out of One, Many Africas, argue that "members of the predominantly white Africanist establishment have long sought to separate sub-Saharan Africa, the object of their study and research agendas, from the African diaspora and issues of race." U.S.-based Africa scholars, they argue, have been on a "mission to produce purer and more objective knowledge on sub-Saharan Africa" and have thus dismissed analytical approaches to Africa that transgress the geographical parameters they established during the Cold War. I do not intend to disparage the vibrant contemporary field of African Studies, nor to suggest that all Africanist scholarship of the late 1950s and 1960s must be viewed as racialized and therefore suspect. However, Martin and West's critique, discussed at length in chapter 2, is powerful. Readers should not, therefore, mistake American representations of Africa for reality. Continental perspectives and those of the Black Atlantic have a manifest reality and importance that no cadre of scholars or officials and no American discourse could ever erase.[10]

Missionary Position

Why, then, the title *Secular Missionaries?* I have already noted the missionary impulse shared by much of the world in 1960 as it contemplated the independence of poor African nations. Students of American history will not find surprising a missionary zeal in American foreign policy, no matter how much material interests actually drive it. The title, in this case, attempts to grapple with complex layers of meaning in America's relationship with Africa. Writing in 1960, two anthropologists revealed the chasm between a "literary" Africa—found in Western nonfiction as much as novels—and "the Africa we knew as anthropologists." The former Africa had, they argued, attained "so patterned an internal consistency" that it yielded "a master image of Africa," one "disturbingly unrealistic" yet deeply influential. Literary tradition systematically reduced Africans to "inferior, exotic, and alien" peoples who required Western supervision or control. Central to this system of representations was the invariable invocation of "The African," a singular type bearing collective, usually tribal, characteristics and customs. Indiscriminate labeling of "The African" blotted out diversity and individuality, paving the way for authoritative statements on Africans' mental inferiority and "Stone Age" way of life. Figuring Africans both savage and childish, this literature reflected and reinforced the judgment of the famed Christian medical missionary Albert Schweitzer: "Without the white man they would no longer be in existence because they would either have slaughtered each other or ended in the Pahouin cooking pots."[11] This criticism of Schweitzer—an icon of colonialism and the "white man's burden"—reflects the urgency with which postcolonial Western scholars sought to distance themselves from the corrupt racialism of their predecessors. Nevertheless, like them, the postcolonial liberals invoked their authority as credentialed academics—"the Africa we knew as anthropologists"—in ways that privileged some voices (white, policy-oriented Cold War liberals) while excluding or at least muting others (political dissidents, activists, African Americans). Would the Africa of W. E. B. Du Bois constitute a "literary" or an "anthropological" Africa? What would be at stake, and who may judge?

   We can now explore such questions with the aid of rigorous African thinking. What Edward Said did for understanding Orientalism as a system of Western institutional authority and representations of Arabs and Muslim, V. Y. Mudimbe accomplished in *The Invention of Africa* (1988) and *The Idea of Africa* (1994). Exploring the production of knowledge and discourses about Africa,

Mudimbe found that in virtually every intellectual, religious, and aesthetic endeavor "until now, Western interpreters as well as African analysts have been using categories and conceptual systems which depend on a Western epistemological order." Western anthropologists, explorers, colonial officers, and missionaries all contributed—despite their different avocations, ideologies, and personalities—to enduring images of Africa that relegated its peoples to the status of an inferior other. Missionaries were the greatest founders of discourse. Not only had their work paved the way for conquest and colonization, they indelibly shaped Western knowledge of Africa even as they created a new, Christian epistemology for Africans. The missionary, Mudimbe argues, had been "the best symbol of the colonial enterprise" as the committed believer in "the ideals of colonialism: the expansion of Civilization, the dissemination of Christianity, and the advance of Progress." No one more earnestly or comprehensively sought African transformation. "Missionary speech," he observes, is inherently "colonized" and rests on "a normative discourse" of "the authority of the truth." It reflects the European God's will that Africa undergo "cultural and socio-political regeneration, economic progress and spiritual salvation." What missionaries and their colonial collaborators began in the nineteenth and early twentieth centuries could not be entirely swept away in 1960, not even by well-meaning anthropologists.[12]

My title invokes this missionary experience and bids us remember how direct a part American proselytizing has played in shaping American "Africas." For most of American history, the Americans who traveled and worked in Africa were mainly missionaries or teachers. This included a significant contingent of African Americans, eager to bring what they believed their black brethren on the continent lacked: civilization. Though outnumbered by the combined presence in Africa of European missionaries, teachers, and colonial officials, for many years Americans experienced the heady sensation of those who believe they are remaking others at least partially in their own image. One missionary in 1927 wrote, "As we write on the tablet of the hearts of the youth, we are determining the future of the nation."[13] In a provocative recent critique of American overseas teachers, including the Peace Corps, Jonathan Zimmerman emphasizes how "post–World War II teachers, often including missionaries themselves," reacted viscerally to the term and concept "missionary." For postwar idealists, "these terms assumed an almost demonic connotation." Christian and secular missionaries desperately sought to distance themselves in word and deed from the cultural imperialism and racial arrogance of earlier generations of overseas missionaries. Zimmerman's study suggests they came to frustration in this noble effort, a conclusion also indicated by the title of one of Julius A. Amin's articles on the Peace Corps in Africa, "The Perils of Missionary Diplomacy."[14]

Above all, the title borrows from Immanuel Wallerstein. The world-systems theorist, in an earlier academic incarnation, was part of the first generation of U.S.-based African Studies scholars. Wallerstein authored many books and articles in the 1960s, and his early work fit in well with most of the political science and sociology of the decade, with its emphasis on African nationalism and the state in the context of nation building and development. By the 1980s, African Studies had been transformed. Wallerstein, in a retrospective essay, argued that 1960s Africa scholars had more in common with their colonial predecessors than they had realized. Colonial-era European anthropologists—"university-trained scholars on the one hand or colonial administrators or missionaries (with a scholarly bent) on the other"—did field work, learned local languages, and disseminated their findings about African "tribes" to the colonial state and anthropologists back home. "In political terms," Wallerstein argued, "the anthropologists of this period were essentially secular missionaries, liberal mediators between the tribe and the Colonial Office (plus metropolitan public opinion)." African nationalism in the 1950s shattered this colonial arrangement, opening Africa to an influx of researchers from the United States, the Soviet Union, and other countries. Scholars replaced "tribes" with nationalist movements and nation-states as the object of their inquiry. However, though explicitly granting Africans agency as historical actors and openly sympathizing with nationalism, "their basic political stance in the period 1950–1970 was not as different from that of the pre-1950 anthropologists as one might have expected." The new Africanists, "self-congratulatory about . . . overcoming 'ethnocentrism,'" continued to act as "liberal mediators" and "secular missionaries." They "mediated between modern Africa (represented first of all by the nationalist movements) and the Western world in general," attempting to interpret "modern African behavior" in a way that would make "Western policy-makers" more sympathetic to African leaders. Wrote Wallerstein, "The very same Africa scholars who engaged in the interpretive political tasks turned right around and assigned themselves the role of counselor and advisor to African institutions, overtly and covertly, explicitly and implicitly, invited or uninvited. And they played this role with the best of conscience, pursuing their appointed tasks in the spread of rationality and progress as decreed by the Enlightenment and transmitted via science and scholarship."[15]

As a prominent contemporary Africanist has commented, Wallerstein's "secular missionaries" is apropos, for it captures "the belief and the personal commitment, but also the unavoidable internal feeling of cultural or 'theoretical' superiority."[16] I adapt Wallerstein's term, broadening it to include other scholars who, while not specialists on Africa, sought to apply to Africa the tenets of modernization theory. Social scientists in the 1950s and '60s who congratulated themselves on the originality of their theoretical insights into the process of economic development were heirs to an old concept. Historians Michael Adas and Michael Latham have demonstrated the continuity between the Cold War–era development discourse and earlier, colonial-era discourses of civilization and race. Though disavowing its racism, mid-century interdisciplinary theorists of modernization shared with these earlier Western traditions a faith in linear historical progress propelled by technology. Just as "civilizing mission rhetoric" justified colonialism in the nineteenth- and twentieth-century age of empire, so, too, did modernization theory legitimate the persistence of Western (and especially American) global predominance. The postwar American cornucopia of abundance became, like industrial Britain before it, the presumed universal model for poor societies to emulate. Ironically, American avatars of modernization theory, for all their secular rationalism, were also zealous missionaries. The historian Nils Gilman notes that "development promised to exorcise the secular demons of the postwar world—poverty, Communism, and colonialism." Social scientists, backed by substantial government, foundation, and university funding, and "armed with sacramental science and technology," brought to their scholarship and policy advocacy a "proselytizing zeal." The United States, one scholar declared, had to offer Asia and Africa a positive model of development to counter the Soviets; "We must be missionaries." As Gilman writes, modernization theory sought "to 'modernize' the postcolonial world, to deliver its members to the secular heaven that the United States had pioneered." American experts described themselves as "apostles of modernity" and "crusaders." Late in his life Walt Whitman Rostow, high priest of modernization theory and counselor of Presidents Kennedy and Lyndon B. Johnson, admitted that "as individuals, most of us felt, I suspect, some kind of moral or religious impulse to help those striving to come forward through development. In that sense we were in the line that reached back a century and more to the missionaries from Western societies."[17]

I trace the impulse of "liberal mediators" and secular missionaries beyond academe. Intellectuals and Peace Corps volunteers were not alone in viewing themselves as victors over ethnocentrism and friends of African nationalism. American travelers, journalists, and policymakers, too, proffered advice to governments in Washington and Africa intended to forge a mutually beneficial partnership in a world divided by the Cold War and "North-South" economic disparity. In so doing, they carried on an ideological legacy of American exceptionalism in the implicitly imperialist formulation of Henry Luce's "American Century." His essay in Life envisioned benign American global dominance. The son of missionaries himself, Luce anticipated the spread of U.S. culture, in his sole African reference, "from Zanzibar to Hamburg." The inevitable exportation of the American model around the world would find its ultimate expression and, potentially, vindication in the transformation of "Zanzibar," a signifier of African obscurity and distance. The colonial world, in fact, is virtually invisible in Luce's picture of the future. As historian Stephen J. Whitfield notes, the essay "did not even envision national sacrifice or heavy civic demands" to achieve his goals of world power and Americanization. Indeed, "Luce could not get beyond the pleasure principle," a fact powerfully illustrated by the presence of several advertisements for women's underwear and a plethora of other consumer goods in the same issue of Life. Two decades later, American advocates of aid to Africa, too, understood America as a consumer society and envisioned no large sacrifice.[18]

Luce's essay (and media empire) can be understood as an expression of lifelong interests and zeal derived from his birth in China, to missionary parents, in 1898, the year of American overseas imperialism. Yet "The American Century," as Whitfield shrewdly notes, contains "no hint of piety." As a prophet of power and cultural expansion, Luce was the quintessential secular missionary. The fact of his ignorance of Africa only enhances his standing as an archetype for much of the self-referential hypothesizing about the region that later characterized American commentary. Whitfield, in an otherwise incisive analysis, insists Luce's vision of a pax Americana reflects American "exceptionalism rather than . . . domination," noting the absence of explicit references to military power. Amy Kaplan, however, observes how Luce's Americanization promised to "efface the irritating otherness of foreign lands, peoples and cultures with strange names." American culture as the "universal language across the globe" would relieve Americans of the need to learn across cultures, and Luce's formula permitted the United States to enjoy the fruits of neoimperialism without renouncing American exceptionalism.[19]

This proved a powerful formula during the Cold War. Less than two decades after Luce published his article in Life, The Ugly American captured an evolving zeitgeist and mobilized American optimism against the ostensibly complacent U.S. foreign policy in the Third World. Though set in Southeast Asia, the novel inspired such Kennedy-era initiatives as counter-insurgency and the Peace Corps, and spurred on the growth of American influence in Africa. The novelists' portrait of malleable Asians ripe for American tutelage (or Communist exploitation) played so loose with specific Asian cultural traits or circumstances that it could, with little effort, be transposed to Africa.[20] Taken together, the African Studies scholars, modernization's "mandarins of the future," youthful teachers, and avatars of the American Century and Cold War crusades all expressed a concentrated version of American exceptionalism, one with an implicitly imperial mission despite its professed humanitarianism.[21] That some contemporary non-governmental organizations (NGOs) exude a paternalistic attitude while producing marginal results in African development suggests that a study of this impulse and its effects is worthwhile.[22]

In Washington, even self-styled "realists" swooned, at least during the early sixties, titillated by the same essential challenge of remaking Africa that had once enchanted European colonialists. Others were secular missionaries to the bone. No one better exemplified such a condition than G. Mennen Williams, better known as "Soapy," thanks to his family fortune. The Bureau of African Affairs gained influence with Kennedy's appointment of the former Michigan governor as Assistant Secretary of State. Earlier, Kennedy's campaign staff had wooed Williams, an ardent campaigner and outspoken advocate of civil rights, despite its somewhat apprehensive internal assessment of him. Williams, they understood, took "himself very seriously and believes that he is an instrument of God's will in furthering liberal, humanitarian causes." His politics were informed by the reality of being "a devout Episcopalian . . . who sees himself as having been tapped to put the Sermon on the Mount into governmental practice. This is not a pose but reflects a sincere, if unusual, conviction."[23] Upon winning the presidency, Kennedy saw in the Episcopalian crusader—so different from his own cool, cynical, self-consciously "tough" politics—an apropos temperament and demeanor to represent the United States in its new African crusade. As one of the Africa experts in the United States argued in the aftermath of the election, Williams would be ideal for the position, for despite a "superficial knowledge of specific African problems," he seemed "well-suited for bubbling, rough-and-tumble Africa, where 'stuffed-shirtism' is inevitably associated with race consciousness." Such an individual promised "to change dramatically the image of the United States which is beginning to take form in Africa."[24]

Like Martin Staniland, in his intellectual history of Americans and African decolonization, I wish to distinguish between representations of Africa by social and political conservatives, reactionaries, and frankly racist white Americans, on the one hand, and mainstream, middlebrow, and academic Cold War–liberal discourse, on the other. Mainstream liberalism imbued most journalistic, academic, and official accounts of Africa after 1960, and the politics of the two Democratic presidents and the surging black freedom struggle further placed conservative bigotry on the defensive. Liberal representations carried greater weight, and the fact that these borrowed as heavily as they did from colonial imagery is a chief concern of this volume. However, a hard core of explicit racist contempt for Africa remained, sometimes ensconced in officialdom. When Kennedy became president and installed liberals like Williams, Chester Bowles, and Adlai Stevenson as key officials, resistance within the administration and the Foreign Service illustrated the persistence of racism. White House civil rights advisor Harris Wofford, before becoming a passionate secular missionary in Ethiopia, shared with the president an anecdote about "old-school, Europe-first policymakers" in the State Department. "The trouble with Bowles and Williams," one of these men said, "was that when they saw a band of black baboons beating tom-toms they saw George Washingtons."[25] Indeed, racism and the broader cultural politics of whiteness are inseparable from the postcolonial American engagement with Africa.[26]

Whiteness, the subject of a burgeoning interdisciplinary literature, offers an important context for understanding Africa's meaning for many Americans.[27] George White Jr., in a study of U.S. policy toward Africa in the 1950s, provides a diplomatic history of racism. He demonstrates the tendency of officials in the Eisenhower administration to express explicit racism as they deliberated about African affairs. Whiteness remained a factor in American images of Africa, as well as U.S. policy, during the sixties. I argue for a broader conception of where, and how, whiteness operated, even among liberal individuals who are difficult to label racist. Evidence of racial imagery, affinities, and antipathies were not confined to official communications within presidential administrations. The era of explicit white supremacy in world politics had ended with colonialism and, after 1960, American officials consistently condemned the extraordinary South African system of apartheid, as well as racism in such European colonies as Angola, Mozambique, and Rhodesia. Nevertheless, whiteness remained a powerful influence on American and South African identities and perceptions. American elites seldom explicitly associated themselves with white settlers in Rhodesia and South Africa on the basis of race or invoked racial supremacy as a rationale for cooperation with those regimes. However, whiteness is not synonymous with an ideology of white supremacy. Conscious or explicit racism is not necessary for whiteness to preserve privileges for those identified as white.

Whiteness, like other powerful discourses, conceals itself even as it shapes debate and discussion. When white privilege is "normalized, and rendered unremarkable," it subtly shapes perceptions, becoming both an identity (for those classified as white) and a usable tool, for those seeking to make their practices or beliefs seem legitimate and universal rather than unequal or particular. As I have argued elsewhere, American representations of South Africa as a white, modern, consumer society undermined U.S. resolve to confront the apartheid regime in Pretoria. More broadly, whiteness, as a "passport to privilege" in the newly independent African nations, cannot be separated from the conceit of individual American experts and commentators traveling or working on the continent.[28]

The other side of race, of course, is that it provided a bond between some Americans and Africa that, while not entirely in conflict with the Cold War missionary impulse, could challenge or modify it. The growing literature on African American perspectives and involvement in world affairs underscores the black impact on foreign policy. Even when they did not change Washington's actions, their engagement in the realm of ideas meant that representations of weak, exotic, or "tribal" Africa could not circulate without resistance or competition.[29] If African Americans did not experience the same kind of "discovery" of Africa that most white Americans did during the era of decolonization, neither were their reactions to the continent simple or unified. Certainly, African Americans drew inspiration from African independence and added motivation to accelerate their own freedom struggle. "The nations of Asia and Africa are moving with jet-like speed toward gaining political independence," declared Martin Luther King Jr., "but we still creep at horse-and-buggy pace toward gaining a cup of coffee at a lunch counter."[30] As some African Americans sought an enlarged black role in the making of American policies toward Africa (while African Americans such as Ralph Bunche, Carl Rowan, and Ulric Haynes served as U.S. officials), some black activists also looked more broadly to the forging of Pan-African ties transcending the inherently limited perspective of policymakers in Washington. The results of these strivings, like so much of American effort in 1960s Africa, can only be described as mixed. Rather than treat black commentaries separately, by devoting distinct chapters or sections within chapters to them, this book weaves together black, white, and African voices, recognizing that, while some were more powerful than others, none sounded in a vacuum unaffected by one another.

Distinguishing between black and white perspectives is one example of the caution with which we must generalize about Americans and their views of Africa. Throughout this account, readers will note my frequent reference to the "American" perspective. This is not intended as a contentious claim that all Americans shared the same ideology, discourse, or understanding of events, peoples, and individuals in Africa during this period. Nor is it merely an expedient lumping together of disparate perspectives. Readers will understand that, at times, while I discuss policymaking, the designation "Americans" includes such decision-makers as ambassadors, diplomats, government officials, or presidents. In other contexts, it will be clear, at least by inference, that the label "American" will refer to journalists, scholars, volunteers, or the general public (as a consumer of images produced by the aforementioned groups). I am writing about mainstream Cold War–liberal American opinion, the dominant perspective found in the period's journalism, scholarship, policymaking, and popular culture. As many examples in the book suggest, it is not always possible or profitable to sharply distinguish between these genres, as individual Americans often played roles in more than one. Academics poured into the Kennedy administration, for example, and some of the president's appointees came from the press (including an influential ambassador like William Attwood, for instance). Few if any of the individuals discussed in this book approached Africa in ways that derived solely from one disciplinary or occupational perspective. Even presidents know some—often much—of what they know about the world through non-official sources, including films, photographs, and travelogues.

Obviously, many people's sense of other nations comes from crudely conceived racial images, and not all Americans of the sixties shared the premises of mainstream Cold War liberalism. Beyond the corridors of power (in government, academe, and the mainstream media), sixties radicals and left-wing critics who paid attention to Africa had their own images, symbols, and nomenclature, often infused with Marxism and the radical chic of contemporaries such as Frantz Fanon and Che Guevara (two men who knew something firsthand about African revolution). More numerous, of course, were American conservatives. As Thomas J. Noer has shown, conservatives developed a different language for talking about Africa, one that often revealed the connections between American racism and the erosion of white supremacy abroad. That readers of the *National Review* or listeners to speeches by the likes of George Wallace were exposed to a much starker image of Africa is an important point. While not wishing to overlook this phenomenon, I will insist in this account that a focus on the dominant liberal construction of Africa is necessary. Readers will probably find the news of conservative (especially southern conservative) racially motivated pessimism about African development interesting, but less surprising and significant than this volume's emphasis on liberal American discourse, with its mingling of race, colonial imagery, and modernization theory.[31]

Secular Missionaries is not strictly chronological, though readers will discern a general trend, moving forward from the early sixties. Chapters 1 and 2 outline American narratives of innocence and modernization, as Americans greeted decolonization by imagining Africa as a blank slate and the United States as an anti-colonial, selfless development donor. These narratives are disrupted periodically by African American and African voices, as well as American fascination with spectacles of whiteness and consumption in central and Southern Africa. Chapters 2 and 3 trace the rise of U.S.-based African Studies and the prescriptions for African development emerging from Africanists and modernization theorists. Like other area studies, African Studies in the United States was a by-product of the Cold War. These chapters indicate how Wallerstein's secular missionaries established themselves as "liberal mediators" between Washington and the African governments they studied.

The fruits of this collaboration are explored in chapters 4 and 5, which examine Washington's brief, but intense, commitment to using foreign aid to guide African development planning. Here is where readers interested in policymaking will find the most extended discussion of how the ideas of academic experts fused with popular attitudes and official Cold War concerns to make an ambitious, if often incoherent, American policy for developing Africa. These chapters, as well those that follow, indicate some of the policy disagreements within the Kennedy and Johnson administrations, and it should be noted that at all times, a variety of differences arose among decision-makers concerned with the details and tactics of modernizing Africa. What these chapters also reveal, however, is the cultural continuity tying together a shared meaning among American policymakers. Debates over the quantity and formal structure of economic aid, for example, mattered less, in the long run, than shared premises about Africa and development. Cold War liberals agreed that Africa's economic development was a matter of humanitarian interest, a matter of national security (the containment of Communism), and an opportunity to buttress American leadership of the "Free World" (and the legitimacy of American investments and security interests in Africa) by emphasizing the difference between U.S. leadership and European colonialism. Development, therefore, was always a political matter—not merely a technical one—and one infused not only with ideas about American interests, but also culturally specific meanings of American identity.

Plans were the chief instrument used to promote the American vision. Chapter 4 shows the central importance of long-range economic plans in the development doctrines of the period, and takes three episodes as illustrations of the problems beclouding U.S.–African relations. Three of the largest recipients of American aid—Sudan, Ethiopia, and the Congo—confounded the expectations of secular missionaries and Washington policymakers. As chapter 5 demonstrates, so, too, did Nigeria, the most populous African country south of the Sahara. America's largest recipient of development assistance, Nigeria carried the burden of expectations for regional leadership that bore no relation whatever to the country's fragile ethnic, political, and economic condition. Nigeria's dissolution into civil war in the late sixties revealed how little substance there had been to American plans for Africa.

America's hasty retreat from its self-appointed role as mentor to "developing" Africa brought a decline in aid and paved the way for the rise of the World Bank as Africa's key donor and discipliner. Chapter 6 shows how the transition occurred in the mid-sixties, and how Africans, too, pulled back from the optimistic partnership of the early post-independence years. The recognition that Africa's peripheral role in the world economy and its deteriorating terms of trade mattered more than any aid package or development plan marked, as one self-serving American official noted, a new phase in modern African history. It is here, I argue, we see the origins of contemporary Africa's debt crisis most clearly. Along with the economic and political changes, the mid-sixties became a transitional period in the representations of African culture. Chapters 7 and 8 suggest some of the tropes in a pessimistic, denigrating American discourse of African difference that helped Americans make sense of African problems. Development and nation building had failed, Americans believed, because they had encountered insuperable obstacles in African mindsets, traditions, ethnicity, and religion. Even the Peace Corps, the subject of the second half of chapter 8, found its surging idealism insufficient to prevent or overcome "culture shock," as many volunteers discerned an African culture of underdevelopment resistant to the "can-do" optimism of young Americans.

The Conclusion, while not offering a full narrative or analysis of post-1970 developments, does bridge the story of the "Decade of Development" to our own times. In the twenty-first century, Africa, long absent from mainstream American attention, has reappeared. Once again, it is *Africa in Chaos*, to use the title of one influential if depressing assessment.[32] It remains clad in the garb of the poor and desperate. Assured by Bono, Angelina Jolie, and other passionately well-intentioned celebrities that Africa's needs could be met by forthright Western generosity, ordinary Americans and public figures alike vowed to "Make Poverty History" and wage war on HIV-AIDS, malaria, and tuberculosis.

Before the election of Barack Obama, this burst of humanitarianism influenced former President George W. Bush, who made two trips to the continent while overseeing a significant increase in American aid (the utility of which remains a matter of debate). Bush saw no contradiction between this commitment to helping Africans escape epidemics and poverty and expanding American military and covert forces in Africa, ostensibly to counter the spread of extremism and terrorism. In a historic sense, he was correct. His predecessors found none, either, as they deployed the Central Intelligence Agency in a number of covert interventions in cultural organizations devoted to Africa, and in political intrigue in African capitals, some of which resulted in coups or civil wars. American military force—combined with white mercenaries from South Africa—crushed an uprising in the Congo in 1964, and two years later the CIA provided moral support, at the least, in the overthrow of Ghana's Kwame Nkrumah, the father of African independence. How can aid and Peace Corps missions in Africa go hand in hand with support for an apartheid regime? In Washington, D.C., and Langley, Virginia, the answer may seem obvious. Yet, I doubt even cynical officials during either the Cold War or the War on Terror have really understood how such things become possible, how culture works to produce imaginative spaces in which common sense is rendered helpless by tropes with lives of their own. I hope this book has something useful to say about that.

"The Most Innocent of Continents"

Imagining Africa

During a meeting of the National Security Council in 1959, a perplexed President Eisenhower asked, "Did Somalia consist of wild jungle?" As yet another African colony approached independence, the president felt apprehensive. He wondered "whether the Somalia [sic] people were primitive and aborigines." Director of the CIA Allen Dulles pointed out the largely arid landscape of the country, but allowed the second of the president's assumptions to stand. In reply, Eisenhower, "citing his experience with primitive peoples in the Philippines, expressed some wonder as to how the natives of Somalia could expect to run an independent nation and why they were so possessed as to try to do so." Dulles, too, doubted the Somalis could "organize and administer a modern civilized state." Bemused by the rapid emergence of so many small nations, the president declared of West Africa, "the whole area is a mishmash of chopped-up geography."[1]

The aging Republican president's incomprehension and sense of Africa as the "Dark Continent" already seemed passé. While Eisenhower groped uncertainly with a changing world, his liberal critics embraced "emerging" Africa with enthusiasm. Chester Bowles, a leading spokesman for liberal Democrats in foreign policy during the 1950s and early '60s, had already contributed to the transformation of American attitudes.[2] *Africa's Challenge to America* (1956), based on lectures Bowles delivered at the University of California in 1956 following his tour of the continent the previous year, garnered academic attention. Published by the University of California Press, the book was reviewed at length by political scientist James S. Coleman.[3] Bowles, noted Coleman, had written the first book "to deal primarily with America's relation to Africa." An impressionistic look at Africa on the eve of independence, *Africa's Challenge to America* touted the "stupendous possibilities" presented by Africa's natural resources. "Africa is the richest untapped source of mineral wealth still available to a world that is rapidly devouring its resources," wrote Bowles. Arguing that the growing "stream" of U.S. visitors reporting the "complexity" of Africa ensured that the region could no longer be ignored, Bowles insisted Americans had to learn to appreciate Africa's global importance and cease regarding it as a "mosaic of appendages" of imperial Europe. The exercise of world leadership during the Cold War, according to Bowles, required Americans to play a major role in guiding the period of transition in Africa.[4]

Bowles argued that Africa had better development prospects than much of Asia. "A continent relatively empty of people and yet with great economic promise," it offered "a particularly striking contrast to Asia." A single African colony—the Belgian Congo—had immense mineral wealth and land area comparable to those of India, and with a population of just 12 million, compared to India's 360 million. Unaware that Africa would soon experience an unprecedented population explosion that would more than double the number of people within a generation, Bowles believed that abundant land and "the apparently limitless mineral reservoir of Africa" would automatically create more wealth. Moreover, Bowles contended, only Ethiopia and Liberia suffered the burden of the kind of entrenched, landed class that impeded modernization in Asia and Latin America. That these were the two African states that avoided European colonization hinted at his sympathy for the outgoing rulers of the rest of the continent. Bowles praised the "outstanding" British record of colonial administration "in Africa, as in colonial India, Burma, and Ceylon." The Belgians, he opined, took an "understandable pride" in their development of the Congo. In Belgium's racist yet economically successful rule, Bowles discerned a model for African development. Thus, Bowles's distinctly American optimism about Africa' future blended the new Western outlook with the old.[5]

"Mr. Bowles," observed Coleman, "tends to approach Africa as an undifferentiated continent to which a simple formula . . . can be indiscriminately applied." In this, Bowles anticipated the outpouring of writing and policymaking about a more or less unified American policy for an apparently singular "Africa." Bowles never served as an ambassador in an African capital, and his stint at the State Department under Kennedy proved short-lived. However, his ebullient optimism about Africa—"a continent boiling with change"—and confidence in America's right and capacity to shape it neatly encapsulate the newfound American interest in Africa. State Department planners hoped to "demonstrate to Africans that the United States is a truly disinterested friend and that we genuinely and fully support their aspirations to run their own affairs free from outside interference." Viewing decolonization in Cold War and developmental terms, Americans desired "the orderly and peaceful transition in Africa from colonial rule to independence, from primitivity to modernity," in a non-Communist region.[6] Americans became fascinated with Africa, but with an artificial, culturally constructed "Africa." This was an Africa of the mind, not the concrete, discrete, immensely large and diverse Africa of lived reality. Many Americans expressed optimism based on a belief that Africa had no history and thus no baggage: a kind of blank slate, malleable, ready for American tutelage. African Americans and Africans contested some, but not all, of these assumptions. Paradoxically, while imagining an "innocent" Africa, Americans admired much of the economic infrastructure, built environment, and lifestyles they encountered in the Congo and South Africa.

Innocence, African and American

Of the swift achievement of independence in 1960, Immanuel Wallerstein recalls, "It was a wonderful story—full of passion and optimism. Africa believed in itself, in its future, and in its past, and the world took note." That Americans once waxed optimistic seems strange in a post–Cold War world in which "Africa" signifies desperation, absolute poverty, and chaos. Africa today, "more than any other region has had its development problems dissected and analyzed by the World Bank, the IMF, the OECD, or the United Nations," notes a critic of Western aid policies, "although none of the resultant studies has actually made any real difference to what happens on the ground." Africans in 1960 would have deemed impossible such a historical cul-de-sac. As historian Frederick Cooper observes, "No word captures the hopes and ambitions of Africa's leaders, its educated populations, and many of its farmers and workers in the post-war decades better than 'development.'"[7] For Africans, independence meant the dawn of an era of social and economic progress, with the global discourse of development offering them a language with which to demand justice.

Americans understood that. However, they took, as Wallerstein suggests, an anthropological interest in a changing Africa. Social scientists, journalists, and officials traveling in and writing about "transitional" Africa at the dawn of independence imagined a tumultuous, yet ultimately benign, process. Inevitably, it would end with the achievement of modernity (conceived as a kind of Americanization). Africa, Mennen Williams explained, sought "to bridge several centuries in the march of human freedom and in some instances a millennium or more in the economic life of its people." Edward R. Murrow, journalistic icon-turned director of the United States Information Agency, saw Africa as "a continent groping for directions, churning with ideas, surveying our style, sampling our ideals." Such a transition provided fodder for the press. The *New York Times* colorfully declared that "primitive customs are disappearing from the continent almost as fast as its wild animals. The spear, the ostrich feather, the juju mask, the thumping dance with naked breasts and swinging monkeytails—all these soon will be as extinct as the redskin stockade and the pony express." William Attwood, a *Look* reporter who became Kennedy's ambassador to Guinea, recalled a visit "into the bush," where he found "a Bassari village" comprising "a dozen or so huts made of loose stones." There, the ambassador met his African escort's "withered aunt"—a living embodiment of antiquity—and, after photographing her with a Polaroid, showed her the picture. "When the reality dawned on her, she screamed and dropped the print," whereupon her nephew dismissed her belief in the Polaroid's "magic." Expansively, he told Attwood that within three years the village "will be swept away and you will see a modern school in its place." For Attwood, the episode illustrated that "Africa is changing fast, and here, in this remote Bassari settlement, you could see the change in microcosm: the aunt, frightened, illiterate and naked except for a string of beads, and her nephew with his white shirt, Dacron trousers and dark glasses, talking French and listening to the Voice of America on his transistor radio."[8]

Rapid change often produces new narratives. As Melani McAlister has argued in her brilliant study of the cultural history of Americans and terrorism, "Such narratives, born of amnesias, promise to stitch together a patchwork past." Her key insight is that narratives "are forged not just by policy makers, but at the intersection of news accounts, policy developments, and cultural texts such as films, novels and even video games." In fact, scholarly writing, travel accounts, and other texts join this list, and, as McAlister argues, the representations that result "are never distributed evenly or unproblematically. But they *are* powerful."[9] As African nations achieved independence with what seemed to Americans remarkable suddenness, an amnesia of a special kind engulfed memories of American responsibility in African affairs. The long history of missionaries, explorers, safaris and travel narratives, the Firestone empire in Liberia, Marcus Garvey's movement, the presence of the U.S. military in Africa during World War II, and U.S. investment in the mineral industries of Southern Africa: all these encounters were forgotten. Needing a language with which to describe and understand—and shape—the unfolding African drama, American observers' individual accounts coalesced into narratives that told stories and offered morals. While many conservative and southern Americans, viewing Africa through an explicitly racist lens, remained content with traditional images dismissive of Africans, most Americans wanted to articulate a sense of sympathetic understanding. Thus, while some continued to accept narratives of hopeless African backwardness, prevailing narratives mobilized the legacy of American exceptionalism and proclaimed that Africa had only begun to develop, and America had only begun to help. As with Luce's American Century, a discourse emerged that reconciled a neoimperial mission—making Africa safe for Americanization and freedom from Communism—with the truisms of American exceptionalism.[10]

Tarzan did some of this cultural work. As Martin Staniland argues, the novels of Edgar Rice Burroughs and movies based on them had the greatest impact on "established American views" of Africa. Tellingly, Burroughs never visited Africa and used it as a primitive, tropical, colonial setting where Tarzan, after quitting the colonial service, adopts a masculine lifestyle of rebellion against colonialism.[11] As a foreign policy analyst in the 1960s recalled, in Tarzan films, "Europeans in Africa were invariably evil and out to exploit the Africans in the most devious and criminal ways; Africans were innocent and good; and Americans, who were innocent and good . . . would save the Africans from the ruthless Europeans."[12] American professions of innocence not only implied that Americans had been absent from the scene of exploitative European colonialism, but also denied that Americans had known Africa at all. While Tarzan's rebellion represents American masculinity and imperial innocence, the Africans remain frozen in time, with colonialism entrapping them in an ancient, primitive state.[13]

Tarzan made manifest the centrality of whiteness to American cultural constructions of Africa, as part of a broader literary and cinematic tradition. Writings by Henry Morton Stanley and Theodore Roosevelt—chronicles of the white man's adventures in Africa—had established "an American variation on a European theme," and its imprint persisted even after Americans largely abandoned the explicit racism and "white man's burden" affinity for imperialism. As for movies, their reputation for distortions of Africa was so pervasive by 1961 that it became a subject of diplomatic exchanges. Kennedy, during an after-dinner toast in honor of the visiting Nigerian Prime Minister Tafawa Balewa, lamented that "Hollywood" had left Americans with little understanding "of your culture and history and traditions."[14]

Unlike the European colonialists or participants in a worldwide Communist conspiracy, Americans appeared without (imperial) history, bereft of exploitative intent. This narrative of innocence shaped more than fantasy, fiction, and superficial news headlines as Africans achieved independence. Anthropologist Melville J. Herskovits, a founder of modern U.S.-based African Studies who considered himself "engaged in the scientific study of the changing cultures of the continent," claimed that America's innocence of colonialism helped provide him with scholarly "detachment" and a "broad view."[15] By 1960 American journalists and foreign policy analysts had written "a multitude of articles whose typical titles would be "Emerging Africa," "Awakening Africa," "Africa Out of Her Shell." Such reports informed Americans that "Africa, the awakening giant, stands with one foot in the primitive past, the other in the twentieth century." *Time's* Johannesburg bureau chief declared, "The young African giant is on the move," enjoying late-colonial economic gains and a drive for political independence. Africa's innocence, measured in time, suggested potential. "It is as if a great giant stirred for the first time in many centuries, stretching itself, opening his gentle eyes upon an unknown and very disturbing world." Explicit claims that Africa lacked a history were common, though the intention now was to underscore Africa's freshness rather than to denigrate its lack of achievement. One account published by the Foreign Policy Association contended that "the evidence seems strong that in art, as in science, medicine, crafts, religion, language, navigation—in short, across the whole range of human activity— Africa remained until only yesterday at a primitive stage of development."[16] As one journalist breathlessly declared in a book rushed to the presses, "In effect, the Industrial, Agricultural and French revolutions, the Magna Carta, Bill of Rights and the U.N. Charter, the Russian Revolution, the rise of fascism and the H-bomb, all these have been compressed into an emetic mass and forced in *one generation* down the throats of a society no more advanced than the German tribes of Tacitus' day." Fortunately, in spite of its problems, this Africa was "*alive, not stagnant,*" for "Africa is a continent on the move."[17] "Even today," declared the president of the World Bank, Eugene Black, in 1961, "the bulk of Africa's 200 millions are only beginning to enter world society" after centuries of isolation from the West.[18] While a representative of the AFL-CIO wrote of Africans making "a leap from a centuries-old darkness into the light," a historian conceived Africans' having to "jump straight from the jungle trail to the jet plane." Another writer held that "Africans reared in primitive mud-and-dung huts, clustered deep in the shimmering African bush, are today becoming doctors of divinity and medicine." Bowles sympathetically depicted Africa as "an awakening giant, stretching its limbs and opening its eyes to the first faint prospect of freedom." More important, from an American perspective, these colorful, overwrought pronouncements heightened the hopefulness and sense of historic significance of Africa's future, and its impact on the world. Adlai Stevenson, former Democratic nominee for president and U.S. Ambassador to the United Nations during the early sixties, described Africa as "at the threshold of history," and "the most innocent of continents." Evoking the essence of American perceptions of Africa, Stevenson's label suggests the absence of the past, of culture, and of limitations. America's own self-styled innocence, endowed with a zeal to spread "The American Century," seemed a perfect match for such a naïve land. Such an innocent region required American protection from Communism and liberation from the legacy of European colonialism.[19]

Much of the burst of writing about Africa betrayed the shallow trendiness of the topic, generating complaints about its quality from scholars with expertise on Africa. St. Clair Drake, a sociologist at Roosevelt University and former head of the sociology department at the University of Ghana, complained that "the flood of books dealing with Africa continues" displayed a "highly variable quality and the unevenness of style and significance of data and comment even within individual volumes." He added, "The number of factual errors due to ignorance, carelessness, or emotional bias in many of the popular works by journalists is especially disappointing." Political scientist Harvey Glickman agreed, observing, "The first 'wave' of reporting" had been marred by "obvious formats ('from the Stone Age to the Machine Age')" as well as "much triviality (the juju market in Ibadan)." Even Bowles, while pleased that "the flow of books, documentaries, articles, and lectures on African history, politics, geography and culture has reached flood-tide," felt it necessary to refute several "current popular stereotypes" about Africa that questioned the region's prospects for development.[20] Nevertheless, Drake, Glickman, and Bowles shared with glib writers an excitement about the novelty of the postcolonial moment and its global meaning.

Convinced that Africa had emerged naked on the world scene, Americans viewed Africa's "underdevelopment" and silent record as blessings. Waldemar

Nielsen, a political scientist who worked at the Ford Foundation, the Council on Foreign Relations, and the African-American Institute, insisted, "Africa carried into the modern age a less burdensome baggage of history, of self-pride, of destructive ideology and of encrusted social structure to impede progress." This absence of a usable past gave Africa an advantage over "underdeveloped" Asia and Latin America, as Africans enjoyed a blank slate. Another observer declared, "They have no ancient greatness with which to mask their present inequality. The cultural state of the Africans is so low that they are considerably more adaptable to the challenge of Western civilization than the Arab or the Indian. They do not have to defend their past" and they had "fewer 'bad' habits" to break "before acquiring the more productive aspects of Western civilization." Thus, Africa as "tabula rasa," as Stevenson put it. Staniland summarizes the message: "It could have a purely modernizing nationalism, because it had no traditions worth preserving or seriously capable of getting in the way."[21] Even at the end of the decade, an American economist who advised African governments argued that "the absence of so much written history" gave Africa better prospects for development, for "unlike in Asia, history has not yet become an all-but-unbearable burden."[22]

President Kennedy inaugurated the first zestful African policy in Washington. Applying to Africa the same lessons from The Ugly American driving American policies in the rest of Third World, Kennedy dispatched energetic ambassadors to bring the New Frontier to Africa. Bowles, during his brief stint as Undersecretary of State, urged Kennedy to trust Mennen Williams and the African Bureau as his most motivated, loyal, and energetic State Department cohort, officials with a "clear understanding" of his approach to Africa. The ambassadors in Africa, he asserted, "are an able and particularly dedicated group" possessing "excellent" morale and a grasp of "the philosophy and policies of the Administration."[23] Bowles's apt celebration of Kennedy's ambassadors highlighted key secular missionaries of the administration. The novelty of Africa made it an irresistible challenge to those ambassadors. Kennedy's ambassador to Gabon (one of the Francophone countries that gained independence in 1960), Charles F. Darlington, expressed a sentiment common to Americans dispatched to Africa. Of Gabon he recalled, "Remote and almost unknown to Americans, it seemed to offer adventure and all kinds of possibilities for constructive work." Darlington's description of his task as ambassador fit other ambassadors and, more generally, the U.S. presence in Africa. "I knew when I went out to Gabon that aid would be my most important business," he wrote. A poor, newly independent nation of less than a half-million people, Gabon appeared a natural client. "The essence of our relationship, at least for a number of years, would lie in the help we could give them, help over the whole range of their needs: finance capital, equipment, technicians, health care, education and moral leadership."[24]

African American reactions to African decolonization both reproduced and challenged narratives of innocence. Expressions of astonished delight that "Africa was on the stage of history" were joined by a recollection that it had once been on that stage before colonialism. According to James Baldwin, African Americans could now realize "they were also related to kings and princes in an ancestral homeland, far away," an epiphany that became "a great antidote to the poison of self-hatred." African independence disrupted the white American racial imaginary; "the American Negro can no longer, nor will he ever again, be controlled by white America's image of him. This fact has everything to do with the rise of Africa in world affairs."[25] Baldwin discerned an African contribution to the Civil Rights Revolution in the United States. So did Martin Luther King Jr., who concluded, after visiting Ghana's independence ceremony in 1957, that colonialism and Jim Crow had much in common, as both were based on "white supremacy and the contempt for life." He urged his congregation in Montgomery to draw from Ghanaian independence the historical lesson, "The oppressor never voluntarily gives freedom to the oppressed. You have to work for it. . . . Freedom only comes through persistent revolt, through persistent agitation, through persistently rising up against the system of evil." Thus a lesson central to his later letter from Birmingham City Jail came directly from Africa. Africans, too, drew constant attention to the connection between the rights of African Americans and the influence of the United States in Africa. Throughout the 1950s and '60s Africans argued that America, "hailed as the leader of the democratic world," as a Nigerian newspaper put it, "carries with it a great deal of moral responsibility." Racial discrimination in the United States violated that mandate, whereas securing civil rights "would be the greatest possible assurance of America's good faith and sincerity towards the establishment of a true world-wide democracy."[26] Though white Americans professed innocence of empire in Africa, African Americans and Africans seldom missed an opportunity to note the pertinence of American racism to the newfound American mission in Africa. Even after passage of the Civil Rights Act of 1964, the African American director of the United States Information Agency (USIA), Carl Rowan, reported that in Africa, "some evidence exists of an increasing impatience with what is regarded as the lagging eradication of racial discrimination in the United States." At the Cairo meeting of the

Organization of African Unity, Kenya's Prime Minister Jomo Kenyatta "attacked the continued existence of racial discrimination and stated that this was an area in which the United States could learn from independent Africa." Rowan noted that "Africans are keeping a watchful eye on the bill's implementation."[27]

If African Americans had a different perception of African innocence, Africans openly rejected their portrayal as a people without history. The naming of independent nations after ancient West African empires—Ghana and Mali—symbolized the efforts of African leaders to yoke their peoples' traditions to their modernizing, nation-building efforts. At the same time, while most African leaders were moderates eager to avoid entangling Africa in the Cold War, and some were avowedly pro-American, the history of racial discrimination in the United States powerfully shaped African responses to American claims to moral leadership. In the 1950s, newspapers in West Africa often criticized American racism and the hypocrisy of a country that persecuted black people in attempting to spread its anti-Communism agenda in Africa.[28] African scholars began writing a new history of the continent that challenged narratives of innocence. Nigerian historian J. F. Ade Ajayi, in particular, argued that colonialism had ultimately proven a brief disruption in African history, and that independence offered an opportunity not to begin from nothing, but to resume the main course of African development. This perspective, however, made less impression on American observers than the perceived gulf between colonial culture and "traditional" Africa.[29]

Sensing Modernity

Americans, despite their narratives of innocence, openly admired aspects of European colonialism. Staniland points out that most in the late 1950s and early 1960s, though hostile toward the repressive aspects of colonialism, believed that "colonialism had served a useful purpose, by destroying feudalism and firing up the engines of modernization." This influenced the way Americans evaluated individual colonies and colonial systems, for "the greater the material advance and the degree of modernization achieved, the more indulgently was the system judged." The British colonial system often received praise for having made some strides in preparing an African elite to take over the reins of power, and for London's relatively quick acceptance of independence for most of its African territories. The Belgian colonial enterprise in the

Congo, which had been built on an extremely violent founding at the turn of the century, and which never spread education and modern amenities for the vast majority of Africans in the colony, found favor with many commentators. The extent of the Congo's industrialization seemed impressive, though the civil war that erupted immediately after the country won its independence in 1960 postponed hopes for modernization. Only Portugal, the most oppressive and least economically modernized colonial power in Africa, drew consistently negative attention from academic and political commentators.[30]

To understand American fascination with what they perceived as colonial modernity, consider James Ferguson's study of representations of modernity in the Copperbelt industrial region of Central Africa. Social scientists and other Western observers were enchanted by the rapid transformation of Northern Rhodesia (Zambia upon independence). "The overdramatic and exaggerated narration of the rise of industrialism and urbanism here reflected the extent to which the Zambian experience captured something in the modernist imagination and came not only to exemplify but to epitomize the revolution that was understood to be taking place in Africa." To Westerners, "urbanization seemed a teleological process, a movement toward a known end point that would be nothing less than a Western-style industrial modernity. An urbanizing Africa was a modernizing one, and there was no place urbanizing faster than Zambia."[31] Large industrialized cities figured as sites and emblems of modernity. Western excitement over Zambian industrialization overlooked the narrow concentration of that process within the mining sector of the colonial economy. However, representations of Zambian modernity were less about Zambia than about the "modernist imagination" of the West. Though mainly concerned with the influence of Western social science, Ferguson also draws attention to the sensory impetus behind Western fantasies about Zambian modernity. As mining expanded, so, too, did the mining towns founded on the Copperbelt during the early twentieth century. This "urbanization process was a stereotypically industrial one, whose noisy smelting plants and sooty miners seemed to reiterate a well-known chapter in the usual narratives of the West's own rise to modernity." African modernity was "directly observable in the smokestacks." Sight, smell, and sound, therefore, made Zambia seem like the Britain of yesteryear; the Copperbelt sensorium dramatized economic change and, for Western observers and participants, made modernity manifest.[32]

Beyond the Copperbelt, Africans received plenty of unsolicited advice about how to handle the colonial patrimony. "Nothing," asserted one journalist, "would serve rising Africa better than to stop and reconsider objectively its colonial heritage . . . it brought to Africa not only development money but an economic libertarianism that was perhaps the best thing that could have happened to the continent."[33] Beguiled by late-colonial economic growth driven by increased worldwide demand for primary products and minerals, American appraisals of African economic prospects brimmed with optimism. Citing the region's minerals and other natural resources, many Americans believed "Africa's possibilities are staggering," though they also recognized that "obstacles to economic development are enormous," including environmental, social, and economic.[34] To illustrate the claim that "the contrast between the Continent's resource potential and the present economic state of society is staggering," Eugene Black recalled a visit to the Congo River. "A few years ago I stood on a bluff overlooking the Congo River, 100 miles below Leopoldville, while engineers described to me how a series of dams built at this point would create electric power capacity equal to all the power then installed in Western Europe. The only economic activity in that almost uninhabited area appeared to be the collection of a species of caterpillar which was traded across the border into Portuguese Angola where caterpillars are a staple part of the local diet." The Belgian Congo seemed special; as the leading American scholar on the country put it, in the mid-1950s it was "riding the crest of a wave of economic expansion of literally spectacular proportions."[35]

Americans stressed the immense size, mineral wealth, and inherent economic potential of the Congo in language that implied irresistible force. "There are only a few territories in Africa that are as big as the Congo, and none of them is anywhere near as rich," reported one. Its size—"nearly 80 times the size of Belgium, and about a fourth the size of the United States"— and its lack of population density suggested a cultural, as well as an economic, meaning. "The Congo, alone among all the territories of Africa, actually resembles the popular notion of what the Dark Continent should look like. It is covered with thick jungles and is literally soaked with water. Torrential downpours are unleashed almost every day." If it seemed like a natural setting straight from *Heart of Darkness* it also beguiled Westerners as "one of the most fabulous territories in Africa." "There are minerals from one end of the colony to the other," and its future seemed likely to unleash enormous hydroelectric power along the Congo River and the cultivation of unused, "highly fertile" farm land.[36] "On balance, the Belgians can be justifiably proud of their economic achievements in the Congo. Few colonies have developed either so far or so quickly; none has shown such concern for the native inhabitant's share in the growth." The analyst who made this statement conceded, however, that while the Belgians had trained plenty of Africans to drive trains or operate steam shovels, "no Congolese had yet been trained as an engineer" nor had they been placed in upper-level civil service positions, leaving the country unable to cope with, "or even understand" the "managerial problems of an economy as complex as that of the Congo."[37]

Enthusiastic accounts, like the older literary tradition that imagined African otherness in a pure form along the banks of the Congo, expressed sensory perceptions of modernity. Tarzan aside, no source of images of Africa has had more enduring effect than Joseph Conrad's engrossing novella, *Heart of Darkness*. Vicariously journeying with Marlow down the Congo River, Americans had glimpsed both Central Africa's natural resource potential and what Kurtz called simply, "the horror." By 1960, while retaining indelible impressions of African savagery (nature's and man's), American visitors to the Belgian colony saw another world, too. Sight seemed now to confirm the modernity—hence, the appropriateness—of the built environment of the Congo. Profits from mining worked one of the world's wonders of whiteness. One analyst of European colonialism described Belgian rule in the Congo as "honest, efficient, unsentimental and effective," characterized by "planned and steady economic progress and growth" that had benefited the African people of the colony, though the Belgians had also provided woefully inadequate education, political freedom, and racial equality. Leopoldville, the capital, "is well laid out, with broad boulevards, impressive buildings, a beautiful mechanized port, a spanking new university. It is an orderly and restrained city. . . . For the most part, the natives are well-dressed, and thousands ride bicycles."[38] The *New York Times* reported that at night, Leopoldville's main thoroughfare, "the Boulevard Albert I, is lit up like New York's Third Avenue by garish fluorescent units that project sideways and provide a purplish-white glow." The city boasted "touches of Broadway and the Forties" with juke boxes playing Elvis Presley and stores selling the records of Harry Belafonte.[39]

U.S. *News and World Report* published a glowing profile of the "burst of economic development" entailed in Belgium's ongoing ten-year development program. "As African cities go, Leopoldville is the most modern of them all. There are air-conditioned hotels, luxury shops, restaurants, night clubs and sidewalk cafes. You can buy just about anything you want here—from a Cadillac to a Parisian gown to a thousand-dollar movie camera." The frenetic construction promised to give the city "the skyline of an American city" complete with work under way on boulevards, a new airport, and a sports stadium seating 75,000 people. Meanwhile, the Belgians, out of enlightened self-interest, had begun expanding economic opportunities to Africans: "The Belgians now are building what ranks as the first real 'welfare state' in Africa." As a correspondent for the New York Times observed, in economic development the Belgians had "worked a miracle."[40]

Americans celebrated the spectacle of consumption in the Congo, revealing the association between modernity, whiteness, and consumption that also shaped perceptions of South Africa. By the 1960s, consumerism, like whiteness and modernity, was presumed universal and normative. American accounts of these countries repeatedly invoked their miraculous production and consumption.[41] If enchanted with Leopoldville, Americans found Johannesburg even more compelling. Much of the hyper-praise for South African progress and modernity focused on the metropolis of Johannesburg, consistently depicted as a "white city," despite its dependence upon black labor housed in impoverished townships. By 1950, "Jo'burg" had already emerged as a crucial trope in American constructions of a white, modern South Africa. American travelers were awed by the "progressive spirit and dynamism of the Johannesburg businessmen" and the skyscrapers and industrial plants that affected "an atmosphere more like Chicago than Africa." The city reminded one American writer of Houston, Texas, "a rowdy city, tough, raw, confident and energetic," endowed with gold instead of oil. "In quickness of tempo, somewhat crude vitality, and brilliant aggressiveness, Johannesburg is the most American of all cities in Africa," he asserted. By the mid-1960s, Allen Drury recalled "South Africa's Manhattan" and its frenzied construction, which ensured "the sound of the jackhammer and the crash of the wrecking crew will always belong to Jo'burg." Drury insisted, "You have to hand it to Johannesburg, big, vigorous, crude and brawling, filled with the insistent pulse of life that will not be denied." It had, in eight decades, blossomed "from open veld to modernity as vital as any city's anywhere," although one plagued by racial conflict and high rates of crime. An American businessman in Johannesburg declared, "This is the only real industrial complex south of Milan."[42]

Skyscrapers signified South Africa's "miracles of modernity" as no other large African city skyline could. Americans sometimes pointed to Accra, Nairobi, or other cities as evidence of African modernization, but those cities had far smaller populations and much less intensive concentrations of financial and industrial wealth. The city typically figured as an enclave, a harbinger of modernity in countries still primarily rural (hence "transitional," in modernization parlance). By contrast, whiteness and modernity glittered in reports of the "brash and booming city of 1.2 million, whose busy streets and stores hum with a babble of languages" in "the No. 1 business city on the African continent." Noting that white businessmen walked to work on Holland Street, South Africa's "Wall Street," one profile noted that 60 percent of the country's retail business occurred within a thirty-mile radius. "The consumers there represent the largest and richest market on the continent," a condition illustrated by the fact that "private swimming pools and swank golf and tennis clubs abound." "I have never seen a community with so many tennis courts," marveled an American travel writer.[43]

Private displays of wealth and comfort also attracted Americans. A cover story on South Africa in *Time* magazine noted Johannesburg's "expensive northern suburbs," where "artistically wrought steel burglar bars cover the windows of elegant homes, where watchdogs growl on the door mats and swimming pools sparkle on the spacious grounds." These "fashionable" suburbs were also home to many U.S. executives, who enjoyed the service of black cooks and nannies. "Proud citizens," noted the *Christian Science Monitor*, "claim the Johannesburg-Pretoria complex has more swimming pools per capita than any other place in the world." "The swimming pool is no longer a sign of status here," wrote one reporter, "but rather a symbol of what is generally called 'the South African way of life.'"[44]

Pools were important racial and cultural symbols. In the United States, blacks and whites alike imagined swimming a "white" recreation, one in which blacks allegedly underachieved. Swimming pools in suburban America, particularly in Southern California, symbolized economic prosperity and reflected what one architectural historian calls an "ideology of making the desert bloom. . . . The dry should be made wet, the hot should be made cold. The ultimate luxury is to turn the world into what it is not." South Africa's natural and social climate fueled such an ideological drive to turn the world upside down, and the results impressed American visitors. "Airline passengers traveling over Johannesburg's northern suburbs in the late 1960s could not have failed to notice scores of bright blue squares, ovals and rectangles dotting the spacious gardens of the homes," prompting one American writer to pronounce, "white South Africans overtook Californians as the single most affluent group in the world." Certainly, no American observer made similar claims while flying over Accra or Lagos. Such statements were not intended to highlight the shared histories of racial exclusion and residential segregation evident in any comparison of the histories of Southern California and South Africa. They were, rather, uncritical expressions of white identification that undermined the efforts of those Americans and Africans (including the African National Congress, in particular) trying to persuade Americans of the uniquely unjust and brutal nature of apartheid. How evil could a system so well endowed with familiar-looking buildings, suburbs, pools, and (white) people really be?[45]

Of course, the crises of apartheid and civil war captured American headline coverage of South Africa and the Congo, respectively. Americans, though divided about what the United States should do about each crisis (debating economic sanctions against apartheid and the wisdom of military intervention in the Congo), officially repudiated racism. However, spectacles of white consumption and modernity influenced their perception, and Americans hoped both countries' economic infrastructure would remain intact. African Americans came close to a full break with this prevailing American preoccupation with whiteness. The Congo crisis, the preeminent Cold War event that put Africa at the top of the agenda of the United Nations and the superpowers, led to the demise of the immensely popular nationalist leader Patrice Lumumba. Upon the announcement of his assassination, world reaction was strongly negative, and among African American citizens, this took the form of dramatic protests at the United Nations. Lumumba, concluded one activist, had been the victim of "the international lynching of a black man on the altar of colonialism and racial supremacy." However, some black leaders in the United States distanced themselves from the methods and emotional vehemence of the protests. This mixed African American reaction to the demise of Africa's most passionate young statesman—at the hands of the United States, in effect—revealed divisions among blacks on foreign relations generally, and Africa specifically.[46]

The Congo and South Africa provided a template for colonial modernity—one clearly expressing the influence of whiteness on American visions of Africa—enabling comparisons with other countries. Liberia did not fit the description "new nation" and the narratives of innocence that required forgetting the history of American colonization in West Africa. Due to large-scale U.S. investment and apparent political stability, Liberia could impress Americans anxious about African chaos. An Africanist scholar visiting at the end of the 1950s expressed admiration for its "fantastic boom," predicting that its increasing economic diversification suggested "the long-range future is fairly bright."[47] However, the near-total absence of white settlers and the institutions of a colonial state produced a common concern voiced by a State Department official returning from a ten-week tour of Africa who distinguished most African countries from Liberia and Ethiopia, the two nations that "have never had the material benefit of colonial rule and, where progress, in terms of human welfare, is at the lowest level." The Belgians had "done fairly well" in giving Africans in the Congo economic opportunities, while in Liberia, Firestone and other American companies had practiced segregation and had "not developed the African worker as they should have," as one participant noted during an NSC meeting. Meeting with Kennedy in the White House, Liberian President William Tubman claimed his country was "underdeveloped" because of its absence of "a colonial past with hospitals, schools, public buildings and roads constructed by the colonial powers."[48] Thus, for American officials, an African nation's historic ties to the United States mattered less than its material attributes of modernity, a criterion that heightened the perceptions that colonialism had done some good and Belgian colonialism in Central Africa had been largely beneficent.

South Africa and the Congo cast shadows over an "innocent" continent, and American associations of whiteness and modernity with these racist regimes belied American professions of innocence. Yet, as many headlines as the crises of these countries captured, much of American interest in 1960s Africa focused elsewhere. In the dozens of newly independent nations, American representations of a "transitional" continent—whose African inhabitants were "transitional" personalities—framed a new American commitment to impart its missionary zeal. The Africa Eisenhower had dreaded and Bowles welcomed offered opportunities for the United States, and especially for a new field of academic study in close partnership with the state.

"Africa in Transition"

In 1960 Harold Isaacs, a scholar at the Center for International Studies (CIS) at the Massachusetts Institute of Technology (MIT), visited West Africa. Despite his credentials as the author of a major study of American images of Asia, Isaacs, like many other scholars, produced impressionistic writing about the newly awakened Africa. Like others at CIS, Isaacs was interested in modernization as a process that transformed the consciousness of individuals in the Third World. Therefore, he wrote of "the emergent African," an ideal type or composite of Africans embracing change and self-improvement. "The emergent African," Isaacs argued, shared with Americans a goal of "raising his people up and out of the swamps of backwardness." Beyond economic change, development meant cultural and social revolution. Isaacs assured readers that the emergent African "knows that a good part of their traditional culture will have to be swept out of their way." This epic transition he regarded as "the major content of the national and social revolutions now convulsing the greater part of the world. This is what all the shooting is really about."[1]

Decolonization, many Americans believed, would usher in more than independence and political freedom. Nation-states, national economies, national cultures animated by modern scientific knowledge and values would bring Africa fully into the present. This temporal revolution, abetted by American advice, promised to complete the world's transition from the epoch of European preeminence to the "American Century." Americans also believed this was what Africans wanted and how they defined freedom and aspirations for a better future. Theoretical models of nation building crept into middlebrow and official discourse about Africa. Like economic development or modernization, nation building was a process both linear and universal. Looking at the "new nations" of Africa, those Americans who had more or less absorbed the basic tenets and terminology of nation building saw promise. They imagined a modernization of African politics and governance as educated nationalist leaders gained control of the colonial state. Such modernizing leaders would strengthen the state, build a national economy, and above all, nurture a national—rather than ethnic or "tribal," religious or regional—identity uniting the Africans of that territory. As James Ferguson notes, however, there remained a "phantom that stalks 'nation-building'—the specter of premodern resurgences such as 'tribalism.'" The stakes were high. "'Development,' in such a view, is the natural reward for successful national integration, just as nation-building is the characteristic rhetoric of the developmental state."[2]

African nationalists shared many of these preoccupations, without, of course, the West's patronizing view of emergent or transitional Africans simply emulating Western modernity. Nation building and development were central to the stated goals of leaders and attained heightened importance among leaders of the most diverse African countries, such as Nigeria. Kwame Nkrumah and other nationalist leaders, upon taking the reins of the state, sought to consolidate their power. Chiefs or other regional, religious, or ethnic leaders beyond the central state represented a potential threat to both the political ambitions of the national rulers and the stated objective of nation building. Yet Africans often perceived nation building differently than Americans. For Western scholars, nation building meant transferring loyalty and identity from a tribe or region (for example, Asante) to a nation-state (Ghana). "For us," writes one African scholar, "the process of nation-building does not involve the transfer of 'commitments and loyalties' from narrow or parochial levels of ethnic groups to a larger political unit such as Nigeria. That you are an Igbo, a Yoruba, or a Kikuyu, is a matter of identity. You cannot transfer it. . . . For us it involves the widening (rather than transfer) of horizons of identity of parochial units to include larger units such as the state."[3]

The American misperception of African identities represented part of a larger confusion now evident after two generations of scholarship. As Ferguson observes, "Academic and nonacademic understandings of African societies and cultures have long misunderstood Africa's difference from the West as anachronistic relic; as somehow not really of the present; as a symptom of backwardness and incomplete development—in short, as 'tradition.'"[4] In the era of decolonization, American representations of Africa measured the presence or absence of "tradition" and "modernity," two abstractions the meanings of which were believed to be self-evident. The archetypal American news or travel account (often echoed in academic and official papers) during the "Decade of Development" stressed the manifest contradiction between modern dress, machines, buildings, cities, and other expressions of modern material and cultural progress, on one hand, and persistent "tradition" in many of the same categories. These contrasts struck American observers not merely because they offered snapshots that seemed to neatly encapsulate a narrative—"changing Africa," "Africa in transition," "Africa on the Move"— although that served the immediate purposes of quite a number of journalists, writers, and analysts. The juxtapositions resonated deeply because they signified a modernization process that, according to scholars, philanthropists, and officials, was universal, linear, inevitable. The modernization of Africa—entailing economic development, nation building, and the supplanting of traditional values and knowledge—required change in governments, economies, families, faiths.

Reacting to first impressions of Africa as a region of "new nations" with "old" cultures, Americans imagined African modernization in universal terms. As James Coleman argued in a retrospective essay, in the early years of African independence there was "an evangelical, American-dominated discipline of political science." It "launched upon a global quest for generalizations confirming the unity of mankind and the universal convergence toward a common destiny." These secular missionaries romanticized African nationalist leaders amidst "academic euphoria" induced by decolonization.[5] Such a wave of confidence and anticipation prompted grand statements. In 1959 the influential political scientist Karl Deutsch pronounced, "Countries are becoming somewhat less like Ethiopia and somewhat more like the United States." Viewing African affairs through this prism, Americans imagined the achievement in Africa of what "modern" societies elsewhere had. Modernity, whatever it actually is, functions as "a keyword that anchors a host of discussions in and out of the academy about an emerging global social order," writes Ferguson. This, as he acknowledges, has been so since the heyday of modernization theory. The gap in wealth and stability between the wealthy and the poor nations of the world was conceived as a difference in degrees of modernity. Countries in transition from static tradition were en route to modernity, the end point in time and development for all nations. "Modernity figures as a universal *telos* even for the most 'traditional' of societies."[6]

Within this restrictive conceptual framework, Americans understood the vicissitudes of African politics, economics, and society as part of the overall transition to modernity. Political scientist Rupert Emerson, a longtime analyst of comparative politics, argued that modernization was Westernization: "What makes 'modernization' modern is the ability to live, to think, to produce, to organize, in substantially the same fashion as the Western countries whose imperial hold has now been almost totally broken." Leaders of poor nations must adopt "modernization as defined by the Western model." Whatever else Africans pursued upon achieving independence, the "pressing need is to make a plausible adaptation to modernity. Survival is at stake, and in addition the climate of rising expectations can be satisfied only if there is development along modern lines." Emerson provided a succinct definition of modernity. While it might or might not entail Western-style democracy, it would "include a rise in material well-being, an expansion of education, and a political and administrative system which can maintain order at home and have some modicum of power in relation to the outside world even though the armed forces may well have more significance at home than abroad."[7]

African modernization required dynamic leaders, Americans believed. As one foreign policy analyst put it, Africa's "period of jet-speed" changes and "political telescoping" would propel the ascent of modernizing leaders. "Tribal chiefs who resist change are being shorn of authority by modern-minded politicians, who, before they have had time to develop into nineteenth century liberals on the Western model, find themselves already being crowded off the stage by trade-union leaders like Sékou Touré and Tom Mboya."[8] Indeed, Mboya appealed to Westerners to embrace the momentum of African nationalism and development. The Kenyan labor leader and charismatic politician, who toured the United States in 1956 and 1959, expressed the same determination and optimism about development. African political independence would, he argued, enable Africans to "meet the technological and scientific challenges of the twentieth century." For critics of rapid decolonization, Mboya offered a retort: "To suggest that this would lead to an overnight reversion to barbarity shows an utter disregard for history and the fact that Africa, despite her many temporary handicaps, lives in the twentieth century, receptive to all the influences of the attitudes and developments of the present."[9]

Many African Americans also found African tradition less captivating than the emergence of the continent's "modernizing middle class." Nkrumah and other "cultivated Africans," as *Ebony* referred to Western-educated elites, symbolized black progress. Most African American accounts of Africa during the period shared with whites' a fascination with what one contributor to the black journal *Phylon* neatly summarized as the "juxtaposition" between an "Old Africa" and a "New Africa." Decolonization and nationalist fervor had "created a 'New Africa'—without as yet destroying the old Africa." Their juxtaposition would persist, he predicted, "for a long time thanks to the many problems that hamper industrialization, impede Westernization, and retard the process of modernization." Like modernization theorists, the African American visitor to the continent was apt to perceive an Africa with a split temporal consciousness: part "clinging tenaciously to the past," part "wed to the present and looking hopefully to the future to which they appear doggedly oriented." Hugh and Mabel Smythe exemplified this interest in their research on the rising educated elite of Nigeria.[10]

If a source of pride for African Americans, men such as Mboya fascinated and inspired white Americans, too, often because of their perceived moderation and ability to transcend ethnicity. *Life* declared, "Tom Mboya is not only the outstanding political personality in Kenya but among the most important in all Africa."[11] Mboya's popularity in the United States owed a good deal to the image he cultivated as a political leader who had transcended ethnicity (tribalism). A Luo politician whose following came mostly from the Kikuyu in the Kenyan capital, Nairobi, he was seen by Westerners as "a rational, secular, thoroughly demystified" nation builder, particularly compared to the Kikuyu leaders, including Jomo Kenyatta, whom the British had accused of triggering the Mau Mau rebellion of the early 1950s. As General Secretary of the Kenya Federation of Labor from 1953 to 1963, and as a Parliamentarian representing Nairobi, Mboya in fact, used ethnicity rather than renounced it. His biographer David Goldsworthy argues that Mboya remained proud of his Luo ethnicity and "positive tribalism," by which he meant the "communality and generosity of traditional African life." What he rejected was a "negative tribalism" in which politicians used ethnicity for divisive purposes. Nevertheless, Americans saw Mboya as a straightforward repudiation of African tribalism and thus an exemplar of modernization, and this is largely how they reacted, at least initially to such African leaders as Nkrumah, Léopold Senghor of Senegal, and Tanzania's Julius Nyerere.[12]

The sociologist, pan-African, and peace activist St. Clair Drake argued for optimism about Africa by offering comparisons with the European experience of modernization.[13] Drake admitted that "social change in Africa has been traumatic and sometimes tragic." However, he argued, "There has been nothing anywhere to compare with the massive dislocation of social bonds and its consequences that Europe suffered during the Industrial Revolution" that had generated revolutions in France and Russia. African cities were not in "so bad" a shape as those of England during the era of Charles Dickens. Africans would not explode in revolutionary anger during the 1960s, predicted the sociologist Drake, because foreign aid and investment would provide "new schools and clinics, expanded scholarship programs, Africans occupying posts once held by white men, and similar gains to offset moods of disillusionment or doubt about the value of independence." Africa's transition to modernity, though bumpy, would not produce coups or "mass revolts" in the form of "crises of the kind that periodically shake the Middle East, Asia, and parts of Latin America," in part because African leaders could, for years to come, blame their nations' problems on the West, distracting their people. Like Chester Bowles, Drake argued that social upheaval in Africa would be tempered by the fact that African societies had no "landed aristocracy (except in isolated spots in Uganda, Nigeria, and Ethiopia). There is no poverty-stricken landless peasantry waiting to revolt." That a prominent black scholar advocated aid to Africa was unsurprising. However, the congruence between Drake's arguments and those of white Cold War liberals suggests the breadth of early 1960s American optimism and the widespread acceptance (beyond policy-oriented circles) of a popular version of modernization theory.[14]

Despite the perceived absence of feudalism in Africa, American optimism was never unalloyed. The New York Times Sunday Magazine published an essay on the African transition with the alarming title, "Africa Is Poised on the Razor's Edge." It analyzed recent events by relating them to Africans' "great promise" and the danger that "unresolved problems may lead them from crisis to chaos." Africa emerged from this overwrought account as "tremblingly poised on the razor's edge between peace and calamity—between one of the most inspiring possibilities of human liberation and progress in all history and one of the ugliest eventualities of chaos and international danger." If true, such claims implied an urgent need for American expertise on Africa. There would be no shortage of experts to step forward, eager to perform the function of "liberal mediator."[15]

Making African Studies

If modernizing, transitional Africa was undergoing a special version of a universal process, the kind of phenomenon requiring experts' guidance. Americans, too, needed expert guidance to understand the new Africa. Mennen Williams and others enjoined his countrymen to learn about Africa, to become expert about its needs. This need arose concurrent with the maturation of American Studies in the United States. "The disciplines within the field of American studies," notes Donald E. Pease, "intersected with the United States as a geopolitical area whose boundaries field specialists were assigned at once to naturalize and police." Just as American Studies cultivated a parochial interest in American exceptionalism and the nation-state, African Studies defined and regulated the boundaries of its object in ways that suited U.S. foreign policy.[16]

The postwar growth of area studies, combined with African decolonization, provided the spark for a rapid growth of African Studies programs. Ten new programs emerged in the United States during the 1950s, with forty in place by 1967. By that date, 260 professors in a number of disciplines specialized in Africa at U.S. colleges and universities and supervised over a thousand graduate students. Scholarly interest in the subject found support from an equally intrigued federal government, which funded the programs to the tune of $76 million for four hundred research and training projects from 1949 to 1964, and many millions of dollars from philanthropic foundations, especially the Ford Foundation. The African Studies Association, founded in 1957, included 1,400 members by 1966, and contributed to the growing number of academic publications covering Africa.[17] Moreover, the cross-fertilization between foundations, government agencies (some of the early Africanists had worked in Washington during or after World War II), and academe provided personnel as well as resources and ideas that made academic African Studies a prosperous field for nearly a generation.

A recent insurgent critique within African Studies by William G. Martin and Michael O. West draws our attention to the role of whiteness, the Cold War, and personalities in the making of this new field. The founders of the new African Studies programs were nearly all white men possessing Ph.D. training in disciplines such as history, anthropology, political science, and sociology. Martin and West expose the emergence of the Africanists' "creation narratives"—conventional accounts that declare Melville Herskovits and his colleagues the founders of American scholarship on Africa—which conceal the previous history of African American research and teaching, primarily at historically black colleges. W. E. B. Du Bois, Carter G. Woodson, William Leo Hansberry, and Ralph Bunche exemplified a tradition of writing about Africa to "vindicate" black culture and history. In essence, this search for an inspiring past—one that typically looked to precolonial empires such as the West African states of Ghana, Mali, and Songhay—illustrated the pan-African linkages any African history evokes. Moreover, it challenged the colonial-era conceit on both sides of the "White Atlantic" that Africans, as European imperialists claimed, had no history and no record of cultural achievements before their conquest in the late nineteenth century.[18] The "vindicationist" tradition posed a challenge to the narratives of innocence—both American and African—emerging in the era of decolonization. This intellectual tradition had long insisted that Africa had a history of material, cultural, and political achievement, one brutally interrupted by European colonialism. As one proponent of this understanding of African history put it in 1961, Africa had been "the cradle of civilization."[19] This, Martin and West suggest, is one reason why the foundations and the U.S. government found the rise of white-dominated African Studies so appealing, and why black scholars of the Pan-African or vindicationist tradition were excluded from grants, academic positions, and leadership in African Studies.

Africanists defined their field, and the political object of U.S. attention, as sub-Saharan Africa. In a pointedly programmatic statement, Herskovits, in the preface to his *Human Factor*, defined his subject as "the Subsaharan continent," a region demarcated by its common material and cultural "realities." North Africa, though geographically part of the continent, lay outside the essential cultural unity of sub-Saharan Africa, and Herskovits's analysis stressed cultural unity, not diversity.[20] Herskovits, "U-Thantish-looking, of medium height, perky and humorous," according to an admirer, founded the first major U.S. African Studies Center at Northwestern in 1948. Less than a decade later he became the first president of the African Studies Association (ASA), which continues to be the organizational home of American-based academic study of Africa. Founded in 1957 as an ostensibly "nonpolitical" organization, the ASA would "focus upon the problems of sub-Saharan Africa," according to a news release issued by the United States Information Agency.[21]

Herskovits took credit—"I was the hatchet man"—for blocking funding for W. E. B. Du Bois's ambitious project, *Encyclopedia Africana*, claiming, "Dr. Du Bois was not a 'scholar;' he was a 'radical' and a 'Negrophile.'" When Herskovits assumed the presidency of the ASA, he wrote the director of the

Central Intelligence Agency, Allen W. Dulles, to offer service: "The Association," he assured Dulles, "which represented the combined strength of those concerned with Africa in this country . . . would be happy to aid you in any way it can." Citing this letter from the Herskovits papers at Northwestern as evidence, Martin and West argue that the actions of the ASA's first president illustrates "the creation of a set of shared assumptions, agendas, and interchanges at the higher levels of the academy and private and public agencies."[22]

Something of the Northwestern scholar's commitment to American interests came through in his statement of motivation. "As far as I am concerned," he said, "I am interested in Africa not only because it is Africa, but because as a student of human behavior it provides me with a laboratory for the study of problems" evident around the world. Thus inspired by a vision of Africa as a laboratory, in September 1958 "the largest meeting of African specialists ever held on this side of the Atlantic" occurred at Northwestern. The first annual meeting of the ASA attracted over one hundred fifty U.S. scholars. The leaders of this new field agreed that more Africanists were needed for both academic and governmental tasks.[23] As Wallerstein recalls, he "was at that very moment in West Africa doing research on my dissertation with the aid of a Ford Foundation Fellowship."[24] Martin and West note that in 1983, Wallerstein, a former ASA president, contributed to the Africanist "creation narrative" by claiming that Herskovits had been "virtually" the only American scholar of Africa before 1945. As Martin and West comment, "Conspicuously absent from these narratives is any mention of more than a century of work by African American scholars" in the "vindicationist" tradition.[25]

African American anthropologist Elliot Skinner noted that when the ASA began, twelve of its thirty-six charter members were from foundations, government agencies, and missionary societies, individuals who "must have known that the ASA would involve more than scholarship." He also skewered Herskovits's claim, in his presidential address at the meeting, that Americans were ideally suited to study Africa objectively because they possessed "no territorial commitments in Africa" and enjoyed "a certain physical and psychological distance from the problems we study." Skinner marveled at Herskovits's ability to ignore how black members of the ASA had basic ties to Africa, as "Africa was in their skins." The ASA president also seemed to ignore "that as a white American he was a citizen of a country with a fatal flaw for continuing to discriminate against people with African skins. No commitments?"[26]

Herskovits and the white-led ASA divorced their subject from the African diaspora and defined Africa as sub-Saharan Africa, "a sharp break with the earlier generation of pan-African scholarship, which stressed ties across the boundaries of North Africa, sub-Saharan Africa, and the wider African world," according to Martin and West. This paradigm shift was more than academic, as it matched the reorganization of the State Department, which in 1958 created the African Bureau to focus on new independent nations as development aid clients and partners in the Cold War.[27] Indeed, Herskovits, seeking to seize the opportunity to gain for African Studies a voice in foreign policy and security in the form of federal patronage, submitted a study to the Senate Foreign Relations Committee in 1959 offering a series of recommendations for Africa policy. He urged the United States. to deepen its involvement in Africa—it "must treat Africa as a major policy area"—and "move beyond the compulsive preoccupation with Communist penetration that has so strongly motivated our actions." He suggested that "U.S. Government agencies should make maximum use of the growing body of knowledge about African societies gathered by nongovernmental institutions."[28] The Cold War orientation of the early American Africanists came through. "As every American with specialized knowledge of Africa has stressed," the report proclaimed, "there is little question that though Soviet advance in Africa has thus far been negligible, the countries of the Communist bloc can be expected to take every opportunity to fish in troubled waters." The United States therefore had a vital interest in taking steps to ensure that African leaders, inherently committed to a benign form of neutralism, "will remain friendly" and not "drift toward the Soviet orbit."[29]

Growing from its original membership of 35, the ASA by 1960 claimed 866 members, including 291 in the elite "College of Fellows" who alone could vote and serve on boards. By 1970 the total rose to 1,400, and the United States boasted approximately three dozen "major" African Studies programs, while such journals as *African Studies Bulletin* (renamed *African Studies Review*) emerged as major outlets for Africanist scholarship, joining such British-based journals as the *Journal of African History*. How did African Studies grow so rapidly? Funding from the foundations and Washington. Ford Foundation fellowships for African Studies, beginning as early as 1954, as well as Ford's ample donations to the ASA during its earliest years, joined the $76 million Washington devoted to African Studies in 1949–64. This growth was, as Martin and West note, "only one small part of a much larger agenda" of building expertise on world regions (area studies) during the Cold War. One ASA founder later admitted that the early African Studies programs were "originally designed somewhat as crash programs to create requisite numbers

of young African specialists for posts in government, industry or in international public and private agencies."[30]

That the ASA's research interests dovetailed with the strategic interests of
Washington seemed natural. According to Immanuel Wallerstein's summary
of the 1966 annual ASA meeting, the major research topics featured in panels
included contemporary politics, economic development (with an emphasis
on plans and projects), and such aspects of "modern social change" as nation
building and race relations.[31] U.S.-based Africanists' "construction of 'Africa'
as an intellectual object" differed greatly from the perspective of Europeans.
For Americans, the study of Africa would not be "part of larger imperial or
orientalist networks" but of Cold War–inspired area studies. By sealing off
Africa from European empires, this analytical shift to area studies—"sub-
Saharan Africa"—also severed historical, cultural, and political connections
between Africa and its diaspora. Africanists would not study or encourage
such ties any more than they would larger imperial systems. Theirs was to
be an Africa of smaller units, "the emergent nation-states model preferred by
political science and the other social sciences dedicated to national integration and development."[32] The Africanist fascination with the process of modernization and the analytical task of evaluating African societies and individuals in terms of their modernity shaped the relationship between the
"liberal mediators," Washington, and Africa. As late as 1966, the president of
the ASA could address his colleagues and "assume that there would be general
agreement that one of the fundamental issues—I am inclined to think that it
is probably the fundamental issue—is adjustment to the modern world." Such
adjustment, for Africans, was "not really a matter of choice for the new countries but an essential condition for survival, or, if not quite of survival, at least
for doing more than sullenly vegetating and perhaps rotting away in some
remote corner."[33]

As African Studies expanded as an academic field and consolidated its linkages to the state and foundations, individuals could move from one sector to
the other. An example of this is Waldemar A. Nielsen. A Rhodes Scholar,
economist, and political scientist in New York, Nielsen worked in the 1940s
as a researcher in the U.S. Department of Agriculture, the State Department,
the Commerce Department, and the Marshall Plan before joining the Ford
Foundation. In 1961 the 44-year-old executive of the Ford Foundation "and
a specialist in the problems of world educational and cultural development"
became president of the African American Institute (AAI).[34] The AAI, founded
in 1953, was a predominately white-led private organization devoted to

assisting African education and training. It created in Washington an "Africa House" to accommodate African students as it expanded its scholarships and exchange programs. A recipient of grants from the Ford Foundation, the Rockefeller Brothers Fund, and the Carnegie Corporation, AAI conceived of itself as "the central private American agency in African-American relations." At the Ford Foundation in the 1950s Nielsen worked on grants for the development of the U.S. social sciences and academic exchange programs. In 1961, he worked as a consultant to the State Department on cultural and educational issues before assuming the AAI presidency. An active participant in the Council on Foreign Relations, Nielsen carried his official contacts and access with him to AAI, where he succeeded Emory Ross, a missionary in Africa. This marked a transition for AAI. Nielsen approached his AAI work with a Cold War perspective, having published an article warning that Soviet and Communist Bloc technical assistance programs in the Third World seemed moderately effective in promoting Soviet prestige and influence, a message that— sharing the secular missionary premise of *The Ugly American*—implied the need for a vigorous American response.[35]

Africa Report, begun in 1956 by AAI, became in the 1960s the major Africa-related publication in the United States. By the mid-sixties, the magazine had become a kind of *Life* for Africa, combining its core of semi-academic articles and book reviews with abundant photos and advertisements. The monthly by this time ran approximately fifty to sixty pages per issue, carrying articles from an array of academics, journalists, and other close observers of what was then known as "the African scene." Reportedly selling 10,000 copies per month worldwide, the magazine, according to editor Helen Kitchen, relied on financial support from the AAI, but its contributors' views did not necessarily reflect those of the organization. *Africa Report*, she asserted, remained "primarily concerned with reporting the facts and understanding the dynamics of political, economic, and cultural developments in present day Africa." Kitchen, a member of the ASA, eschewed an explicit ideological framework, arguing "it is unrealistic to try to fit the countries and personalities of a transitional, revolutionary Africa into solidly fixed ideological or operational categories." The magazine, therefore, set as its primary goal promoting an understanding of African change without "projecting into them American stereotypes, mores, or expectations."[36]

While many of the articles and reviews in *Africa Report* expressed the conventional viewpoint of modernization theory and the Washington-oriented outlook, the magazine received strong praise from South African writer Lewis

Nkosi. Noting the transformation from a four-page newsletter in 1956 to a magazine that, less than a decade later, included subscribers "from Dean Acheson and Walter Lippmann to students and scholars, from African militants to" Soviet scholars, Nkosi admired the quality of writing and depth of coverage found in *Africa Report*.[37]

The growth of such a publication reflected the intensity of American interest in African affairs, though its content failed to challenge the mainstream perspective. *Africa Report* carried an ASA-inflected news coverage, political analysis, and cultural criticism to an audience fluent in the conceptual vernacular of the foundations, academe, the arts, and foreign policy. Yet the magazine also—in spite of Nkosi's encomium—illustrated the power of whiteness in America's discovery of postcolonial Africa. By the end of the decade, however, *Africa Report* seemed less benign to critics on the Left. When a group of insurgents within African Studies published a withering attack on the field, it mocked the AAI publication—a "slick establishment journal all fitted out with airline adverts and a subsidy from a para-government agency"—in a pamphlet called *Africa Retort*. To these critics, radicalized by the Vietnam War, the magazine offered little but "pseudo-reportage . . . a pretentious editorial or two, or perhaps the latest views of the CIA."[38]

Although such critiques ripened only at the end of the 1960s, AAI met more immediate resistance from black critics. Despite its efforts to promote African education and American knowledge of Africa, AAI drew criticism from some African Americans for its overwhelmingly white membership. In 1959, the *New York Age* attacked its nearly all-white leadership and lamented "the appalling lack of an effective antidote to the African-American Institute," as no large or active black-led organization could match AAI's resources and influence to offer a distinctly black perspective on Africa.[39] Such a complaint reflected the frustration of those critics who recognized that African American visions of Africa could not emerge untouched by a white lens. W. E. B. Du Bois lamented, "Today the American interest in Africa is almost confined to whites. African history is pursued in white institutions . . . while Negro authors and scholars have shied away from the subject" as a new generation of black leaders distanced themselves from Du Bois's brand of Pan-Africanism.[40]

Black Diplomacy

African Americans did, of course, attempt to influence Washington's African policies. However, the absence of a powerful, unified black perspective or institutional setting limited the African American impact on Africa discourse in the United States and on African policy. One of the few U.S.-based black organizations devoted specifically to African issues, the American Society of African Culture (AMSAC), created in the mid-fifties and affiliated with the Paris-based organization that published *Presénce Africaine*, evolved as "a more culturally oriented" organization devoted to raising sympathetic awareness of African culture. Among the Society's founders were Duke Ellington, Langston Hughes, James W. Ivy, editor of the NAACP's *Crisis*, and Thurgood Marshall. A key figure in AMSAC, political scientist John A. Davis of City College of New York, explained the group's interest in promoting awareness of what he called "the high culture of Africa. . . . This work has aimed at providing a sense of worth among American Negroes and Africans, a basis for respect from whites, and a basis for continental pan-Africanism." As historian James Meriwether observes, such a cultural enterprise—"an intellectually elite organization"—could exert little influence even among African Americans on African policy issues. Moreover, AMSAC received—without many of its members' knowledge—funds from the Central Intelligence Agency for over a decade. It became, therefore, a victim of Washington's ongoing and covert cultural Cold War, as the agency funded also AAI and the Congress of Cultural Freedom.[41]

In 1962 a group of top civil rights leaders, including Martin Luther King Jr., A. Philip Randolph, Roy Wilkins, and James Farmer, founded the American Negro Leadership Conference on Africa (ANLC). They intended to help shape American policy. As Farmer argued, "As Americans of African descent, we felt we should take the lead in interpreting for America what was happening in Africa and also in explaining to Africans what was happening in America." Although this sounded like a black version of the liberal mediator role of secular missionaries, ANLC proved not very ambitious. Though it urged a "Marshall Plan for Africa," it did not dissent from the basic premises of the Kennedy approach to Africa or the prevailing American vision of modernization and Americanization in Africa. ANLC sought more high-level attention and more money for Africa, differing from Kennedy by degree, not in kind. Moreover, ANLC lobbied as much for greater racial diversity within the Department of State as it did for a more forward African policy. This priority was well founded. As Michael Krenn has demonstrated, the whiteness of the State Department changed little through the eight-year tenure of Secretary of State Dean Rusk. Beyond Ralph Bunche, few blacks implemented American foreign policy. The situation in the field was little better. In 1966 a USAID official traveling in Africa reported to Washington the continued paucity of minorities working in USAID, USIA, and State Department positions in Africa. As an internal report in 1965 pointed out, "At the 40 AF posts to which Americans are assigned there are a total of 21 Negro officers in State, 25 in USIA, 36 in AID, and 21 in the Peace Corps. Twenty-six of the 40 posts have no Negro officers at all. At the 4 posts visited by Bill Hall, we have 2 Negro officers in the Congo, 1 in Nigeria, 2 in Ethiopia and none in the Sudan."[42]

Ultimately, ANLC wielded little influence. Distracted by the freedom struggle at home and then by Vietnam, it never developed momentum and a clear agenda to institutionalize a distinct black voice in American policymaking. As Brenda Gayle Plummer notes, even Bunche could do little to promote such a goal. His status as an American representative at the United Nations and his opposition to militant African American politics in the mid-sixties left him out of touch with rapidly evolving African American sentiment.[43] Perhaps the biggest reason ANLC and Bunche failed to create a black lobby was that President Lyndon B. Johnson staunchly opposed the idea. The president who shepherded the Civil Rights and Voting Rights Acts through Congress also demanded black support for the Vietnam War and other Cold War policies. When Roy Wilkins told a White House aide that black leaders wanted to meet with Johnson to give him some advice on how to avoid missing "opportunities" in Africa, he learned of Johnson's aversion to the symbolism of such a meeting. Wilkins agreed to "explore the matter quietly and discreetly" with administration officials.[44] In response, Johnson told aides to talk to the black leaders but to discourage their identification with African issues. One aide summarized the president's views:

> He doesn't think it at all a good idea to encourage a separate Negro view of foreign policy. We don't want an integrated domestic policy and a segregated foreign policy. The President recognizes the American Negro community's natural interest in African affairs but doesn't think they should make it their special province. They shouldn't become a special interest group but should be interested in the totality of US policy as Americans. In short, I get loud and clear that the President wants to discourage emergence of any special Negro pressure group (a la the Zionists) which might limit his freedom of maneuver.[45]

When it appeared that African American leaders would form a new organization devoted to lobbying the U.S. government on Africa policy, Ulric Haynes argued, "If there is an inevitable trend toward the emergence of a major private organization interested in US policy toward Africa (which may be the case), we should guide this toward a non-racial outcome, i.e. it should include whites as well as Negroes."[46] Thus, well-positioned African Americans supportive of Johnson helped delay the inevitable rise of a vocal black lobby on Africa. In so doing, they eased pressure on Washington to accede to African demands for economic sanctions or other measures to promote black liberation in South Africa, Rhodesia, and Portugal. Historian Kevin Gaines points out how the Cold War liberalism of the Kennedy-Johnson years undermined black solidarity across the Atlantic. George Ball, one of the architects of Kennedy and Johnson's diplomacy, spoke for Cold War liberals when he dismissed blacks' interest in Africa and their own African identity as a "cruel joke" on a people who should identify wholly with the United States. Those who shared Ball's views, writes Gaines, "arrogated to themselves the role of prescribing normative Negro American civic identities, seeking to delegitimize and discourage transnational solidarities for black Americans," a move that "epitomized the racially circumscribed nature of the citizenship extended to African Americans during the 1960s."[47]

While African Americans struggled to organize, the predominantly white ASA had no trouble being heard in Washington. With the election of Kennedy, the identification of African Studies with the U.S. state reached its zenith. Africanists served in a variety of official and unofficial capacities as the New Frontier set its sights on Africa, and Washington joined the foundations in cultivating the maturation of African Studies. In 1962 Kennedy sent the ASA a telegram in honor of the fifth annual meeting. The president's message declared American support for "African goals and aspirations," particularly self-determination and economic development. "We Americans," Kennedy explained, "must seek to understand their reasonable needs and their problems. We must explain to Africans our rational policies and interests." The ASA's research "has helped to illuminate the African continent," making possible the U.S.–African collaboration sought by Washington.[48] The president of the ASA, political scientist Vernon McKay, heaped praise on Kennedy's point man on Africa, Assistant Secretary of State Mennen Williams, as "a good friend of our association." Endorsing Williams's agenda and method of diplomacy, McKay celebrated him for having "the kind of warm and outgoing personality that the administration needs for its dealings with the young leaders of Africa." Williams's "genial and unorthodox shirt-sleeve diplomacy," McKay assured Africanists, "has won many African friends for the United States." Williams had made a member of the ASA's College of Fellows,

Wayne Fredericks of the Ford Foundation, his Deputy Assistant Secretary while naming "twenty Fellows of this Association to a new forty member non-governmental Advisory Council on African Affairs," illustrating the partnership between Washington, the foundations, and the ASA. No wonder that McKay declared Williams had "done more than any other American to establish the kind of rapport we need in order to deal effectively with the new leaders of Africa."[49] The ASA shared with U.S. officials a felt need to "deal effectively" with the societies that constituted their object of study. In no way did McKay or other ASA officers seem to consider their collaboration with Washington as reminiscent of imperial ties between missionaries, social scientists, technicians, and colonial officials.[50] McKay was right to note the significance of Fredericks, a former executive for Kellogg's whose business and travel experience in Southern Africa led him to the African program of the Ford Foundation. There, he developed policy expertise on Africa, feeding information and ideas to Democrats such as Bowles, Stevenson, and Kennedy. When in 1961 he joined Williams at the State Department, they shared a determination to establish the African Bureau as a major voice in the Kennedy administration.[51]

African scholars did not uncritically accept the concepts of their American counterparts, and many rejected or ignored works that propounded modernization as a universal process unaffected by local culture.[52] Nor did African political leaders, artists, intellectuals, students, or other citizens merely embrace modernization as an unalloyed American import. No one could have more eloquently refuted Western claims that Africa lacked a rich precolonial heritage than the Nigerian novelist Chinua Achebe, in his deeply influential debut, Things Fall Apart (1958). Achebe's classic postcolonial novel brought home to Western readers the cultural disruption and casual violence caused in Africa by missionaries and colonial officials. African literature flourished during the 1960s, and it boasted new periodicals such as the Kampala, Uganda-based journal Transition, which featured essays and creative writing by East African writers along with African and American notables such as Achebe, Baldwin, and Tanzanian leader Julius Nyerere.[53]

In politics and diplomacy, Kennedy and his successor would find African national leaders—Nkrumah is the preeminent example here—anything but malleable, "innocent" Africans ready as clay to be molded on an American wheel. As soon as the Gold Coast won its independence from Britain, Nkrumah redefined Ghanaian nationalism. "From now on it must be Pan-African nationalism, and the ideology of African political consciousness and

African political emancipation must spread throughout the whole continent, into every nook and corner of it."[54] The constitution of Nkrumah's Convention People's Party, Africa's first effective nationalist political party and the spearhead of Ghana's independence, declared the party's international goals unequivocally. It sought the end of "imperialism, colonialism, racialism, tribalism, and all forms of national and racial oppression and economic inequality among nations, races and peoples and to support all action for World Peace." African leaders may have sought modernization, but this was not deemed incompatible with revolutionary struggle.[55]

Despite African resistance, the importance of the achievements of the cultural work of (primarily white) Americans interested in Africa at the beginning of the 1960s must be grasped. In just a few years, this body of writing, teaching, and speaking about Africa—derived from increasing travel and other forms of personal experience, Cold War concerns, and the rise of a new institutional intertwining of foundations, academe, and the state—had invoked a broad (if not deep) consciousness of African affairs in a country that had historically devoted scant explicit attention to the region. This newfound interest, bolstered by institutional development, publications specializing in Africa, and distinctive tropes of a rising, "transitional" Africa ripe for transformation and American tutelage, framed the emergence of a new American Cold War mission in Africa. To clear the path for Washington policymakers, America's "mandarins of the future" and Africanist secular missionaries needed to articulate how modernization theory and nation building could become an American "foreign policy doctrine."[56]

Mennen Williams's memoir, *Africa for the Africans*, featured on the cover an image of a black man wearing a Western suit, a brief case in one hand and a spear in the other, adorned in African ear hoops, necklace, and pendant and shod in sandals. Here was the "transitional" African, the "man of two worlds," as first-generation educated Africans were known.[1] Secular missionaries like Williams earnestly sought the salvation of this transitional African. American expertise, technology, and capital, they believed, could ensure the successful African adaptation to modernity. That the transitional African was an archetype based on sweeping generalizations rather than a specific, concrete knowledge of Africans bothered few Americans. This African's homeland represented, for Americans au courant with modernization theory, nation building and the imperatives of Cold War diplomacy, an ideal laboratory.

"A 'Doctrine' for Africa"

American scholars offered a wide array of suggestions, recommendations, and proposals in fulfillment of their mediating role. Modernization theory, having coalesced into a powerful worldview, complete with ambitious academic (theoretical) and policy (foreign aid) agendas, supplied the overarching context for American prescriptions. Even as late as the 1970s, a critic in *Comparative Studies in Society and History* could complain of "modernization" that "the popularity of the term does not appear to be matched by any widespread consensus concerning its precise meaning."[2] Modernization theory and its profound impact on the social sciences and American foreign policy have, over the past decade, been exhaustively investigated by historians.[3] Economic change in poor nations prompted the attention post–World War II scholars in several disciplines devoted to devising an inclusive theory that accounted for growth across cultural and temporal divisions. At its most basic level, the modernization theory that crystallized in the late 1950s offered an explanation for the quantum leap from stagnancy to what became known as "self-sustaining growth," a dynamic condition also called modern. Modernization theory figured newly independent nations as "transitional societies," countries that had experienced halting steps toward development (evidenced by their Western-educated elites, nationalist—rather than tribal—politics, and "modern" sectors of the economy such as mining or cash-cropping). These societies, however, continued to feature "traditional" economic and social institutions and practices such as low-productivity patterns of work (particularly subsistence farming), the authority of chiefs or landlords, and seemingly timeless beliefs and customs incompatible with individualism and a cash economy.

Beyond economics, modernization theory encompassed broader change. Frederick Cooper refers to "the most incisive tenet of modernization theory; its insistence that modernity constituted a package." This, perhaps, accounts for the popularity of the theory and scholars' sense that it could provide an overall paradigm. For "modernization signified a series of co-varying changes, from subsistence to market economies, from subject to participant political culture, from ascriptive status systems to achievement status systems, from extended to nuclear kinship, from religious to secular ideology." In fact, "Modernization theory was both analytic and normative, its insistence on the historical inevitability of modernization its most powerful argument for jumping on the bandwagon."[4]

Among modernization theorists, none articulated this sense of modernity as "a package" more clearly than the sociologist and international communications expert Daniel Lerner. The author of the influential study *The Passing of Traditional Society: Modernizing the Middle East* (1958), Lerner invoked Karl Marx's assertion in *Das Kapital*: "The country that is more developed industrially only shows, to the less developed, the image of its own future." For the American social scientist a century later, Marx's vision—if not his philosophy—rang true. The future of what were commonly known as "underdeveloped," "less developed" or "Third World" countries must, Lerner and his colleagues believed, eventually converge with that of the United States and other wealthy nations at a common level of economic, social, and political modernity. Lerner defined modernity as the national possession of five "salient characteristics" (operational values). These included "self-sustaining growth" in the economy; "political participation;" "secular-rational norms in the culture;" personal "mobility in the society—understood as personal freedom of physical, social, and psychic movement;" and a "personality transformation" appropriate to a society that rewards "striving," as well as "empathy."[5]

Though emanating from academe, modernization theory was, from the first, a project important to the state. In 1951 the federal government gained a powerful new weapon in the intellectual Cold War. At MIT, the government's ongoing efforts to fund projects in psychological warfare against the Soviets culminated in the establishment of the Center for International Studies. Former CIA official and MIT economist Max F. Millikan founded CIS and gathered an all-star lineup of cutting-edge social scientists eager to participate in a think tank motivated by academic ambition and anti-Communist zeal. Such luminaries of the 1950s and '60s social science as Lerner, Walt Rostow, and political scientist Lucien Pye developed their theories collaboratively at CIS. While receiving CIA funds for research that could be applied to anti-Soviet initiatives, CIS also drew support from the major foundations for what became the centerpiece of its mission, studying and prescribing U.S. policy toward the "developing" or "underdeveloped" world. An economic historian, prolific writer, and successful self-promoter, Rostow imparted the greatest confidence and accessibility to the ideas percolating at CIS. "No other living economic historian," commented a colleague, "occupies a similar position. Indeed, one would probably have to go back to Karl Marx—with whom Rostow likes to compare himself—to find an equally prominent member of our profession, and Marx achieved his greatest fame posthumously." His most crucial contribution posited five "stages of economic growth," a successive series of transformations for societies surging forward in time from a traditional stage to the "preconditions stage," then the pivotal "take-off stage," followed by the happy "drive to maturity" and, ultimately, the conclusive "age of high mass consumption." *The Stages of Economic Growth* (1960) cemented this ambitious concept at the heart of modernization theory, and provided policymakers an accessible framework for thinking about economic change in the "underdeveloped" world. Rostow's opus served as a capstone to a productive decade in which he emerged as the most influential modernization theorist.[6]

The pivotal stage of growth—and the one enjoying the greatest notoriety in the 1960s—Rostow labeled "take-off." He defined this as the historic stage in which a nation, having achieved the "preconditions" for self-sustaining growth—ample industrialization, growing investment—makes its definitive break with its traditional past. "Take-off," writes Mark H. Haefele, "was a twenty-to-thirty year process of industrial revolution that led to the final stage, self-sustaining growth." At least, that was what Rostow first claimed. In later works, he shortened the process to a "decade or two," which raised hopes that the United States need only provide aid for nations at that stage of growth for a brief period. As historian Nick Cullather notes, Rostow's invocation of an aeronautical metaphor "highlighted not only his sense of the sharpness of the transition, a change in both the kind and direction of growth, but also the dangers of this stage, for it is at the moment of takeoff that crosswinds, mechanical flaws, or pilot error are most likely to prove fatal." A transitional society entering this stage could be disrupted by nationalist or Communist upheaval caused by the sudden and disorienting changes wrought by the early phases of modernization.[7]

The Emerging Nations (1961), largely the work of Millikan, distilled the CIS vision of modernization theory as the "conceptual framework" for American Cold War policy in "transitional nations." While Stages of Economic Growth garnered a wide readership and popularized Rostow's version of modernization theory, Emerging Nations more directly bridged the gap between theory and practice. First submitted as a report to the U.S. Senate Foreign Relations Committee, the book reflected the collaboration of several CIS scholars, a kind of state-of-the-art treatise.[8] The book's preface offered a bold assertion intended to provide a Cold War rationale for a major new American commitment to foreign aid: "Outside the Communist bloc, more than a billion human beings accustomed to life in the setting of traditional society are now learning to adapt themselves to the requirements of modern life." Awakened, apparently, from an immemorial slumber, "more than a billion human beings" lived in transitional societies adapting to modernity. This, rather than their struggle to end vestiges of colonialism and racism, and economic inequality in the world, mattered most. Since "the passing of traditional societies seems inevitable," what mattered—particularly for the United States—was "the results of the transitional process." To ensure that the process would not be derailed by Communist subversion, an active American intervention was needed, and Washington could draw on its extensive economic and cultural resources. "American technology penetrates the most remote areas. American political philosophy is studied widely; its culture and values are carried by modern communications into every society."[9]

Where did Africa fit in this vision of American-led modernization? According to Millikan and Rostow in *A Proposal* (1957), some "African regions" would require "a decade or more before the preconditions for effective investment on any scale are established." If a correct assessment of African conditions, this ruled out the utility of a massive infusion of Western capital: Africa lacked "absorptive capacity." Instead, the poorest countries needed Western personnel, assistance in education and developing policy planning, and other "basic infrastructure facilities" (the latter, however, sounding suspiciously like a job for capital).[10] As Haefele notes, one of the great appeals of Rostow's stages theory is that it solved the "bewildering complexity to U.S. foreign relations" caused by the sudden emergence of so many independent nations. He gave policymakers "a system that imposed order on this chaos because, in his model, all nations were merely at different points on the same development path." The dozens of African nations made this a pressing matter. *Stages of Economic Growth* devoted little space to Africa, aside from its observation that the Belgian Congo and white-ruled Southern Rhodesia were "enclave economies" featuring two of the three "conditions" necessary for economic "take-off." Both colonies possessed export-oriented industries that fueled "a rise in the rate of productive investment . . . to over 10% of national income," and "the development of one or more substantial manufacturing sectors, with a high rate of growth." However, most of Rostow's arguments were intended to apply to the entire "developing" world. "The non-Communist literate elites in these transitional societies bear a heavy responsibility for the future of their peoples," Rostow declared. While right to expect aid from the West, these leaders "must focus their minds on the task of development" and eschew international adventures and "the distractions of the Cold War."[11]

Rostow spoke on African development in an address before AMSAC, published in the liberal periodical *Africa Today*.[12] Before an audience far better versed in African affairs than he, the self-confident modernization theorist offered advice in the best fashion of a secular missionary. Invoking the optimistic theme of African innocence, he contended that Africa had entered "the world of modern technology relatively late in the game," and therefore could learn from the experiences of other nations. Studying these "Lessons of History," Africans could "make the transition to modernization a more humane and efficient process than it has been in any of the other parts of the world where this has occurred or is now taking place." Africans in "transitional societies" needed to begin "training quickly and massively a new modern generation of African men and women," meaning education must be the top priority. The next priority should be agriculture. Raising food production would feed the cities and give farmers the cash to become consumers. "An industrial revolution without an agricultural revolution," warned Rostow, "is a dead end." Here the American theorist dismissed the aspirations of most African leaders to promote rapid industrialization. This, perhaps, was unsurprising, as Rostow had previously criticized Communist nations' neglect of agriculture as a prerequisite to industrialization. In the long run, African industrialization should follow the unlikely example of Sweden. Rostow argued that the Scandinavian country had become wealthy "by exploiting to the hilt a few rich natural resources," such as timber and iron ore, which it exported but also refined. That the Swedes had not had to overcome a heritage of colonial exploitation and massive cultural disruption caused by foreign invasion and conquest Rostow did not acknowledge.[13]

Not content to proffer this unusual advice, Rostow insisted that African leaders embrace the depoliticization of development. Africa's "newly released energies" should be channeled into modernization and not world politics. Taking a lesson from post-1868 Japan, Africans should avoid the temptation to become embroiled in the Cold War and focus instead on "concrete tasks of modernization" that would culminate in national unity and national identity. As a "historian," Rostow advised African leaders: "make modernization the first order of business." Since African societies were mostly in Rostow's "preconditions" stage of development, their eventual economic take-off first required a strong government, and that meant leaders serious about development. Those African leaders fascinated with continent-wide African unity must realize that unity could not be "a substitute for the hard tasks of modernization at the local level." Development, according to Rostow, was a national affair, and only after its success would the unity of African nations be meaningful. That this meant reifying Africa's artificial national boundaries—relics of colonialism—and the handicaps they imposed on transportation and communication (at a time when it was easier for Africans to make phone calls to Britain or France than to their African neighbors) Rostow did not admit. The political and cultural case for African unity meant little to the economic historian. "Although the impulse towards African unity may have deep emotional, racial, and cultural roots," lectured Rostow, only economic criteria mattered.[14]

Rostow's prescriptions, drawn from a highly selective reading of economic history, presumed African development required material and cultural modernization; education, farming, strategic industrialization, he suggested, all required sober statesmanship from the top. After becoming a policymaker himself, Rostow continued to insist upon the value of the "non-capital side" of aid, arguing that Western technical assistance rather than capital would best promote Africa's thrust through the "preconditions" stage. "If we can get first-rate scientists into the foreign aid program," declared Rostow, "we may give it a very important new look." Nevertheless, in Africa "and other relatively primitive cases," there must be "rather extensive dams, transport facilities, and other elements of the foundation for a modern society." That this kind of investment would necessarily prove costly for any donor—to say nothing of African governments attempting to pay for them—proved a contradiction so near the heart of Rostow's prescriptions for Africa that he seems to have been unaware of it.[15] Rostow's mixture of great confidence in the utility of American development assistance and a general apathy toward Africa ultimately shaped the contradictory U.S. aid policies of the decade.. Surveying the prospects for new nations in 1961, Rostow believed "the West has some chance of developing over a period of years an Africa which would present us with only modest military and political dangers, and which might, in time, form a constructive part of the Western system."[16]

The Kennedy administration, many of whose members—Rostow, in particular—came to power with considerable experience with modernization theory in academe and the foundations, believed development and nation building the solution to the problems that seemed to make "underdeveloped" regions vulnerable to Communism. As Kennedy stated in an address to Congress, "the economic collapse of those free but less-developed nations which now stand poised between sustained growth and economic chaos would be disastrous to our national security, harmful to our comparative prosperity and offensive to our conscience." Fortunately, he argued—drawing directly on the confidence and jargon of modernization theorists—the 1960s provided "an historic opportunity for a major economic assistance effort by the free industrialized nations to move more than half the people of the lesser-developed nations into self-sustained economic growth, while the rest move substantially closer to the day when they, too, will no longer have to depend on outside assistance." To "move" that mass of humanity toward the economic goals identified by modernization theorists, Kennedy proposed a reorganization of U.S. economic aid (the creation of the United States Agency for International Development, USAID) to oversee a major new aid effort. That aid effort would help "the southern half of the globe" achieve progress and "help make a historical demonstration that . . . economic growth and political democracy can develop hand in hand." The president thus promised "the crucial 'Decade of Development'—the period when many less-developed nations make the transition into self-sustained growth," at which time the new nations would no longer require aid.[17] Thus committed to modernizing much of the world, the Kennedy presidency naturally became the first to devote significant attention and resources to Africa. During the presidential transition after Kennedy's election, a group of his advisors concluded that development could be conceived as an answer to "the most important job facing us," which they defined as "developing a 'doctrine' for Africa—an integrated approach responsive to long-term trends, rather than a hit-or-miss reaction to particular problems."[18]

Development discourse certainly provided such theoretical content and accompanying jargon appropriate to a "doctrine." The Kennedy administration hoped to use development assistance to "provide incentives to the new African leadership to involve itself constructively in the evolution of the free world community rather than either withdrawing into isolation" or, of course, succumbing to Communism. American officials and intelligence analysts in 1961 approached this task with a mixture of missionary zeal and apprehension. As one internal assessment warned, "moving almost overnight from tribal to modern societies" would be a wrenching process for Africans. A major memo within the African Bureau at the beginning of Mennen Williams's tenure called on the administration to draw on the expertise of the best "sociologists, anthropologists, political scientists, psychologists, economists" and others to help manage "the explosive, volatile and underdeveloped aspects of African societies."[19] This belief that Africans in "transitional societies" had only just begun to escape "tribal" life reflected the influence of the "stages of growth" criteria for ranking national development. As one Harvard professor and advisor to the Kennedy transition pointed out, India and some Latin American nations were generally held to be significantly more developed than most African countries. Therefore, their needs for economic aid would differ considerably from those of "a primitive country like Libya, Somalia, or the non-urban, non-mining parts of tropical Africa."[20] What mattered, then, was to use the Rostovian categories to determine what modernization theory described as a nation's "absorptive capacity"; those with greater capacity should receive more capital.

Though Rostow sought some limits to American aid to Africa by linking it to the criteria of absorptive capacity and seeking burden-sharing contributions from other Western nations, the narratives of innocence and faith in modernization theory so characteristic of the early 1960s ensured that a big effort would be attempted. Political scientists, in particular, imagined aid for African development as inevitable and crucial. In political science, Africanists contributed to modernization theory in some of the early classics of the field.[21] As one political scientist noted in 1961, an "early consensus" had been reached among American observers on Africa's need for major external aid for development, "and on the massive effort which the United States will have to make to get things rolling in this post-colonial era." America's Cold War interests in Africa depended upon the U.S ability to inspire Africans as a symbol of modernity. Another political scientist argued, "If the United States is to retain any influence on that continent, it must become synonymous with hope and with progress." American aid must help Africans attack "poverty, disease, illiteracy" by moving "from puny, piecemeal and political measures to massive developmental programs of true war-effort proportions."[22] Such an effort meant mobilizing political science. In 1964, the theme of the American Political Science Association's annual meeting was "Africa in Motion." Addressing scholars interested in transitional Africa, Edmond C. Hutchinson, Assistant Administrator for Africa in USAID, gave a talk titled "American Aid to Africa." Hutchinson, himself a Ph.D., illustrated the tendency among scholars and officials to substitute impressionistic rhetoric for precise analysis. Decolonization, he argued, "reinforced by new dignity and national pride, has released great new energy. It has spawned a drive for modernization and better living. Nearly everywhere in Africa progress is being made in nation-building. . . ." While deploying such middlebrow rhetoric about African "energy," Hutchinson also invoked the high priest of modernization theory, stating that most African nations belonged in "that grouping which Walt Rostow describes as 'societies at a relatively early stage of what I would call the preconditions period.'" American aid would flow to these nations as they focused their abundant "energy" on modernizing their social, economic, and political institutions.[23]

Mennen Williams, in particular, repeatedly sounded the call to act. African governments were, he argued, "in a race with time and the expectations of the African peoples." Development had to satisfy rising demands for a better life to provide the new national governments with legitimacy.[24] "Every single government" in Africa, argued Williams, "is going to stand or fall" based on the "belly," meaning a clear demonstration of an "improvement of the standard of living." He warned, "Time is running out on us. We have some six to eighteen months to demonstrate by action our commitment."[25] This time frame, considerably smaller than that of Rostow's "take-off," imparted a sense of urgency. Williams groped for "a 'big idea' for Africa," such as an "Education for Africa" package designed to ensure at least four years of schooling for "every child in Africa." This matched civil rights aide Harris Wofford's message that "Africa requires the kind of enlarged, concentrated support that the Alliance for Progress was designed to give Latin America." The key, he argued, lay in "a massive program of education on all levels" to eliminate illiteracy and establish sound educational systems in Africa. That no such program ever emerged did not mean that the impulse to think and act on such a scale made no difference. Precisely because African nations tended, in most cases, to be smaller and at ostensibly lower "stages of growth" than their counterparts in other world regions, Americans imagined themselves capable of making a profound difference even with aid on a scale something short of an Alliance for Progress or a Marshall Plan for Africa.[26]

Something was at stake for American interests. In words of an earlier administration policy paper, "the United States . . . probably cannot 'win' Africa" as a regional ally, though it "could, by failing to put forward a major effort, 'lose' Africa by default."[27] Wofford developed a particularly strong urge to activism in Africa. In a memo to the president, he argued that if the United States moved "on a big scale" in Africa, it would discover that "there is literally a continent to win—not to win as allies, necessarily, but to win for freedom and the world community."[28]

"Things African"

Herskovits, in an editorial on the opening pages of the first issue of *African Studies Bulletin* (the ASA organ later renamed *African Studies Review*), declared the Africanist mission. The organization's basic "assumption," he explained, was "that for the social sciences and the humanistic disciplines, Africa is a veritable laboratory, in which the dynamics of human experience can be studied under optimum conditions of understanding and historical control."[29]

First published in 1958, an influential collection of essays entitled *The United States and Africa*, found widespread use as an introduction to African policy issues. Funded by the Carnegie Corporation, the volume's contributors included leading Africanists, many of whom characteristically moved in and out of government positions. Among the authors were James Coleman, Vernon McKay, and Elliot J. Berg, a Harvard economist and consultant to the State Department and the Agency for International Development (AID) during the Kennedy administration. The book touched on all the major issues in U.S.–African relations, and encapsulated much of the theoretical and practical academic thinking that imbued Washington's policymaking at the time.[30]

Berg 's contribution on African economies explained the reasons for an optimistic outlook on African development, building on the basic case advanced several years earlier by Chester Bowles. The ratio of available land to inhabitants in most of Africa remained favorable, leading Berg to predict (wrongly) that "the 'population explosion' is less of an economic menace than elsewhere in the underdeveloped world." A growing population might even assist economic development by allowing for more intensive cultivation and making investments in roads "more economical." Socially and politically, the relative abundance of African land meant that "unlike most of Asia and Latin America," there appeared no "landlord problem." Moreover, in spite of his criticisms of African leaders' socialist proclivities, Berg cited the "dedicated, honest, moderate, responsible, and intelligent" quality of most African leaders. Given the lack of colonial preparation for the transition to independence, and in spite of instances of corruption and extravagance, overall, he found it "a remarkably able leadership." Most important, "it is a leadership practically everywhere dedicated to rapid modernization," another point of contrast with other "underdeveloped" regions of the world. On economic policy, despite an often-radical rhetoric, most African leaders followed cautious paths, issuing development plans with "little fat or waste." Wisely, they had focused on "transportation, education, agriculture, and public health," and had rapidly expanded access to secondary and university education since gaining independence. Berg also complimented African leaders' efforts to promote the virtue of "manual labor" and "technical and vocational training," as well as their relatively limited spending on military budgets. "They are trying to spread literacy and the gospel of modernization throughout their countries," cooed Berg, and the only "real danger is that they will try to do too much, too quickly." Africa's chances for development seemed better in many ways than those of either Asia or Latin America, regions with population problems or social upheaval not found in Africa. This prospect justified major U.S. and Western aid to Africa, for, "in the long run, the economic and political pay-off for our aid efforts may well be greater in Africa than anywhere else."[31]

The task of applying new foreign aid programs to the rapid modernization of African economies thus seemed a large yet manageable task. Analysts whose writings addressed theoretical and practical questions together had the opportunity of marketing their ideas as solutions to America's Cold War problems. One individual who did this, described by an admirer as "The Reasonable American," summarized the elementary beliefs of development scholarship as it related to Africa. He also set the tone for much of American foreign aid planning and played a personal role in translating academic theory into governmental practice. Born in New York, Arnold Rivkin studied economics at Brooklyn College, was wounded in the Battle of the Bulge during World War II, and then graduated from Harvard Law School. An Anglophile who married in London, Rivkin was "a shortish, solid figure, hospitable, gregarious and friendly," and "above all, reasonable, and always ready to listen and to learn."[32]

In 1950 the Assistant General Counsel of the European Headquarters of the Marshall Plan in Paris made his first trip to Africa. Rivkin, with responsibility for coordinating United States economic aid, visited the French colony of Madagascar. Years later, writing as an influential Africanist scholar and advisor to the World Bank, he recalled, "I was completely taken with the experience, and ever since I have had both a professional and personal interest in all things African." That abiding interest took a specific form, however. The Heart of Darkness, according to Rivkin, "was still very much in evidence in 1950" on the distant Indian Ocean island. Rivkin found it fascinating that "Conrad's 'prehistoric' man who lived in the heart of darkness" now lived alongside "a small but growing elite of educated Malagasy." These he described as "transitional Malagasy, hovering between traditional and modern society," a new class destined to lead the colony to independence, and perhaps to modernity. Working in African Studies, the U.S. government, and the Bank, Rivkin devoted the rest of his life to studying, and even attempting to mold, this African transition.[33]

Rivkin, his enthusiasm borne along by the thrill of discovery in Madagascar, expressed the quintessential cultural and intellectual traits of 1950s modernization theory and the new field of African Studies. From 1950 to 1956, working in Paris and London for the International Cooperation Authority (ICA, the forerunner of USAID), he combined official trips to African colonies with "a rich diet of reading and discussion of things African wherever and whenever possible." Rivkin cultivated knowledge and, perhaps at least as important, a reputation as an astute expert on "things African." The first U.S.

Ambassador to Guinea declared later, "In the period 1950–1958 there was probably no American who had more intimate economic, political or cultural knowledge of Africa than did Arnold Rivkin." The scholarship of social scientists such as Herskovits, Coleman, and Bunche gives the statement a fantastic implausibility. Still, it represented a distinct theme in Rivkin's career as he contributed to American representations of Africa.[34]

In 1957 Rivkin carried his self-made Africanist cachet and government contacts with him to MIT, where he had accepted an invitation to be a research scholar. There he established the African Economic and Political Development Project at CIS. His books *Africa and the West* (1962) and *The African Presence in World Affairs* (1963) drew on the substance of a number of journal articles he had previously published, and illustrated American modernization theorists' ambition to transform Africa through American foreign aid. Joining CIS at Millikan's invitation supplied him with the resources to undertake research trips to Africa over the following years and apply the ideas of Millikan and Rostow to that region. Rivkin, upon his arrival at CIS, said his Africa program would focus on "international relationships and the interactions of economic growth, political development, and social change in Africa and the consequences of the differing rates at which these processes proceed." African issues would be studied in the context of "their significance for United States policy."[35] Rivkin by 1967 had "worked and traveled in some 30 African countries and territories, particularly Nigeria, the Congo (Kinshasa), Rhodesia and Kenya."[36]

Rivkin in 1960 served as a consultant to the ICA on its new technical assistance program in sub-Saharan Africa while overseeing field work by two economists and two political scientists studying development in several countries.[37] He helped design training for American personnel to "provide some sense of what it is to work and live among Africans," and "the very taste and feel, the adventure and challenge, of working in Africa and bringing technical assistance to evolving nations anxious and determined to move forward in their economic development plans."[38] Seeking to emphasize the urgency of Africanist expertise, Rivkin declared, "Not only are the African peoples the newest and in some ways the least familiar claimants on American assistance; the whole vast African area is one in which Americans have had comparatively little depth of knowledge or experience."[39]

Rivkin described himself as "a political economist" and called his *African Presence in World Affairs* a product of "the special structure" of the CIS program. This, he explained, "has been an attempt to apply the general research philosophy of the Center to African development" by analyzing economic and political change and its relationship to African diplomacy. Working "on a multi-disciplinary basis, drawing principally on the disciplines of economics and political science," Rivkin, an early member of ASA, became known as "a pioneer in the development of multinational aid."[40] Rostow, on the eve of assuming a powerful position as an advisor to the new president, consulted Rivkin during the formation of Kennedy's transition task force on Africa. Rivkin thus joined the swelling ranks of modernization scholars playing multiple roles in and out of government. As Millikan noted in his foreword to *The African Presence*, Rivkin "interrupted his researches on frequent occasions to perform negotiating missions for the United States government."[41]

Africa and the West argued that African leaders themselves had made development their highest priority. Independence had begun "a fundamental transformation in their outlook on the use of wealth." In a sweeping summary of this change, Rivkin wrote,

> Economic development is the number-one priority to many leaders in independent Africa. . . . With this priority has come an awareness and appreciation of the role of productive investment in development. Development plans, mobilization of local resources, and solicitation of foreign private investment and external aid have become the order of the day in one independent African state after another. Modernization of traditional agriculture, development of basic infrastructure and social overhead facilities, exploitation of mineral resources, and stimulation of secondary industry have all become part of the new African credo of growth.[42]

For Africans to achieve development through a free-enterprise economic system, individuals had to rationally respond to "economic incentives in agriculture, industry, and commerce." Rivkin believed this crucial modernization had begun to speed up with the growth of cash-crop farming, wage labor, and entrepreneurship. While acknowledging that all African nations still had "geographic hinterlands with relatively insulated tribes" largely untouched by modern amenities and economic practices, he remained confident in the inevitability of progress through modernization. "In the end," he assured readers, economic incentives and appropriate governmental policies would incorporate such areas "into the modern orbit, where incentives will supply the normal inducement to perform economic tasks." Insisting that this was "not a statement of faith," Rivkin argued that "the African" would find it in his best interest to settle on "other forms of investment in preference to hoarding cattle," for instance, or switching from subsistence farming to industrial wage labor or growing cash crops for export.[43] Like Rostow, he proposed that Africa simply elaborate on its colonial heritage in the mining sector, the major engine of wealth transfers to the West in mineral-rich countries in Central Africa. These colonies had exported huge quantities of copper, gold, and other minerals and had "the largest national incomes" and "the highest rates of capital formation in sub-Saharan Africa." The reality that wealth and technology had been very narrowly concentrated in the hands of small white minorities in these nations, and that income disparities, poor education and health care, and other basic problems plagued Africans, did not intrude on this academic vision. Nor did he seem concerned by the implausibility of the idea that the path to development in mineral-rich countries would work in agriculture-oriented West African nations. Instead, his proposal—greater exploration of possible mineral resources throughout Africa—required Africa to seek even more Western technical assistance and had the potential to benefit Western economic interests more than African.[44]

One of the key arguments Rivkin hammered home was the need for African leaders to ignore the siren call of Pan-Africanism from Nkrumah. Ghana advocated African unity, a United States of Africa that could consolidate the continent's resources to efficiently pursue both development and economic independence. The charismatic Nkrumah, nothing if not bold, inserted Ghana into the major Cold War issues of the day as well, seeking to vindicate the "African Personality" on the world stage. This, eventually, caused the estrangement of Ghana from the United States. Rivkin ridiculed Nkrumah's pretensions, insisting that African rulers had to "choose between bread and circuses, between building viable economies to sustain their new political structures or waging the fight for independence long after it has, in fact, been achieved." Populist regimes with neutralist Cold War orientations like Ghana's could be dismissed as sideshows, relying on "bread and circuses" in lieu of the hard work of development. In The African Presence in World Affairs, Rivkin contrasted Ghana's policies with what he considered the more rational approach of Nigeria, "to look inward and find stability in internal growth." Nkrumah had squandered too much of his nation's "energy" and scarce "trained manpower" and foreign exchange savings on quixotic foreign policy goals. To blunt the appeal of Nkrumah elsewhere in Africa, Western economic aid had to reward countries like Nigeria. If the West provided "adequate external assistance, including technological transfers," a sound aid program for Africa was "likely to influence the decision for internal economic growth and *against* irredentism and other brands of political adventurism."[45]

While advocating "ample amounts" of aid to Nigeria, the "oasis of democratic development in an arid desert of authoritarian-inclined African states," Rivkin also urged the West to aid "many, perhaps most, African states." Development and nation building must succeed everywhere, and aid should be available regardless of a nation's political orientation, "short of a clear-cut commitment to the Communist orbit or to a headlong plunge down the road to authoritarianism or totalitarianism and anti-Western neutralism." Forcing African governments to make an all-or-nothing choice of accepting aid only from the West or from the Communist Bloc could drive some nations into the enemy camp, he warned.[46] "Nation-building and economic development in Africa are twin goals and intimately related tasks," argued Rivkin, "sharing many of the same problems, confronting many of the same challenges, and interrelating at many levels of public policy and practice." Development, according to Rivkin, was "a precondition for, factor in, and consequence of nation-building," as well as a means of promoting nation building. As the state pursues economic development, making it the top priority, its economic measures create a national economy and an accompanying national identity. Working together to build the economy, citizens from different ethnic groups and regions would create "national cohesion" and unity. "There is a clear correspondence," declared Rivkin, "between the stages of growth and the levels of nation-building."[47]

Reviewers offered a mixed reaction to Rivkin's books. Vernon McKay praised Rivkin's discussion, in *The African Presence*, of "the modernization of agriculture" and other "internal problems of economic growth" in the first chapters, "original and valuable comparative material on African development problems and policies both before and after independence." McKay, however, found Rivkin's discussion of international politics "controversial in both substance and tone," particularly his "oversimplified presentation of Ghana and Nigeria as polar opposites."[48] Political scientist Harvey Glickman, book review editor for *Africa Report*, expressed disappointment with the failure of *Africa and the West* to live up to its author's academic and official credentials. Rivkin had provided "a vision rather than a systematic analysis" of the problems of development. More troubling than the "nearly random relationship among chapters," poor editing, and "needless repetition," was that Rivkin seemed naïve in his belief that African leaders were committed to tolerating political opposition and protecting minority rights. Rivkin's "central" concern—preventing Africa from embracing Communism—seemed to reflect "the notion that Africa still 'belongs' in the Western orbit."[49] While one reviewer hailed Rivkin as "one of the leading authorities in the world on the subject of economic development in Africa," a less charitable critic mocked his "badly written" book, his "very uneven" expertise, and the "special pleading" for Nigeria, "for which his greater familiarity has apparently bred esteem." Another critic astutely discerned "a certain moralizing tone" in Rivkin's prose and suggested that Rivkin and other Americans "must take into consideration Africans' desire to develop in their own way, not in ours." Scholars less closely affiliated with the policy-oriented modernization paradigm responded coolly to the certainty and air of inevitability Rivkin exuded.[50]

Despite academic criticisms, Rivkin translated his expertise in African development into policymaking within the World Bank, serving as economic advisor to its Africa department. In 1963 he expounded upon the important growing role of the World Bank in Africa. Noting that in the previous decade the Bank and its affiliate, the International Development Association, had "become the principal development bankers of the under-developed areas of the world," Rivkin argued that the Bank's growth and the coincidental emergence of independent Africa had the potential to "prove to be of decisive importance to African economic development" as well as "a critical test" of the multilateral institutions in "large-scale development lending." The Bank's role in Africa began to expand in 1960 with two loans for Sudanese irrigation and smaller loans to several nations for other agricultural projects, and Rivkin felt this constituted "something of a quiet revolution," given Africa's dependence on agriculture. The Bank's Development Advisory Service, according to Rivkin (a member), had become "the nearest thing that exists in the economic development field to a professional career foreign service of economic and financial advisors." Expansion on several fronts had created "a population boom in the Bank's new Africa Department," founded in 1962. The department now boasted thirty-five staffers (Rivkin served as its Economic Advisor), and the Bank anticipated "a constantly increasing level" of activity in Africa.[51]

Policy-oriented American social scientists such as Rivkin and Berg applied to African Studies the Cold War preoccupation with American-inspired modernization. Their emphasis on modernization was not unique, as scholars in other countries shared this interest, including those in Africa and the diaspora. W. Arthur Lewis, born in 1915 in St. Lucia in the British Caribbean, studied at the London School of Economics. Turned down by the Colonial

Service, "presumably on grounds of race," Lewis became an academic star. Earning a Ph.D. at London, he served in the Colonial Office during World War II. Lewis "early in his career wrote pamphlets denouncing colonial rule and the planter class in the West Indies." In 1951 he became a member of the UN Group of Experts on Under-developed Countries. "A founding father of development economics," Lewis produced books, including *The Theory of Economic Growth*, which gave him academic cachet to rival that of any American modernization theorist. Like them, however, he focused his interest in the modern sector of the economy. Writes Frederick Cooper, "He looked to liberation in a dual sense: from the backwardness of colonial capitalism toward a more dynamic variant and from the backwardness of tradition into a modern world now open to all." Lewis, active in British Socialist politics, became one of Nkrumah's economic advisors in the 1950s before eventually becoming a professor at Princeton. Sympathetic to African aspirations and condemning racism and colonialism, Lewis' politics and economic analyses were moderate and posed no serious challenge to the prevailing American conception of modernization.[52]

That consensus, in fact, for all its self-styled novelty, recycled economic and cultural assumptions central to the European colonial experience in Africa and other colonized world regions. Inheriting colonial anthropological representations of African women as helpless and oppressed victims of patriarchy, Western development experts in the 1950s–60s (typically white men, of course) "overwhelmingly lumped women in post-colonial societies with the peasantry as repositories of tradition and potential obstacles to their transformative schemes." Modernization theorists, as historian Michael Adas notes, devoted little attention to studying women and tended to rely on "vague impressions that frequently recycled colonial stereotypes." Women were seen as loyal not to the nation or state, but to their family and community only. These gendered assumptions translated into development policies that privileged men and their involvement in the modern economy. Modernization planners failed to include in their calculations women's contributions to subsistence farming and other activities. Development projects usually focused on cash crops and exports, areas with few opportunities for women who had been involved in local marketing and subsistence farming. Educational opportunities continued to go mainly to males, as in the colonial era.[53]

Nevertheless, Americans who shared the assumption of women's helpless oppression sometimes envisioned African women playing a special role in modernization. The president of the World Bank, citing the importance of the recent employment of women in wage jobs such as telephone operators, declared: "When women begin to get rights in Africa, you won't be able to keep development down!"[54] This self-congratulatory refrain at a time of persistent inequality in Western gender relations added a cruel twist to the traditional trope of effeminate Third World men. Now the allegedly unique chauvinism of African men and the patriarchy of African societies were invoked to account for African underdevelopment and to legitimate American efforts to modernize African values. Mennen Williams, too, expressed an interest in women's role. Receiving three "militant feminists" from Africa in his office at Foggy Bottom, Williams was surprised to hear that voting rights were less vital to African women than "a supply of water in the village." What women needed, they told him, was more equitable working conditions. After a 1961 tour of several African nations, he urged "sympathetic understanding and guidance" in aid programs for "the education of African women in order to improve their social status and to inculcate a desire for a better standard of living."[55] "African men," he remarked, "are being caught up in the world of the twentieth century," while African women are "left behind" as a result of chauvinism and a gender-based division of labor. He suggested "a sociological study of the possibility of making the women of Africa" more interested in "raising the standard of living of their families." Williams speculated that once awakened to new material opportunities, women would urge their men to seek employment in "the cash economy" so they could purchase "sewing machines, clothes, radios, education" for them. This trend would create African "consumer economies" and a strong middle class.[56]

Williams's suggestion, like other American visions of gender decolonization in Africa, has to be viewed in the context of American plans for African modernization. Like their colonial forebears in the 1940s–50s, the period sometimes known as the "Second Occupation" as a result of the influx of European technicians and development experts, self-confident Americans from the World Bank, USAID, and African Studies centers descended upon the continent with a mission. Modernization theory and the narratives of innocence born of American exceptionalism vested American experts and officials with cognitive and moral authority to examine, diagnose, and transform Africa. Since modernization of a society entailed more than just economics—investment, trade, production, and such—but also changes in incentives, attitudes, and aspirations, nothing about African societies or cultures was irrelevant. When Americans lamented African male chauvinism and the plight of women, they underscored their basic view of Africa as a land of "preconditions stage" societies where culture had to be modernized. Nevertheless, for all Rostow's emphasis on "non-capital" aspects of American aid, the core concern of secular missionaries lay in the realm of economics, and many imagined that timely infusions of American capital and expertise could prove decisive. All that remained, they believed, was for Africans to have ready a plan to use this largesse.

Four

"The Moral Equivalent of Anti-Colonialism"

In 1961 Vice President Lyndon B. Johnson made his only trip to Africa, a memorable one. Crude yet flamboyant, the consummate American politician visited Senegal on the first anniversary of its independence. Intending to signal the newfound interest in Africa of the United States, Johnson's trip took him beyond the capital, Dakar, to a "fishing village some 25 miles NE of Dakar" called Kayar, site of a proposed Peace Corps project. Johnson "promised to send the Village Chief of Kayar a Johnson outboard motor upon his return to the U.S." The U.S. Embassy in Dakar reported that, while "some of the more extravagant U.S. press accounts of the jubilant public welcome" the vice president received "must be taken with a grain of salt," Johnson did meet "thick crowds" and "frequent bursts of hand-clapping and smiles of obvious pleasure" from Senegalese who had never seen such a "veteran American political campaigner." Accustomed to the formality of French officials, they delighted in Johnson's "smiling, shaking hands and greeting pleased and astonished bystanders." The embassy termed "the high point" of his visit his and Mrs. Johnson's arrival at the Senegalese Artisanal Village, captured in a "widely reproduced AP photograph" of the vice president "presenting an attractive Senegalese baby with a pencil."[1] Johnson thus applied to West Africa the politics of touch so central to his electoral success in Texas. His diplomatic touch signified America's self-proclaimed sincere motives, in contrast to the exploitative colonialism of the Europeans.[2] As Johnson told the village chief, "I came to Kayar because I was a farm boy, too, in Texas. It's a long way from Texas to

Kayar, but we both produce peanuts and both want the same thing: a higher standard of living for the people." His comments erased cultural differences with a vision of Americanization.[3]

Did they ensure Americans and Senegalese would share a vision of development for the small, peanut-exporting nation? Johnson's encounter with top officials in Dakar suggested that problems of communication and ideological differences might not be dispelled by handshakes. When Johnson agreed to meet Prime Minister Mamadou Dia to discuss Senegal's development plan, an American embassy official called the result a "rather curious interview." A socialist and the leading thinker on development within the government, the prime minister explained that Senegal had postponed its requests for aid until it could complete its plan, a draft of which he handed the vice president. Johnson expressed admiration for Senegal's seriousness about development and promised to lobby Congress for immediate use of $3 million the country had requested. While Johnson explained the need for the two countries to reach "a general agreement" that met the criteria of the U.S. International Cooperation Authority and Congressional requirements, as well as "the importance of timing," his interlocutor's response "was vague, if not evasive." The prime minister merely repeated his country's desire to receive aid from all of its "friends." The U.S. embassy was left to wonder whether Johnson's goodwill diplomacy had mattered. "It remains to be seen," the staff noted, whether Senegal would agree to a bilateral aid arrangement "which is a prerequisite to an actual U.S. aid program."[4]

Johnson's "rather curious interview" at the beginning of the "Decade of Development" proved a harbinger of things to come. When in 1963 Johnson was elevated to the presidency, Mennen Williams assured Africans that they could trust him. Noting that Johnson had "campaigned Senegal as he might have campaigned Texas," Williams claimed that the new president "had been to Africa, and more than that he had been able to associate himself with them in a kind of free moving brotherhood."[5] Williams and other Americans striving to empathize with Africans relied on analogies to American geography, history, or politics. During Johnson's presidency, as the White House prepared for a state visit by the president of Upper Volta (present-day Burkina Faso), an aide informed Johnson that the country "resembles Texas in many respects," as "flat, rather dry, cattle-raising."[6] Somalia, in one briefing for Johnson, became "a semi-arid land, much like our South-West," with a commitment to peace and development that had begun to "exceed our most optimistic expectations."[7] American efforts to imagine Africa in terms of American geography

and American understandings of communication ("free moving brotherhood," informality, and instant intimacy) reflected and reinforced American
ignorance of African affairs at the very moment when Washington assumed
the burden of directing the transformation of the region.

Planning emerged as a trope in American and African visions of economic
development. Social scientists and officials saw planning as a safe way for peoples in "developing" countries to divert their energies from politics into the
technical aspects of economic growth. Poor nations could not, it was widely
believed, attract sufficient foreign aid and private capital (foreign or domestic)
to finance development projects in such areas as infrastructure, industrialization, agricultural reform, education, health and other social services, and public administration. Only the government could mobilize the necessary resources
for sustained development. As CIS stated in *The Emerging Nations*, the "rather high
degree of coordination" necessary for orderly development of a transitional
economy could not rely alone on "the market mechanism," for its "imperfec-
tion renders it incomplete and slow," and inappropriate as a coordinator of
investment.[8] Indian Prime Minister Jawaharlal Nehru, whose country drew
deep interest from CIS as a prime candidate for economic "take-off," believed
his nation's industrialization and political stability alike required the presence
of national economic planners: "a staff of economists directing public investment, regulating prices, and setting production goals," thus guiding economic
growth "through technical rather than political means."[9]

Thus, even African leaders committed to a free market orientation acknowledged the need for significant government involvement in the national economy. Taking their cue from Soviet, Chinese, and Indian progress through
Five-Year Plans, African rulers regardless of ideological orientation supported
the drafting and promulgation (if not always the implementation) of national
development plans that established targets and some criteria for allocating
resources (including foreign assistance) to propel the nation forward through
the "stages of economic growth." Planning development not only enhanced
the likelihood of economic success, it placed key decisions beyond politics,
thus beyond ethnic strife and Communist subversion.

"The Plan"

From the beginning of the Kennedy years, the administration attempted to
base African modernization on "sound economic plans." Economists and

political scientists had been advocating various forms of domestic economic planning for many years, and the postwar emphasis on Keynesian economic policy underscored the American belief that governments could set and reach target growth rates. Modernization theorists added the crucial thought that "underdeveloped" nations must efficiently allocate their modest resources—and the external aid and private foreign investment they received—by implementing detailed, far-sighted development plans. In turn, American allocations of foreign aid would flow most freely to those nations, like India, believed to have the most sophisticated plans. Increasing the amount of aid to those countries would reward their leaders for preparing good plans and ensure that essential development projects received adequate levels of funding, thus speeding the modernization process.

The State Department's African Bureau fully embraced this logic and rhetoric, and an early internal memorandum to Williams argued that development planning would turn Africans "away from the sterile arguments of past colonialism to the best methods of developing prosperity in freedom. The moral equivalent of anti-colonialism could become 'the plan.'" This formulation had two striking meanings. It suggested that Washington could burnish its credentials as a friend of African independence by touting its support for effective planning, and that African leaders had to adopt the "planning" mantra in order to maintain their credibility as suitable recipients of U.S. assistance. The same memorandum called for an active American role in drafting and implementing African governments' development plans. Since these "new nations" lacked adequate skilled manpower, Washington would have to help with all phases of the process, at least in the short term. Thus the "planning" theme of U.S. aid promised to essentially de-politicize discussions of African political economy. All economic policy issues would now be reduced to technical matters, with the Americans enjoying extensive influence in the details of African governments' budgetary affairs. Furthermore, African leaders would be discouraged from pursuing political, cultural, or diplomatic ventures that deviated from this narrow concentration upon (free-market, Western-oriented) economic development and (democratic, Western-style) nation building.[10]

Planning, according to some modernization theorists, promised political, as well as economic, development. Max Millikan made broad claims for the efficacy of planning. In one meeting of USAID's Advisory Committee on Economic Development, Millikan joined other prominent scholars in arguing that planning could promote "political development" as well as economic development. Planning, according to Millikan, helped "underdeveloped" nations reduce the "identity crisis" inherent in such "transitional societies." As heterogeneous, newly independent countries groped for a national ethos and unity, Millikan found encouraging the evidence that "much political debate focuses on the plan" for development. Proper development planning and Western aid could bolster the national government's control over communication with the population and eventually increase popular participation in the political process by getting more local groups involved in plans for development projects.[11] Millikan's suggestion reflected his experience with Indian planning and development, as CIS had played a major role in supporting what it and Indian leaders envisioned as a technocratic, apolitical planning process to achieve rapid economic growth.

However, the American emphasis on planning for development entailed contradictions and frequently produced dilemmas. In July 1961, the State Department's Policy Planning Council already glimpsed some of the difficulty ahead. The United States had embarked upon a strategy of offering multi-year commitments of aid to countries that seemed promising candidates for rapid modernization. The problem, as the policy planners perceived, was that once commitments had been made, only with great difficulty and diplomatic cost could Washington subsequently "hold back on them because of unsatisfactory performance." In addition, they feared that aid commitments that were intended to encourage African planning might create excessively high expectations that the United States would provide all the external funding to implement development plans. Once extended, in other words, aid commitments based on an American endorsement of an African nation's five- or six-year plan could spiral out of control, leading to a wasteful foreign aid policy.[12] Making "multi-year aid commitments in African states" risked putting the U.S. government in a bind, as "it will be difficult to hold back on them because of unsatisfactory performance by the aid recipient without causing serious political friction and ill-will." A further problem lay in the realm of expectations: the new "emphasis on planning" might give Africans the impression "that if a country comes forward with a well-thought-out economic development plan we are prepared to provide all of the required external funding."[13]

American observers like the prominent economist John Kenneth Galbraith (who served as Kennedy's ambassador to India) believed that past Western aid and planning had failed to achieve results because they had not successfully targeted the "decisive barriers to development," such as illiteracy and lack of trained manpower. Galbraith, an influential proponent of liberal domestic and international economic policies, argued that poor nations remained poor not because of a lack of capital or foreign aid per se, but because they lacked a real plan for devoting resources to the most important development objectives, education and human resources training.[14] In short, better planning, not an alternative to planning, offered the best hope.

Washington's concerns about the quality of African planning cast a shadow of doubt over the new aid strategy. Though the amounts were small compared to its aid efforts in Latin America, the United States quickly established a significant presence in Africa. As early as the summer of 1962, USAID had 1,310 Americans working there, mostly in Nigeria, Ethiopia, Liberia, and the Sudan.[15] When Kennedy took office, several African nations already had development plans, including the influential West African states of Nigeria and Ghana.[16] Unfortunately, American officials believed, most plans exhibited "a confused, un-coordinated welter of aid and development activity, usually with a proliferation of unrelated projects or programs." Few "underdeveloped" nations in Africa or elsewhere actually devoted most of their development planning to long-term projects deemed suitable by American observers. Noting the troublesome fact that "there is no internationally accepted definition" of what constituted a good "long-range economic development plan," State Department officials lamented that the authoritarian governments of Ethiopia and Ghana had development plans that amounted to little more than random spending on a variety of projects.[17]

Africans, whatever deficiencies Americans discerned in their plans, shared the general enthusiasm for planning. Nigerian economist Adebayo Adedeji recalled of early African governments' desire to raise living standards, "All were virtually convinced that the most rational way ... was through economic planning."[18] Much of the work of coordinating African resources and projects was supposed to be done by regional and international organizations. Founded in 1958, the UN Economic Commission for Africa (ECA) seemed an obvious candidate to ensure the overall symmetry of African planning and external assistance. However, the organization's role became less clear when, five years later, African leaders meeting in Addis Ababa, Ethiopia, founded the Organization of African Unity (OAU). The growing role of the World Bank in Africa, too, represented a challenge to those who would attempt to define the role of any single institution or national government in planning African development.[19]

Americans and post-independence Africans were not alone in trying to apply development planning to Africa, as Western European economic aid programs increasingly focused on the theme. In a more intriguing case explored by Michael Mahoney, Portugal, notorious for its retrograde colonialism in southern Africa, adopted modernization theory as the basis for renewed efforts to develop Mozambique. In the 1950s and '60s Lisbon issued three Six-Year Plans, backed by unprecedented levels of funding, in an attempt to reduce local dissatisfaction and undermine the liberation movement. Like many African development plans favored by the United States, the Third Plan of the Portuguese featured a massive dam. The Cabora Bassa project along the Zambezi River would generate hydroelectric power and stimulate industrialization and, Portuguese officials hoped, symbolize their staying power in Africa. Borrowing from American dreams of "TVA-style" development in Africa, even an explicitly colonial state viewed planning as the key to the future, the source of economic progress and political stability, goals shared by Americans and most African leaders.[20]

Moreover, some African intellectuals and officials articulated a vision of development and planning that, while sharing fundamental premises with that of the West, implied different courses. Mamadou Dia, a socialist, advocated the coordination of African national development plans under a continent-wide plan intended to achieve "a continent-wide industrialization." His The African Nations and World Solidarity, translated by African American Francophile scholar and diplomat Mercer Cook, asserted the necessity of planning in a context quite unlike that resonating in Washington. Planning would be done on a geographical scale far beyond what officials in USAID or scholars at CIS would find prudent, and its goals—quick progress on African unity and an emphasis on industry over agriculture—jostled American officials' go-slow approaches to both.[21]

Ultimately, as Frederick Cooper observes, the postcolonial preoccupation with planning fit in neatly with an authoritarian impulse among Africa's new ruling classes, who distrusted groups such as farmers' organizations and labor unions that held the potential to undermine their hegemony within the state. "The developmentalist state," writes Cooper, "in its post-colonial as much as its colonial manifestation, was thus a peculiar entity: it exercised initiative, yet it suppressed initiative, too, and it above all encouraged citizens to think of the state as the prime mover for raising the standard of living." Planning, then, while deemed essential by American modernizers, appealed to African modernizers as a method to achieve progress toward modernity and consolidate a form of political rule, many would argue, not altogether consistent with modernity.[22] Those African planners and visionaries such as Mamadou Dia with different intentions found themselves marginalized if not penalized, as African democracy proved short-lived.

Sudan: A "Case History"

Even before implementation bedeviled foreign aid, the very process of negotiating aid agreements revealed the importance of politics. In 1961 the
Kennedy administration encountered an embarrassing and perplexing problem in negotiating a development assistance package with the Sudan. Though
only one of a number of instances of miscommunication within and between
governments, the Sudanese incident illustrates the larger problems that
bedeviled American and African attempts to forge a productive partnership
for development. Unique in its straddling of the ostensible division between
sub-Saharan and North Africa, the Sudan emerged from a complicated history of British rule with a deeply divided population and economic challenges. Independent in 1956, the vast country has endured chronic conflict
between northern and southern Sudan, broadly reflecting Muslim/Christian
and ethnic rivalries nurtured by the British. The violence and political instability, along with vast geographic distances separating cities from one another
and from the Red Sea coast, gave the Sudan, despite the presence of the Nile
and colonial irrigation projects, an uncertain economic future.

The Sudan's geographic proximity to the Middle East gave it a new significance to Washington during the waning days of the Eisenhower administration. From 1958 to 1964 General Ibrahim Abboud presided over a conservative regime, following a cautious foreign policy that largely shielded the
country from major international risks. The United States had greeted
Abboud's seizure of power with cautious optimism, viewing his regime as
ideologically moderate and relatively stable. According to U.S. intelligence
analysts, the Sudan enjoyed "modest prosperity" but had "no comprehensive
plan for economic development."[23] At the outset of the Kennedy administration, a National Security Paper warned that the country remained politically
"untenable" under Abboud, despite "promising economic potential."[24] The
country thus appeared a suitable candidate for American economic aid,
though Washington's vision of Sudanese development lacked specificity.

So, too, did the Sudanese vision. In a meeting with Secretary of State Dean
Rusk, the Sudanese Foreign Minister Ahmad Muhammad Kheir expressed a
desire for U.S. loans for three or four development projects that had "seemed
acceptable" to U.S. embassy officials in Khartoum. The Sudanese had, therefore, "brought with them certain items 'in their bag' and hoped and believed

that they would return to Khartoum with the bag full."[25] The Kennedy administration decided to invite General Abboud to Washington in 1961, to reward his moderation and discuss his interest in American aid. In preparation, the U.S. Embassy in Khartoum attempted to teach the Sudanese the new U.S. aid concept of "planned development." Embassy officials noted Kheir's "pessimistic" outlook on his country's ability to plan, his conception of aid as "essentially political," and his wish to avoid long, drawn-out negotiations in Washington. The embassy feared its repeated insistence on the primacy of planning could backfire if the Sudanese concluded "that their present planning is so inadequate that it would be useless to talk about the subject." More important, the Sudanese hoped the Washington visit would yield an American agreement to help build a road from Khartoum to Port Sudan, the country's primary city on the coast of the Red Sea. U.S. officials, however, believed the road project lacked sufficient feasibility data to be worthy of a commitment, and a survey of its feasibility might take several months and $26 million. The Foreign Minister warned that his government would compare U.S. and Soviet aid in terms of "the speed at which agreements in principle were implemented." Fearing such competition, the embassy urged Washington to agree to a loan of over $18 million. However, it noted as an "especially troublesome aspect of the Abboud visit" that few Sudanese officials had prepared for it, due to their preoccupation with a diplomatic conference of non-aligned nations. Embassy officials worried that "we must expect that the visitors will arrive in the United States without having had the opportunity to give more than brief consideration to what they want from the visit and how they expect to obtain it." The State Department, they warned, should "not expect too much precision in the Sudanese presentations."[26]

In his October meeting with Kennedy, General Abboud invoked his country's poor communications, noting that the six-hundred-mile distance between Khartoum and Port Sudan was inadequately traversed by the existing railroad. The president assured the general that he was "fully aware of the importance of establishing a highway" between the capital and the Red Sea.[27] Meanwhile, George Ball, economic specialist of the State Department, chaired a meeting, attended by Rostow, on economic aid between American and Sudanese officials. The Sudanese listed several development projects and asked the Americans to produce "general figures for loans and grants," with the details to be worked out during subsequent talks. Taken aback, Ball observed that such figures would be difficult to offer without first completing surveys of the projects to determine their costs. The United States, he said, would be pleased to underwrite such a survey for the Port Sudan road, though it would need time to find a firm to conduct the survey and determine what kind of road should be built and at what cost. When the Sudanese urged the Americans to "give a commitment in principle to build the road," Ball and his colleagues refused, noting that U.S. law prohibited such commitments prior to feasibility studies. For their part, the Sudanese insisted that the road project was their "number one priority." Rostow pointed out that the United States would have to ensure that if it built the road there would be Sudanese who could maintain it.[28]

The meeting went from bad to worse when Ball asked about the Sudanese application for a loan to build a sugar factory. An American official noted that the Sudanese had put in applications requesting loans for airports and sewage systems and not the factory. Ball flatly rejected the Sudanese request for financing of a fiber bag factory that would use British machinery. When asked if the United States could provide a Boeing aircraft, Ball insisted that "this type of item is not financed through the aid program." When Rostow asked about the status of Sudanese planning, the embassy official declared, "The Sudanese have a plan to have a plan."[29] As Rostow reported to Kennedy, the meeting proved "one of the worst shambles I have ever seen in the Government since arrival." He urged the president to limit the damage by telling Abboud of America's strong desire to help Sudan and its recognition of the importance they attached to the road project. Kennedy should tell the general, "We feel a sense of adventure about the development of Sudanese resources on behalf of its people and look forward to playing a helpful role in making a new future for the country."[30]

In a phone conversation with Ball later that day, Rostow blamed the "shambles" of a meeting on a breakdown in communications among U.S. officials. Ball believed the Khartoum embassy had failed to provide the Sudanese with sufficient information before the trip, saying "there was no serious conversation with these people in Khartoum. They came over here totally unprepared." While Rostow concluded that "the big thing is the road" and that the president would have to show the Sudanese that he understood their priorities, Ball called the episode "a case history" of failed coordination among the embassy, USAID, and the State Department that should be preserved to prevent such a frustrating and embarrassing meeting from happening again.[31] While Kennedy met again with Abboud on 6 October to reassure him, Rostow assured the president that Ball had begun investigating the matter to prepare a "case history" to prevent a repeat performance.[32]

The White House concluded that the confusion at the Sudanese meeting had been caused by a lack of coordination between the State Department and USAID, as the latter "apparently ignored the political relationship between the loan applications and the visit." The Sudanese did not present the applications until Abboud's arrival in Washington, and when they gave them to USAID, the agency failed to inform the State Department which projects were involved. Thus, "the basic cause of confusion is the difference in State and AID philosophies. AID refuses to budge an inch toward using economic assistance for political impact in conjunction with state visits," and it had insisted that the Sudanese made out their applications incorrectly. The incident seemed to suggest the need for the agency to "loosen up a bit" on its criteria of careful planning so Washington could "get some political mileage from aid we are going to give anyway."[33]

Rostow called USAID administrator Fowler Hamilton to urge the agency to complete its survey of the road project by early February 1962 to fulfill Kennedy's pledge to Abboud. If the sugar factory proved feasible, the president wanted its "construction as quickly as possible." National Security Advisor McGeorge Bundy learned that his subordinates had "lowered the boom orally on State and AID, but AID bureaucrats tell us that a piece of paper would oil the AID wheels." Bundy promptly provided it.[34] Meanwhile, the embassy reported the fallout from the visit, noting that Abboud and his advisors were ecstatic about their reception in New York and Washington and the attention of the U.S. press. The Sudanese reaction was unsurprising given that Abboud received a tickertape parade up Broadway and the judgment of a New York Times editorial that his statements on diverse world issues had "won him respect" as a serious figure from the nonaligned world. However, they were "clearly disappointed" by what the Foreign Minister "considered negative results of discussions." Days later, the U.S. Ambassador reported that Abboud believed U.S. aid to build the road had been "assured," a mistaken belief the ambassador feared "could account" for the general's elation about his American experience. The ambassador urged Washington to come through with that aid, for despite its shortcomings, the Abboud regime "is far more likely to hold this disparate country together than any of its sectarian competitors," but to do so, it needed "impact successes" in the economy.[35] Finally, Rostow, in a letter to Kheir, admitted the Sudanese visit "certainly had one clear effect: it focused the minds of our people firmly" on the road project.[36]

Whatever lessons Washington gleaned from this "case history" proved of little value to the Sudanese. The Abboud regime fell to a left-wing coup in

1964, and the new rulers tweaked the United States by allowing the Sudan to become a conduit for weapons to left-wing rebels in the Congo, a turn of events doubly disappointing to the Americans.[37] American aid had not gotten very far by that time. USAID financed a technical feasibility study of a road from Khartoum to Port Sudan while construction began with the shorter road between the capital and Wad Madani along the Blue Nile. Beginning work with a USAID grant in 1962, the Sudanese paved the 183-km-long asphalt road through the desert, though not until 1970 was it completed.[38]

In the midst of technical difficulties and miscommunication between the governments, the Khartoum embassy bemoaned, "In essence, we are asking GOS [Government of Sudan] to put up their own funds and borrow more in order to bail us out of a situation resulting from our failure to fulfill our commitment to provide them with a complete highway as a grant." The dilemma had resulted from American "technical failures and inadequacies, not theirs." The embassy explained that Sudan had initially doubted the U.S. plan, "but we persuaded them we know best how to do the job, or at least they acquiesced in the face of superior American technology." Sudan accepted the U.S. plan and grant, anticipating "a serviceable road" that would be "critical in their prospects for economic development." However, U.S. engineering experts failed, experts now agreed, in their road specifications. The project's failure created a diplomatic danger that Sudanese "disillusionment" might lead them to look for Communist Bloc aid at a critical moment in the evolution of Sudan's government, which leaned West but faced popular discontent, stirred by Communist propaganda, with AID.[39] As NSC staffer Ulric Haynes lamented, the road, "publicized as a demonstration of U.S. technological know-how," had shown something else about U.S. aid. Noting that "construction was a disaster," he seconded the embassy's view that the failure to quickly build a functional road damaged the American reputation for "know-how and good faith." Poorly built, the cracked road would now take a great deal of money to fix.[40] The more ambitious road connecting the capital to Port Sudan was eventually built in the 1990s—by the construction empire known as the Bin Laden Group.

Ethiopia: "A Textbook Case"

A neighbor of the Sudan, the ancient Horn of Africa kingdom of Ethiopia garnered abundant American interest. Though not a "new nation," Ethiopia fascinated Americans. It was one of only two African nations to elude European colonization, and its sovereign, Emperor Haile Selassie, enjoyed a reputation in the United States as a heroic defender of his people during the Fascist Italian invasion of the 1930s. He possessed staunch anti-Communist credentials and impressed many as a bulwark of stability in East Africa. Welcoming American aid in the absence of a former colonial donor, the emperor hosted the most important U.S. military base in Africa at Kagnew Station, in Asmara, Eritrea (formerly a British territory), where the Americans operated key communications and tracking facilities. Ethiopia during the 1950s received Point Four technical assistance worth $27 million focused on agriculture, education, and health, as well as small loans and a military aid package, and agreed to a treaty granting the United States the use of military facilities. Nevertheless, America's embrace of Ethiopia, already well established during the Eisenhower years, remained ambivalent. The antiquity of the kingdom, long dominated by the Amharic Christians, suggested political stability, but also, beneath the tranquil surface, potential trouble. Continuity in Ethiopia also meant a lack of economic change. A 1958 National Intelligence Estimate called the Horn of Africa "one of the most backward areas in the world."[41]

Nevertheless, by 1961 many American officials and observers saw Ethiopia as an important nation because of its status as a large East African state, one of sub-Saharan Africa's most populous, and never been colonized by the Europeans (aside from the brief Italian occupation). Having no former metropolitan power, Ethiopia's conservative imperial regime naturally looked to America for economic and military aid. A 1963 survey of the country in *Africa Report* argued that "Ethiopia's economic prospects can be viewed with some optimism," as the Ethiopian highlands comprised "one of the most fertile areas in Africa."[42] The editorial page of the *Washington Post* believed that in Ethiopia, "the balance is highly favorable, and few African nations have brighter prospects." Greater hyperbole came from a market analysis by First National City Bank of New York. Its enthusiasm for Ethiopian development prompted the claim that "Some day this area could become a breadbasket for the arid Middle East and one of the leading grain-and-meat-producing areas in Africa."[43] Much of this enthusiasm—ignoring the persistent poverty of Ethiopia's mostly rural masses—resulted from visible signs of progress achieved through increased exports of coffee and American collaboration with the emperor in concentrating investment in Addis Ababa (the only Ethiopian city visited by most foreigners). The often extravagant imperial spending on large roads and buildings provided a "semblance of modernity" that attracted ambitious and acquisitive Ethiopians and foreigners alike, fueling naïve optimism about the country's future.[44] The emperor's expansive claims to leadership of Africa, buttressed in 1963 by the hosting of the conference that established the Organization of African Unity, further deluded American reporters.

A more tangible U.S. interest lay in Washington's "principal goal" in Ethiopia, maintaining the right to the Kagnew military communications base. This mutually advantageous relationship suffered, however, from the weakness of the Ethiopian imperial regime. Washington worried that its close political identification with Haile Selassie would harm U.S. prestige, particularly if, as many American observers feared, a revolution eventually swept the emperor out of power. The emperor's "best bet to forestall a possible coup," major political and economic reforms, seemed long overdue, yet Washington sensed that it could not press too hard, lest the Ethiopians allow the military base rights to elapse. The United States found itself stuck with Haile Selassie's "archaic government," which functioned like a "police state" that generated considerable popular discontent, "for better or worse," as the American embassy in Addis Ababa reported.[45] American ambassadors in Africa agreed that U.S.–Ethiopian relations caused "problems calling for special attention because of the serious threat to US strategic interests caused by the large and unpopular US military presence and increasing anti-Americanism in that country."[46]

Unlike most African nations, Ethiopia struck American observers as a land plagued by historical baggage and a rigid social system; as the economist William Hance put it, "feudal landholding" led a list of several "serious inhibiting influences for modernization and economic development." The nation's main export, coffee, and its other agricultural endeavors remained "primitive" and inefficient. Yet the United States hoped to promote modernization through education. USAID sponsored the Haile Selassie I University in Addis Ababa, with the assistance of American universities and foundations. Washington initially regarded it as "one of the better examples of what American assistance—both material and cultural—can accomplish in Africa," for it seemed to provide a pro-American center for the training of a new class of Ethiopian leaders who could promote their country's modernization. Washington could not know that in the years ahead the university would serve as a hotbed of anti-government radicalism.

In February 1962, Chester Bowles, in one of his at-large diplomatic missions overseas for the president, visited Ethiopia in an attempt to convince Haile Selassie to accept American technicians to direct some of the country's development planning.[47] The lack of "a planning organization" seemed one of the most pressing problems with Ethiopian reform, and it came up later in the month when John Kenneth Galbraith arrived in Addis Ababa for three days of talks with the emperor and other officials on military aid. The Ethiopians had requested a squadron of F-86 combat aircraft—at a time of rising tensions with neighboring Somalia —in exchange for allowing the United States to continue to use the Kagnew base. Galbraith interrupted his service as ambassador to India to conduct the discussions for the administration, and afterwards he advised against granting the Ethiopian request. To supply Ethiopia with weapons that might be used against another African nation would, Galbraith reasoned, undermine the American intention to reduce military aid to poor nations and urge them to focus instead on economic development. To soften the blow, he urged Washington to increase its offers of economic aid, "tied to Ethiopian performance," aimed at land reform, development planning, and training for public administration. American aid would also focus on supporting the new university, road construction, agricultural reforms, and public health. All of these and other reform ideas met with resistance from segments of the Ethiopian elite, and the regime remained fragile until a Marxist revolution swept it from power in 1974.[48]

For nearly fifteen years before that, American officials frequently discussed the problematic nature of the regime. In 1961 an economics officer in the U.S. Embassy in Addis Ababa noted that the Five-Year Plan failed to push "land and tax reforms" and was in fact "more a statement of aspirations than a plan, and even so has been given scant consideration by the individual operating ministries." The development projects the plan envisaged were intended to boost the prestige of the imperial regime rather than the requirements of "sound economics." Nevertheless, Americans remained at least cautiously optimistic that they could influence the emperor and achieve some degree of modernization. In 1963 Haile Selassie met with Kennedy, Williams, Ball, Ambassador Edward Korry, and other American officials and pressed for assurance the United States would "commit itself to projects" in the Five-Year Plan. The emperor noted that "several promises in the past had not been fulfilled," and asked for "definite replies so he can adjust his plans for the future," pointing out that other African governments criticized him for continuing to allow the U.S. military access to the Kagnew station at Asmara.[49] Kennedy told the emperor of his admiration for "the role played by Ethiopia in Africa and particularly of its leading role at the recent Addis conference," and expressed gratitude for the country's warm reception of the Peace Corps.[50]

When Ethiopia made new requests for aid, Washington felt compelled to grant some, though nowhere near what was asked. The administration expressed a willingness to study a small dam on the Finchaa River, bridges, meat processing facilities, and malaria and other health programs.[51] The United States found itself in "a bargaining situation over the price we will pay, in increased economic and military aid, for highly classified new intelligence facilities (for monitoring Soviet space communications)" and keeping the emperor happy.[52] This was hardly the coherent policy of rewarding careful development planning the Americans had intended.

Throughout the sixties, American officials feared that their embrace of Ethiopia, however necessary, could prove a costly risk. As an embassy official put it as early as 1961, if the regime fell while still a large recipient of U.S. aid, "we run the risk that our assistance programs, especially military assistance, have identified us to a disturbing degree as supporters of an archaic regime." The consequences for U.S. influence in a post-imperial Ethiopia would likely prove dire. By the end of the Kennedy years, a National Policy Paper on Ethiopia acknowledged the fundamental contradiction in U.S. policies toward what it considered an archaic state. "Our immediate and short-term goals do not seem at first glance entirely consistent with our longer-term objectives. Some are essentially positive and progressive in character, looking forward to considerable change, while others appear negative, preclusive, or in support of the status quo. The risk is always present that the pursuit of longer-term policies relating to reform could unleash forces which could jeopardize immediate US interests."[53] Rostow summed up the U.S. rationale for rejecting large increases in military aid: "Butter, strategically applied, can make up for many tons of undelivered guns."[54]

American hopes that the imperial regime would reform itself and usher in Ethiopian modernity could not have been more fully confounded. As Harold G. Marcus has argued, Washington's dispatch of "thousands of Americans to Addis Ababa and elsewhere" in Ethiopia (including officials of USAID and the Peace Corps, discussed in chapter 8), though intended to save Haile Selassie's regime, "led directly and indirectly to his overthrow—the ultimate irony." The Ethiopian Revolution of 1974, the culmination of years of blossoming anti-government and anti-American sentiment, offered supporters a different version of modernity. Donald Donham's detailed study of the mobilization of the Ethiopian population during the revolution shows that Ethiopian evangelicals and the educated, rejecting Haile Selassie's top-down modernization, supported the revolution as means of replacing authoritarian traditional institutions.[55] Thus, they rejected American modernization and its narrow, apoliti-cal definition of elite planning, as well as their country's deep dependence on American military protection and economic financing.

By 1965, patience in Washington had run out on Ethiopian complaints about a lack of U.S. aid and what Robert Komer called the "Ethiopian doctrine that they can shake us down for more." The country had, he noted, received more aid in recent years than any African nation other than Nigeria. Less than a year later, however, Komer believed the imperial regime "is in growing jeopardy" due to mounting criticism within Ethiopia and the emperor's apparent detachment. "Don't we have some of the ingredients of another coup?" asked Komer, who wondered if the United States could persuade the emperor to adopt "some quick domestic reforms designed to eliminate the most threatening complaints." He invoked the examples of the Shah of Iran and King Hassan, "modern reformist monarchs." Such short-term reforms would "buy time" while "more fundamental reforms could be started."[56]

In 1965 economist Edward Mason of Harvard, author of brief volumes on planning and foreign aid, visited the USAID mission in Ethiopia and reported that the mission's emphasis on technical assistance—mostly in education, public health, and the surveying of a power site on the Blue Nile—"seems sensible at this stage of Ethiopian development." But while Mason considered this technical assistance necessary, he warned that its development "pay-off" would only occur in the "very long-run." "What is needed," he argued, "is greater emphasis on immediately productive undertakings" in agriculture, such as developing animal husbandry so Ethiopia could export livestock pro-duce.[57] Mason's report from Ethiopia reflected more than just his travel expe-rience. He had already argued in print that planning, while politically neces-sary, might fail, particularly if governments pursued industrialization before boosting agricultural productivity. Mason had also argued that U.S. aid should be based on a national security rationale, the very position (advocated by some in Washington) that threatened to disrupt the planning criteria adopted by Rostow and the Kennedy administration.[58]

By the late 1960s, there was widespread public recognition that, as one press report put it, "Fifteen years of accelerating development efforts have failed to budge the stubborn Ethiopian economy." Rather than a catalyst for African modernization or a showcase of American development assistance, Ethiopia became associated with quite different lessons, "a textbook case of how long it takes the fruits of self-help and foreign assistance to ripen in a backward, newly awakened African nation."[59]

While evidence mounted that Ethiopia had proven a frustrating failure for the American development project, signs of what lay ahead were quite visible at the heart of the U.S. presence in Addis Ababa. At Haile Selassie I University, Ethiopian students' violent demonstrations and radical rhetoric symbolized the failure of American policy several years before the revolution. "For the students," according to Marcus, "the university with its many American personnel and its John F. Kennedy library came to represent the sham of democratic American liberalism allied to despotic Ethiopian feudalism," as student critiques of the regime went hand in hand with those of American violations of national sovereignty. Ethiopian students abroad, influenced like many African students by Marxist perspectives, saw the United States as the imperial foe of progressive forces worldwide, and Haile Selassie's regime appeared an American puppet.[60]

Marcus argues that, having helped Haile Selassie survive the aborted coup of 1960, and determined to prop up his regime to protect access to Kagnew, the United States embarked upon a contradictory and half-hearted development project. Washington, he writes, remained unwilling to accept either the status quo (the inept and increasingly unpopular, archaic imperial state) "nor completely to reoutfit Ethiopia with a Rostowian wardrobe," thus dooming American policy to remain "unprincipled, even amoral, in its pragmatic opportunism." For Marcus, the military base "was the priority."[61]

While sharing Marcus's basic recognition of the incoherence and solipsism of Washington's outlook, I argue that Ethiopia, rather than an exceptional or special case, rather exemplified the self-imposed dilemmas of an ambivalent American neoimperialism throughout Africa. One need not agree with Marcus, for example, that the Americans ultimately did not care about reform in Ethiopia, or that evidence to the contrary comprised merely "some progressive window dressing." Officials—as well as technical experts—can and often do desire mutually exclusive outcomes, such as Ethiopian stability and modernization. It is difficult to see how abandoning military facilities in Eritrea would have hastened democratization. Moreover, the awkward embrace of imperial Ethiopia revealed the fundamental conservatism of a Cold War strategy of building the "Decade of Development." Modernity, as Americans envisioned its expansion in Africa, need not mean emancipation from authoritarian and ethnically exclusive rule such as that of the Amhara Christian hegemony in Haile Selassie's state. Arnold Rivkin, for example, concluded that Ethiopian nation building would necessarily be "difficult, complicated, and relatively slow," as it confronted the same problems as newly independent African states as well as "the problem of overcoming serious entrenched or vested interests," namely, the church, landed nobles, and the monarchy. However, the solution, for Rivkin, was not the elimination of the monarchy, but for Haile Selassie's successor to continue the modernization the emperor had imperfectly begun. A not particularly capacious conception of justice and equality or liberation is evident in this kind of thinking. Ironically, the revolutionary regime that seized power in 1974, caught up in the proxy war waged by the superpowers in the Horn of Africa, drove Ethiopia in the mid-eighties into the famine that killed perhaps a million people.[62]

The Congo: "A Special Case"

Some U.S. economic aid was not for development; it went for "supporting assistance," usually loans or grants to shore up weak or unstable governments, often in times of emergency. The major African example throughout the early 1960s was the Congo (later renamed Zaire, and still later the Democratic Republic of Congo), the huge, mineral-rich Central African nation plagued by civil war after the assassination of nationalist leader Patrice Lumumba. While the Americans had ideas about the long-term development of the Congo, during this period only short-term aid mattered, as Washington supported the national government with loans so it could buy imported U.S. goods. The Kennedy administration's involvement in the diplomatic and military aspects of the Congo crisis completely distracted attention from larger "nation-building" goals for the country, at least during 1961–62, and when the turmoil ended later in the decade, a dictatorship emerged, postponing real economic improvement for many years.[63]

Ironically, the most clearly national vision among Congolese politicians belonged to the leader Americans distrusted the most: Lumumba. The passionate and charismatic nationalist leader alarmed Westerners with the acute intensity of his condemnation of Belgian colonialism. As seen in chapter 1, even the avowedly anti-colonial Americans found much to admire in the visible evidence of Belgian modernity in the capital city, Leopoldville. The wealth of the copper mining industry, largely concentrated in the southern province of Katanga, illustrated Belgian achievement too, and when, shortly after Lumumba's ascent to the office of prime minister, Belgian interests backed a secessionist bid there, many Americans sympathized with a scheme that would have rent Congolese unity. Eisenhower, convinced Lumumba was irrational and either a Communist or a potential Soviet pawn, authorized the CIA to launch operations against him. As the country plunged into the chaos of secession, political instability, and riots, Joseph Mobutu emerged from the officer ranks of the army to seize the initiative. Mobutu was instrumental in the arrest and murder of Lumumba, and by 1963, with the open support of Kennedy, he had emerged as the focus of American hopes for political stability.

Kennedy, less concerned with Communist penetration in Leopoldville than the damage to the Congo, and Africa, should Katanga's secession stand, threw American support behind a successful United Nations military intervention that reunified the country. Despite withering criticism from conservative critics in the United States who preferred the white-dominated, impeccably anti-Communist Katanga to any regime in Leopoldville that could succeed Lumumba, the administration achieved what initially appeared a major success for American foreign policy, blocking an avenue of Soviet influence in the heart of Africa.

Aside from thwarting the Soviets, Washington had acted in the Congo to preserve the economic and political potential of a vast Central African territory that many in Africa and the West saw as a potential catalyst for development and nation building. If the Congo could tap the hydroelectric power possibilities of its Congo River (the second longest in Africa behind the Nile) and develop its mineral wealth and abundant agricultural resources, and if a government in Leopoldville could stitch together the numerous ethnic groups into a united state, a model could be achieved for Africa. Upon independence in 1960, Western economists believed fiscal soundness required the Congo to scale back its leaders' plans for a major increase in social services while offering foreign investors strong guarantees. When Congolese politicians expressed a preference for technical assistance from the UN instead of "paternalistic" economic aid from the Belgians, one economist cautioned, "Never has the UN stepped in to run the whole economy of a country such as the Congo."[64]

Commentators stressed "the potential" if the country could survive its political crisis and short-term economic problems. "Sixty percent of the world's cobalt, 70 percent of its industrial diamonds; and about 10 percent of its copper and tin come from the Congo," and at over a billion dollars, its gross domestic product was "slightly larger" than Rhodesia's and trailed only Nigeria and South Africa. Its other key natural resource, the Congo River, gave it "one of the world's most impressive hydro-electric potentials." Development planners wanted to build a $3.5 billion Inga Rapids Project, "a vast power complex comparable to that of the Ruhr industrial basin," near the Congo's mouth.[65]

Harlan Cleveland of the State Department considered the Congo "under-developed, not in resources, mining or urbanism, but emphatically so in organization, administrative leadership, and technical expertise in every field. 'I was shocked,' a Malayan Army Captain told us, 'to see how underde-veloped these people are.'" Cleveland concluded, "It is clear that the task of making a nation out of the Congo will be long and tough." All the UN had been able to do for it was to have "prevented a complete breakdown in the economy," but no real development program existed or was possible because of the crisis, a problem aggravated by "all the classic symptoms of underde-velopment . . . present, including large numbers of ineffective Congolese in something like forty different 'ministries.'" Food aid and other U.S. aid "has been maintenance, not development." Cleveland declared, "The Congolese Government is in fact not a government; it is heavily dependent on outside assistance and foreign advisors. This will be true for a number of years to come." Though suggesting some short-term measures on the Katangan issue, Cleveland concluded, "The Congo has reached a watershed, and we must move from stop-gap interim measures to more long-range steps" so that the Congolese could assume control over their own nation.[66]

In January 1963 a State Department official, in a letter to President Kennedy, argued that the winding down of the crisis meant "the transfer of the prob-lem of the Congo from that of a threat to world peace to the difficult but more manageable task of building a Congolese nation."[67] Dean Rusk pointed out that the Congo required "'nation-building' programs" so that it "develops rapidly the ability to manage its own government and put its own economy to work."[68] The transition would, however, require a continued American role, for reduced economic aid from the UN, feared the State Department, could harm "the Congo, the sick man of Africa." Its government, hampered by "Katanga's secession, divisive tribalism, and corruption," presided over a serious budget deficit and inflation and needed help. If the UN had to cut back to appease the Soviets and other critics of its favoritism for the West, the United States and other nations would have to scramble to fill the void. Rusk sent Cleveland to the Congo to determine the country's future needs.[69]

After a tour there in early 1963, Cleveland produced a report of over one hundred pages discussing "physical security" problems, inflation, and eco-nomic aid. The Cleveland report began by stating, "The Congo is a paradox: staggering problems in the present, and impressive prospects in the future." With the secession crisis nearing its end, the Congo "enters the nation-build-

ing phase of its young life" as it strives for political and economic development. If the country fixed its administrative, fiscal, and political inefficiencies, with American and other aid, "the Congo should not be a burden on its
friends in a few years' time." Since the United States could not play the role
of "very junior partners" to Britain or France in this case, as in many other
African countries, it would join a wide multilateral aid effort that would
"resemble India and Pakistan" in its combination of bilateral technical assistance and other forms of help. Unlike the South Asian nations, the Congo "is
in no position to negotiate at arm's length with, or coordinate the activities
of, the several relatively powerful nations and organizations which control
chunks of the Congo's future." The UN would have to act as coordinator
because the Congo lacked the personnel and administrative structure to jug-
gle this aid. While encouraging the reorganization of the UN Congo Fund,
the report identified America's "strategic role" in the next two to three years
of the aid effort as one focusing on a stabilization program of technical and
financial aid. U.S. aid "not directly related to" retraining the Congolese army,
"internal security, rapid improvement in key areas of governmental administration, and economic stabilization should be deemphasized or eliminated."
Grants for long-term projects in areas such as human resources should be
postponed until the country achieved stability, while the UN should coordinate the long-term development programs.[70]

The State Department embraced the message of the Congo at a "crossroads," and believed Belgium should become the top aid donor; it "might be
augmented gradually and discretely to render it the dominant partner." As an
official in the Bureau of Intelligence and Research noted, Washington had
placed a great deal of prestige on the line in stopping the secession, and it
would be tarnished in African eyes if American aid was withdrawn too pre-
cipitously and the Congo's economy collapsed, a prospect not unlikely, given
its unemployment, inflation, administrative weakness, and the "deteriora-
tion of the economic infrastructure, particularly of the transportation network which must be rebuilt if productivity is to return to pre-1960 levels."[71]
Four months after the Cleveland Report, a CIA report on the country repeated
the litany of resources such as minerals and rivers that "could generate a fifth
of the world's hydroelectric power." That potential was "threatened by
Congolese financial mismanagement" and the government's tenuous grasp
on "the unruly Congo Army." The Congo thus remained "a poor and underdeveloped country" with a per capita income of $50. "Merely to stay afloat

economically," the country needed $175 million in aid in 1963, though the government would remain too weak to challenge the Congo's major economic problems in the immediate future.[72]

While Washington hoped for the best and feared the worst in the Congo, Arnold Rivkin, unsurprisingly, found a cause for optimism. The Congo's Ministry of Plan and Industrial Development, reported Rivkin, had "imaginatively" published planning guidelines in 1963 that insisted, "A development plan—even one conceived in a period of troubles and confusion—is always an element of stabilization and order." The paper waxed optimistic, arguing, "Planning will have a considerable psychological impact on the nation. It will channel toward concrete goals the attention now focused on political passions." This statement of intentional depoliticization Rivkin cited as "an extreme, but highly illustrative, application of the concept of economic development as an instrumentality for nation-building."[73] By the mid-1960s, however, little had come of such confident assertions, as real planning remained but an aspiration, while political and military upheaval flamed anew. An American anthropologist attempted to refute the facile optimism of economists who expected great prosperity once the Congo crisis ended. Alvin M. Wolfe argued that the rosy economic statistics of the pre-independence years reflected a sobering fact for the postcolonial era: the country's economy grew because it was directed and funded by external sources. No real national economy even existed, he suggested, since "the 'Congo economy'" remained in fact "so tightly integrated with other national economies" as its industry and capital all came from elsewhere. The country's goods had to be exported to a "world market, upon which internal Congo forces had virtually no effect." The country's mineral industry was inextricably bound up with that of other Southern African nations and colonies, and its firms were "integrated with not only the parent firms in Belgium, but with other mining firms in Southern Africa, on which depend the 'economies' of the Rhodesias, Angola, South West Africa and the Republic of South Africa." For the people of the Congo, through their government, to have any control over the direction and destiny of their economy, they would have to challenge the very international basis of their economic growth. Wolfe suggested that one might find "that this is the dilemma of all Africans . . . the dilemma of those who strive for political independence in isolated state structures even while economic realities necessitate interdependence."[74]

Wolfe's skepticism soon resonated. *U.S. News and World Report* brought into the mainstream U.S. press an expression of this perspective in a report provocatively entitled "The Congo after 6 Years and a Billion in Aid." The staff writer Albert J. Meyers, author of articles sympathetic to the white perspective in Southern Africa, conflated American aid and the condition of whites in the Congo. "Economically, the Congo is at rock bottom," intoned Meyers, despite ample direct U.S. aid and contributions to the United Nations technical assistance program. All of that money had proven a poor investment, for not only had it not yielded political stability or economic progress, it had unleashed an inflation that inflicted "outrageous" costs on white patrons of Leopoldville restaurants. Meyers's fascination with the return of Belgians and the critical presence of Americans trying to save the Congo led him to pronounce "a return to a form of colonialism." As the caption to one photo of whites read, "Along with Americans, it's Belgians who are keeping entire country from collapsing." What aid had failed to achieve, it seemed, whiteness and neocolonialism might accomplish.[75]

Acknowledgment that American aid had been wasted in the Congo found official, if less inflated, expression. A 1965 memo on aid to Africa noted that the country remained "a special case," a "rescue operation." "If we could once get the place straightened out, our out-of-pocket costs should drop off sharply and quickly," since the country had its own resources for development and could look to Belgium for any foreign aid it required.[76] Haynes, summarizing the turmoil in the Congo in 1966, correctly identified the problem, but not the future: "General Mobutu is the latest in a series of disastrous Congolese leaders. His heavy-handed rule has made him very unpopular with both Congolese and Belgians (especially Belgian commercial interests); his days are numbered."[77]

During a National Security Council meeting in 1967, Undersecretary of State Nicholas de B. Katzenbach acknowleged that the United States had spent "a half billion dollars in aid in the last few years" in the Congo and did not "know the reason" for its troubles and instability. "We must keep Mobutu in power," he argued, "because there is no acceptable alternative to him." In the Congo, "our aid program is small and any payoff we may get is years ahead of us," he concluded. The State Department paper prepared for the meeting noted that Washington hoped to promote development by keeping the Belgians as the main donor to the Congo and preventing instability from triggering "a mass exodus of Europeans from Katanga," which would halt development by damaging the country's "production, transportation and training."[78] Near the end of the Johnson presidency, Rostow expressed interest in an international consortium of aid donors for the Congo, "now that her worst birth pangs (hopefully) are over." While AID prepared for it, hoping to reduce its proportion of contributions to aid to the Congo, the World Bank began "settling itself into a crucial and long-range problem of Congolese development."[79]

That American decisions played a major role in confounded expectations of Congolese stability and development was seldom acknowledged in Washington. In fact, in a move anticipating American excuses and accusations elsewhere in Africa, officials blamed the people of the Congo for a destructive pattern of corruption. Robert L. West, director of the aid program in the Congo, fastened the blame on local women who carried American food aid— butter—across the Congo River to sell it for hard currency in Brazzaville. "This smuggling," a New York Times report declared, "is one of the most blatant abuses hampering the United States aid program here." West's lament to the press framed the issue as one of myopic greed on the part of uncomprehending African women.[80] USAID officials emphasized local culture and corruption in their postmortems. "Bribery is the basis of Bantu politics," one asserted. Stephen Weissman notes that American officials ignored "the political problems of foreign aid," preferring to imagine nation building as comprising a set of "technical problems." This tendency was evident in the Cleveland report's claim that the key to the Congo lay in training the ANC and reforming the fiscal system.[81]

The Congo collapsed in 1964. A series of rebellions in different parts of the vast country killed many thousands of people. To stave off chaos and Communism, Washington used force. American aircraft transported white South African mercenaries, whose brutality subdued the country, making it safe for Mobutu. From 1965 to 1997 the Congo—renamed Zaire—had the most entrenched African dictatorship, and one utterly uninterested in the kind of modernization Americans had hoped for. Rather than stabilizing the country and getting it off the American dole, Washington absorbed an expensive, erratic client. Mobutu enriched himself until the economy could no longer sustain him. Not only had nation building failed. "Over time, the state became less like a state and more like a mafia."[82]

Rivkin at the end of the decade perhaps best summarized American distress about the Congo, in spite of its safety from Communism. The country's experience had been "a special case," admitted Rivkin, though most of its problems existed elsewhere in Africa. "The Congo, however, has all the problems, and has them all more acutely." Assessing its "prospects for successful nation-building" as "dismal," he believed "this has serious implications for nation-building and development elsewhere in Africa, for as The Economist wryly observed: 'Without the Congo, Africa is like a doughnut—it has a hole in the center.'" The African Decade of Development could not bypass the vast, mineral-rich state.[83]

Rivkin, writing in the late 1960s, noted that Western experts remained divided over "how much and what kind of economic-development planning is appropriate for African countries in their present circumstances." Some advocated "comprehensive planning" to establish production goals for both public and private sectors. Others, "anti-planning 'planners,'" sought plans that focused on "a handful of important projects in the public sector." More troubling, Rivkin lamented, "too many African states" had "adopted development plans which have not served their principal needs" and comprised "elaborate exercises" unconnected to the country's realities and capabilities. Meanwhile, other, more modest plans had been "little more than 'shopping lists' for obtaining whatever external assistance can be found." As a result, "there have been no dramatic breakthroughs" in development, with only Nigeria, Ivory Coast, and Kenya achieving sustained high rates of economic growth. For most African economies, growth would add little per capita income while their population grew at 2.5 to 3 percent per year.[84] By the end of the decade, Rivkin tersely remarked, "Few states have got down to cases." Most had "shopping list" plans and an appetite for foreign aid "without clear priorities and 'hard' projects."[85] Africans' failure to follow development planning principles which Americans themselves could not agree upon, clearly had to be Africa's fault, not America's.

Five

"A Significant Historical Demonstration"

"Going Somewhere"

Though admitting "my knowledge of the history of West Africa is quite inadequate," American economist Wolfgang Stolper enthusiastically embraced the
task of drafting independent Nigeria's first national development plan. In 1960,
the forty-eight-year-old University of Michigan professor, formerly a colleague
of Arnold Rivkin's at CIS, made his first trip to sub-Saharan Africa's most populous nation. Desperately needing expatriate experts and civil servants, Nigeria
had asked the Ford Foundation to help staff the Federal Ministry of Economic Development. Stolper, a Harvard Ph.D., friend and disciple of Joseph
Schumpeter, and an authority on the economy of Communist East Germany,
had joined Rivkin's African program at CIS. In February 1961, Stolper began a
sixteen-month stint as head of the Ministry's Economic Planning Unit (EPU).
He kept a detailed diary. It records his professional pride and ambition, couched
in the language of a classic secular missionary. "I have the most enviable assign-
ment a man can have," one endowed with the aura of nation building. "I have
a chance to help weld the territory into a nation," by "developing an integrated plan for the most important African economy with the biggest and most
hopeful future of any African nation." It felt like being in "peaceful army service," albeit one enjoying "an air-conditioned apartment."[1]

Stolper's excitement reflected a broad optimism about Nigeria. Americans
saw it as the African nation best prepared for rapid development. So did
Nigerians. Since attaining independence in 1960, the most populous nation
in sub-Saharan Africa strove to convert its size and economic potential into

leadership in Africa. The former British colony's large population and immense ethnic, religious, and regional diversity garnered notice. A federal system of government, responsible, "moderate" nationalist political leaders (some of whom, such as Igbo leader Nnamdi Azikiwe, had studied in the United States), an expanding free-market economy and abundant natural and human resources (even before the scope of Nigeria's oil resources were known) beckoned observers looking for a model state in Africa. Nigeria, Americans hoped, would blaze the trail of modernization and nation building for other African states to follow, establishing a bulwark of anti-Communist stability. In 1961 Rostow told a Nigerian economic mission visiting Washington that President Kennedy, in contemplating foreign aid, would "regard certain areas of creative opportunity with the same urgency and priority we accord to crises." "Nigeria was one example" Kennedy "had in mind."[2] The president told the visitors that "Nigeria was of great importance to the whole southern half of the globe," and thus the United States was "extremely interested in and attaches very high priority to assistance to Nigeria." Kennedy explained, "Nigeria's influence, its responsible leadership and its economic potential were of the greatest interest," as the country could perform as a catalyst for African development. "Its position in Africa was comparable to that of nations like Brazil in Latin America. If the pattern for social and economic development could be set in Nigeria where conditions were favorable," other African nations would have something to follow.[3]

Americans "felt the closest affinity" for Nigeria of any country in the region during the First Republic. As a regular contributor to *Africa Report* noted, the two nations were "sprawling, varied, bustling, and eager to be successful," and Nigeria fashioned a federalist political system to contain such "centrifugal forces" as ethnic diversity.[4] Americans interested in Nigeria's apparent "dynamism" often expressed the sentiment that Nigerians were a uniquely hardworking people, and that the capital, Lagos, was unique. According to *U.S. News and World Report*, "A riot of smells, none of them pleasant, greets the visitor on his arrival in Lagos. It's a city, he finds, of slums and filth," an immensely crowded city whose streets feature "hordes of naked children" and women and children carrying "huge loads balanced perfectly on their heads." Yet Americans automatically attributed to the essence of Nigerian culture or existence a phenomenal energy. The same *U.S. News and World Report* article quoted "an American who has lived here for years" as stating, "These people are aggressive in the best sense of the word. I don't know how far they'll go, but they're certainly going somewhere."[5]

In the early 1960s, Americans helped Nigeria draft a National Development Plan and provided substantial economic assistance to implement it. However, their nation-building strategy failed and produced long-term results devastating to Nigerian aspirations. The First Republic, however, collapsed in 1966 with a military coup and the assassination of the prime minister, Alhaji Sir Abubakar Tafawa Balewa. Ethnic and regional conflict exploded into a grisly war, confounding the expectations of Americans.[6] A brutal civil war in 1967–70 scarred Nigeria, and reliance on American aid and economic advice yielded growing inequality and a crushing external debt. Nigeria's distress as a country plagued by economic inequality, governmental corruption, ethnic conflict, and abject dependence on the West constitutes a crucial part of postcolonial African history.[7]

Planning for development had begun in a limited fashion during the colonial era, and the World Bank had already extended its first loan to the country, to help finance railroad construction. Upon the achievement of independence in 1960, Nigeria's three regions—Northern (in which the Hausa-Fulani dominated), Eastern (the Igbo) and Western (the Yoruba)—had development planning under way and anticipated a large degree of autonomy within the new federal system. The federal government in Lagos, meanwhile, began preparation for a new national plan. Many Nigerian and foreign scholars have criticized the National Plan of 1962–68 that resulted, the first of several national development plans promulgated since independence. The plan's reputation has long suffered the stigma of foreign authorship, since American experts drafted it and envisioned copious doses of Western aid and private investment spurring export-led economic growth. One contemporary Western academic labeled the plan "rather unrealistic in its assumptions" because its narrow emphasis on government expenditures for public projects added up to "basically a proposal for growth within the existing economic and socio-political structure," and "not a call for development through structural change."[8]

As Nigerian economist Ojetunji Aboyade observed, Stolper shared his mentor's "great admiration for dynamic innovative private enterprise as a vehicle for generating economic growth." While he imbibed the modernization theory then fashionable, "Stolper's vision of economic development followed that of Schumpeter—a process of creative destruction."[9] As head of the EPU in Lagos, Stolper regarded himself as "a Nigerian civil servant" taking orders from Nigerian superiors, and one who worked "not so much as an advisor, but as an executive officer who would do things rather than advise on how they should be done." However, Stolper was in fact an expatriate serving during an early phase of the Nigerianization of the civil service, and one who began his job with no prior knowledge of African languages, history, culture, or politics. There is no evidence that he had consulted the influential studies by James Coleman, Richard L. Sklar, or other recent Western authorities on Nigeria, and the diary shows he learned but slowly the basic political landscape of regional and party rivalries. Perhaps unencumbered by such knowledge, Stolper recorded breezy generalizations and stereotypes about Nigerians, remarking that, while all Westerners he talked to were "enthusiastic about the Nigerians, their future and their importance in Africa and the world," it appeared that "the African is apt to have ten wives and 60 children." Expressing confidence in "my approach to development," he was "elated" by his growing influence in the corridors of government. By September 1961, Stolper flatly declared, "I am the best economist in West Africa." Feeling as though he carried the entire planning effort, Stolper predicted, "If Nigeria gets money, it will be more because of what I do."[10]

His self-confidence belies the claim advanced by the editor of the Stolper diaries, Clive S. Gray, who asserts that Stolper was "intensely curious" about Nigerian society and culture. Though the diaries document his travels throughout the country and, occasionally, into other African nations, they also reveal his private attitudes. Stolper and other Westerners constantly speculated about "whether there had been organized states" in Nigeria before European colonization, besides Benin, of which Stolper thought: "When the British conquered it around 1900, it was completely degenerate, with bloodthirsty tyranny, cannibalism, human sacrifices on an enormous scale." Pre-colonial states featured "cruelty unmatched until Hitler's concentration camps." If exposure to Nigeria did little to broaden his historical horizons, they did as little to alter his disdain for contemporary Nigerian life. Stolper repeatedly complained about the heat and humidity, and the general lack of amenities. Lagos was his favorite Nigerian city, yet he regarded it as "a hardship post." Sensory perceptions hardened Stolper's disdain. The city of Benin he described as "really a hellhole" and "one of the unhealthiest places in Nigeria," short of water, "dirty, and evidently not yet recovered from the massacres of the last degenerate days of the Empire of Benin," a statement that neatly erased the intervening sixty years of British exploitation. More fundamentally, Stolper decried the "really astonishing absence of aesthetic or artistic values" of Nigeria as a whole, and its loathsome crowds of children impertinently clustering around him during sightseeing forays. Oblivious of the pernicious legacy of colonialism or the potential intrusion and disruptive character of his own presence as a privileged Westerner, Stolper complained bitterly about his lack of privacy as Nigerians sought "dash"—cash payment—in return for permission to take photographs or for performing small tasks. Referring to what was known as "West Africa Wins Again," Stolper considered this a traditional African "exploitation" of white visitors.[11]

Like many Westerners and Nigerians, Stolper was fond of contrasting Nigeria with more "radical" states like Ghana. He termed Nigeria "an oasis of rationality in a sea of unreason" upon hearing stories about the weakness of Ghanaian planning. Yet Stolper's initial enthusiasm for Nigerian leaders rapidly vanished. In its place emerged disgust with Nigerian incompetence, laziness, and corruption. As politicians meddled with his carefully wrought development planning, he bristled at the suggestion that some projects were politically desirable, even if their profitability was questionable. "The fact was that politicians wanted to spend roughly three times as much as there were conceivably resources for," hissed Stolper. Nigerians struck him as inordinately impatient for the fruits of economic growth. His diary records his private view: "If they don't want to work like mad and wait for the results, then they can't be helped." Even among Nigerian officials who worked hard, Stolper claimed they had "no conception of what development means, or that funds are scarce, that you can't borrow from abroad to make up for ordinary budget deficits, that loss-making operations don't contribute to economic development, or for that matter, of just what planning is supposed to do." By February 1962, Stolper's angst over Nigerian corruption had become acute. "It isn't the stealing itself so much," he wrote, "as the effect it has on priorities, on costs, and on the morale of the people who know." From his point of view, in particular, "This makes the problem of enforcing the Plan priorities so important, fascinating, and probably impossible. . . . " The sense of ironic detachment in this statement recurs in many others in his diary and published writings about Nigeria.[12]

The Rivkin Report

Before disillusionment set in, Stolper experienced the thrill, along with Rivkin, of wielding power and making history. Turning to his MIT associates Rivkin and Stolper for insight into Nigeria's development prospects, in March 1961 Rostow set in motion a collaboration between the Kennedy administration, MIT, the Ford Foundation, and the Nigerian federal government that produced Nigeria's Six-Year Plan of 1962–68.[13] Rivkin, responding to Rostow's request for an appraisal, declared that Nigeria "may play a role in Africa as important as India in Asia."[14] Millikan relayed Rostow's message to Stolper that the White House had "selected Nigeria as the African country which it is important for us to deal with in a successful way." Rostow wished to know if MIT had anything on hand with which to quickly estimate the kind of five-year plan Nigeria could or should produce.[15]

In May 1961, the Nigerians (and Stolper) learned that the Kennedy administration would send Rivkin to lead an economic mission to determine the status of Nigerian development planning and Nigerian needs for assistance. Stolper briefed the Nigerians on "what kind of fellow Rivkin was" and what the American mission would want to know. Meanwhile, the American economist collaborated with U.S. officials in exchanging information and views on the Nigerians. When an officer at the U.S. Embassy informed Stolper about the mission's intention to pave the way for a major U.S. aid commitment, an exuberant Stolper recorded: "What they want to know and what they are prepared to offer is something of a triumph for me: it is just what I have been arguing we should do. This is perhaps not too surprising, because I was after all at MIT," he noted with wry satisfaction. The Rivkin mission's interest in obtaining data on Nigerian financial resources, "what we can finance ourselves, how many grants and loans we need," and the Nigerians' commitment to placing all specific development projects firmly within the framework of a detailed plan all meshed with Stolper's efforts within the Planning Unit. Stolper's strategic position within the Nigerian government made Rivkin's negotiating task easier. In a May 24, 1961 meeting with Nigerian officials, Rivkin "was taken aback" by the ease with which they agreed that an international donor consortium modeled on the World Bank–inspired group for India should be created. Though Rivkin had girded himself for a long conversation "to convert the Nigerians to the Kennedy point of view" on multilateral aid funding, Stolper's influence within the Nigerian government made a meeting of minds almost automatic. The foundation had been laid, almost casually, for the future dominant role of the World Bank and multilateral lending processes in Nigeria's economy.[16]

During a June 1961 meeting between the U.S. mission and the Nigerian planners, Rivkin gave a detailed assessment of the mission's impressions of the economic activities of each Nigerian region. Rivkin also told them that everything depended on "the structure of the plan," and "that a carefully integrated approach might cover items which were less attractive in themselves." This meant specific projects; the United States would fund a quality plan, not quality projects.[17] Rivkin, in a letter to his former MIT colleague, wrote that he enjoyed working with Stolper "in the exciting atmosphere of Lagos."[18]

The report Rivkin submitted in the summer of 1961 stated confidently, "Nigeria, perhaps more than any of the new independent African states . . . meets the new aid criteria of the President, and offers a good opportunity . . . to achieve economic development in a democratic framework." Nigerian leaders exhibited an "all pervading spirit of determination" and a "seriousness, a thoughtfulness, and an earnestness" about achieving modernization within a capitalist framework. Thus, the Rivkin Report urged Washington to offer substantial aid to help Nigeria implement its development plan and to coordinate assistance with the World Bank, especially in sponsoring a $189 million Niger River hydroelectric dam.[19]

The Rivkin Report's outlook took firm hold in official Washington. The African Bureau of the State Department believed a long-term aid commitment to Nigeria would "demonstrate the advantages of long-term development planning," and that with U.S. help, "the moral equivalent of anti-colonialism could become 'the plan'" throughout the region. Nigeria "should be given special treatment as the most populated state in Africa with excellent prospects for economic development, i.e., the India of Africa."[20] Fowler Hamilton, head of USAID, advised the president of the "extraordinary" character of Nigeria's development plan, which he described as the "first development plan of such scope and magnitude on the continent of Africa" and "truly national in scope and purpose." Two days later, on 24 November, Kennedy approved a directive, supported by Hamilton, to commit to a long-term aid package for Nigeria. Nigeria, according to another report by USAID, provided America with "an excellent opportunity . . . to demonstrate to the newly independent African nations that the best way to achieve their economic and political aspirations lies in developing institutions and cooperating with the Free World." Thus, although "no major American trading or investment stakes" or "major strategic or military interests" seemed evident in Nigeria, it remained "the most important country in Africa." For its potential impact on Africa's development decade, Nigeria would remain relevant to Washington "in a way [in] which most other typical African countries are not."[21]

Before Prime Minister Balewa's arrival in Washington in July 1961, Rostow summarized for the president the importance of this "key visit from a key country." Balewa, "an intelligent and able politician," had, Rostow noted, "consistently reiterated his belief in good U.S. intentions but has expressed concern about the slowness with which our aid arrived." Rostow "strongly" urged the president to read a five-page summary of the Rivkin Report before the meeting.[22] During Balewa's visit, Kennedy said he was "extremely interested in Nigeria's economic development and he had read the Rivkin report." The United States, Kennedy explained, had "grouped" Nigeria together with India, Pakistan, and Brazil as exemplary countries deserving substantial aid. Expressing gratitude, Balewa replied that Nigeria sought to be a model for Africa.[23]

In Lagos, Stolper received a preliminary version of the Rivkin Report, ahead of the Nigerian government. He enjoyed the "very complimentary" description of the Nigerian plan in the report, and observed, "Most of it plays into my hands very nicely in stressing the need to avoid inflation and exchange control at any cost." In the relatively minor areas of the report where Stolper "disagreed" with Rivkin, he was able to contact him immediately to seek amendments.[24]

Rivkin noted that his report "has been very well received" in Washington as had his testimony before the House Foreign Affairs Committee in June. "All of this is most gratifying and promises well for the future."[25] Stolper wrote to Rivkin that the World Bank's recent visit and the Rivkin Report "will strengthen our Ministry's position quite considerably and will help the concept of overall economic planning." These Western-authored reports would back his side in the internal Nigerian debate over how to balance specific projects with the overall plan and how much flexibility should be built into the plan.[26] In a series of letters about the Rivkin Report in August 1961, Rivkin expressed that he was "delighted" that only a few technical points in his report "bothered" Stolper, and Rivkin assured his friend that he remained open to continued discussion of changes that should be made.[27]

When the second Rivkin mission arrived in Nigeria in September, for negotiations to pave the way for the precise amount of American aid, Stolper met the Americans at the airport in Lagos and shepherded them through customs. It came as no surprise to Stolper that Rivkin insisted that the Nigerians understand the cardinal rule of the Kennedy approach to aid: the amount given depended wholly on the nature and quality of "the plan." He wanted the Nigerians to see that Washington now extended grants and loans to help implement development plans, and not, as before, "on a political basis." Rivkin intimated that private American investment would begin to flow more fully into Nigeria if and when Nigerian politicians ceased public statements hinting at nationalization. He even brought up the sensitive issue of what he called, "the general problem of, let us say, dash," much to Stolper's delight. In subsequent discussions Rivkin was, as Stolper put it, a "broken record" in reiterating the American refusal to consider individually the value of specific Nigerian projects in a field such as education outside of the context of the overall development plan. The Americans had clarified their agenda and indicated their insistence on its acceptance.[28]

During a September 1961 meeting, Rivkin urged Nigerian planners to focus on public relations; more needed to be done to show Westerners that Nigeria was not unstable like other African nations, and "that the Nigerian personality should be more widely broadcast and that U.S. investors did not wish to be suspected of neo-colonialism or economic imperialism."[29] In October Rivkin and Ambassador Palmer met with Balewa to discuss U.S. aid and the plan. Rivkin told the prime minister that while he was impressed with Nigerian planning efforts, the plan was "not as far along as one might hope," a statement that led to a "frank and friendly conversation," according to Palmer. When Balewa declared his acceptance of the idea of a donor consortium for Nigeria the Americans found it "completely satisfactory."[30]

In linking U.S. aid to the Nigerian plan, the men from CIS had sealed a crucial relationship. Stolper found many Nigerian ideas about development disturbing, as his diary records numerous instances of what he perceived as wasteful spending, politics intruding on planning, and wrongheaded development priorities. Echoing Rostow's advice that Africa focus on agriculture before industrialization, Stolper urged Nigerians to accept that "industrialization is a long way off, and in any case only makes up the visible seventh of the iceberg. The important six-sevenths represent less spectacular agricultural development and general improvement in productivity."[31]

In November Stolper admitted to Max Millikan that he tended to "alternate between extreme despondency and conservative hopefulness" about the plan.[32] Stolper declared in his diary that he still liked Nigeria, "in a sort of exasperated way," but he had given up hope for Nigerian politicians learning the true meaning of development, or the value of implementing his plan. Instead, he hoped "to use the application process" for American foreign aid (an increasingly Byzantine one much resented by Nigerians by 1963), as a tool "to monitor Plan execution and respect priorities." Though he eschewed politics, Stolper's interest in forcing Nigerians to accept, learn, and master the complex paperwork required by the U.S. Congress in order to receive aid promised in support of his plan constituted a major intervention in Nigerian politics. Characteristically, he evinced no awareness of this, nor would he likely have been concerned by it.[33]

By the end of his tenure in Nigeria in 1962, Stolper felt satisfaction with his handiwork but, as always, pessimism about Nigeria's capacity to make the best use of it. He concluded that "the Plan was very good, and could have been superb" had it not been for the meddling of politicians. Political, economic, and cultural aspirations for organized expressions of African unity he dismissed as "paper-thin" and "a purely negative reaction to colonialism." Furthermore, only "Commies" were responsible for the African allegations of "neo-colonialism" that were increasingly leveled against the West. Though Stolper believed Nigerian economic growth would exceed the projections made in the plan, he had become disillusioned about Nigerian corruption. A Nigerian official told him that few federal ministers really sought development, just "contracts and kickbacks."

When an official from the American Agency for International Development mission in Nigeria revealed his bleak view of Nigerians as a people lacking "discipline" and whose complete corruption left them with "no shame," Stolper merely agreed, though he mused that his plan, a dose of "market discipline," and God's charity could still help Nigeria move forward.[34]

As he prepared to wrap up his Nigerian mission Stolper weighed a number of professional options. Tempted to accept offers from the Ford Foundation, Harvard, and Michigan, he wrote to Ford's representative in Nigeria, "I have to keep telling myself that I am basically an academic," and thus that he should pause in his official duties and "write my books on Nigeria."[35] He did. Stolper wrote *Planning without Facts*, an account of how the paucity of economic statistics had impaired his work in Nigeria intended to caution planners elsewhere to be less ambitious. That it might mitigate his responsibility for the plan's failures would probably have been all right, too.[36]

In Nigeria, Rivkin displayed the skills he shortly thereafter put at the disposal of the World Bank. As an admirer noted in 1963, the Bank's staff "are hard-hearted people, all from 'the West,' who ask penetrating questions, pour cold water on much-favored projects, suggest unpopular measures. Their secret is that nobody can doubt their sincerity and objectivity, and that they really know not only the technicalities of their job . . . but also the nature of the country and the people with whom they are dealing." Hiring Rivkin as Economic Advisor to the African Department demonstrated "how determined the Bank is to recruit expertise." The methods Rivkin used in steering Lagos to accept his and Stolper's conception of an American-Nigerian economic partnership in development found a natural home in the Bank, the institution that, as the biggest external influence on African economies from the 1970s, has poured an infinite amount of cold water on African ideas.[37]

In 1962–63, Rivkin zealously brought his message about Nigeria's importance to a wider audience with *Africa and the West* and *The African Presence*, and two articles on Nigerian planning in the periodical *Current History*. In these writings, he declared his scholarly judgment and quasi-official statement of U.S. policy that Nigeria would serve as the model, what he called "a significant historical demonstration" that Western-style development worked in Africa.[38] Nigeria, according to Rivkin, stood out as "a unique nation." He described it as "the only state in Africa to date to come to independence as a single unit with a fully operating federal system, chosen by the democratically elected political leadership of the country and successfully negotiated by them with Great Britain *before* independence." In his July 1961 testimony before the U.S. House Committee on Foreign Affairs, Rivkin spoke of the "very impressive" Nigerian quest for development. "This is a society very responsive to economic incentives," he stated. Unlike such authoritarian and interventionist states as Ghana and Guinea, Nigeria boasted an "open, private-sector economy growing in an atmosphere of democratic tolerance." Thus, Rivkin placed it "at the opposite pole from the African and Arab socialism" found elsewhere on the continent, and made Nigeria his favorite example of the apolitical essence of proper development planning. By concentrating its resources and attention on internal economic development, Nigeria had avoided the wasteful "diversions of external adventures" that had preoccupied Ghana and Guinea. Rivkin underscored the importance of Nigeria's success at maintaining democracy and accelerating economic development. "Much is at stake in Nigeria," he wrote. "For the country itself, in its growth and development; for Africa, in producing a vivid example of development and democracy existing together for economic growth and political stability; and for the free world, in the emergence of an important state with a system and interests compatible with those of other free-world states."[39]

Nation building would ensue. "Economic development in Nigeria is likely to strengthen the federation and the multi-party political system," maintained Rivkin. Eventually, economic growth would create "a national economy" that would allow Nigerians to transcend their ethnic, cultural, and regional differences and forge common national interests and identities. Already Rivkin saw hopeful "signs of a political realignment—on the basis of interest rather than region or tribe" that would pull Nigeria together. He predicted the endurance of Nigerian unity, citing the colonial inheritance: a "common language, similar university education, similar concepts and practices of modern jurisprudence, a common system of administration, a common currency, and expanding market system, a uniform system of weights and measurements, a telecommunications system, and one could go on."[40]

To ensure that this progress continued, the United States and other wealthy nations needed to provide aid "in ample amounts, in timely fashion, and in an order of priority best designed to facilitate economic growth and political stability."[41] The country had "the second largest economy on the African continent" after South Africa, he noted, and possessed "the capacity to receive and utilize productively significant amounts of capital, including external assistance and private investment." In addition to its good "absorptive capacity," Nigeria's development plan would, he argued, correct such problems as the shortage of trained manpower and the paucity of credit and extension services for agriculture. "Since Nigeria stands out as an oasis of democratic development in an arid desert of authoritarian-inclined African states," Rivkin declared, it would be the West's model, as "the economic development of Nigeria in democratic circumstances would make a significant historical demonstration that 'economic growth and political democracy can develop hand in hand' in Africa."[42]

Ultimately, according to Rivkin, Nigeria's drive for development offered the promise of "social justice" for nearly all Nigerians. He believed Nigerian leaders, especially Prime Minister Balewa, had committed to development as "a way to pull more and more people out of the subsistence economy and into the market economy where reward is based on performance, rather than status." Development would bridge "tribal, cultural and sectional differences" while serving as "the key to financing the technological revolution which Nigeria is about to embark upon" to create jobs for the next gen-eration of educated young people. The plan's emphasis upon agriculture "almost automatically insures that it will affect the economic status of most Nigerians," since 75 percent of the population worked in that sector. Finally, "in the goal of education for everybody, one finds in a sense the Nigerian answer to social justice for its people," as the nation strove "to improve everybody's status, including that of women." Thus, he concluded, "The Nigerian Development Plan reflects the society for which it was drawn and this is one of its chief assets." It did not strike Rivkin as ironic that he had described a plan "for," but not prepared "by" Nigerians.[43]

Second Thoughts

Despite Rivkin's absolute certainty that Nigerian planning would produce development and national unity, the plan written by his friend received criticism early and often. While it was still being prepared, Yoruba political leader Obafemi Awolowo criticized Stolper in the Nigerian legislature. Soon, Western and Nigerian scholars began to critique the plan in public debates and in print. Ojetunji Aboyade, a Cambridge Ph.D. and an economist Stolper respected, debated him publicly in Northern Nigeria in 1962. Aboyade devoted much of his book in 1966 to a sympathetic, yet sharp, critique of the premises of Stolper's plan. Western planners who did not share Stolper's conception of planning dismissed the plan as timid.[44]

Still, in America, broad-based optimism about Rivkin's "unique" African nation persisted. Americans repeatedly invoked Nigerian energy and dynamism; as CBS newsman Eric Sevareid put it, the consensus held that upon attaining independence, "a compressed boiler of Nigerian energy will be released."[45] David E. Lilienthal, former chairman of the Tennessee Valley Authority and an ardent proponent of government planning for economic development throughout the world, agreed that Nigeria was a unique nation. In 1961, after a month's tour of West Africa, he wrote a glowing profile of the country in the New York Times. Lilienthal's avid interest lay in Nigeria's largest development project, the Niger River dam. Damming West Africa's longest river would generate inexpensive electricity to spur development and "could within half a generation transform the lives of Nigerians." "Undertaking a task so large" as the Niger Dam would, according to Lilienthal, create national priority "that can provide an authentic unifying force for a new nation." Harnessing the Niger via modern technology and planning would inspire other African nations to follow suit. Lilienthal urged the West to generously fund the project, which would be less costly than the kind of spending needed "just to keep a modicum of order in the Congo, for example."[46] Such a suggestion implied that economic planning and development lay along the same continuum as military intervention in Africa.

Yet, not all American observers confidently predicted Nigerian nation-building success. Representations of Nigerian culture as primitive, exotic, or incompetent were never absent in American press coverage. Sevareid, whose curiosity was sufficient to motivate him to visit the country in 1960 to work on a television documentary, declared, "I hope the Nigerians make it," though he had doubts. "I could not help but like them, could not help being moved almost to tears by the remaining evidence of a slavish mentality, the inheritance of centuries of slavery—to the Moors, to the Westerners, to one another. It is both embarrassing and exciting to see such a people trying to adjust to a new civilization, and a technological one, to make it all the harder." Though he hoped Nigerians would retain some of their traditions, he insisted, "All Nigeria needs a cleaning, a strange thing to say of a fresh, 'new' country. But it isn't new; it is ancient—ancient in its tribalism, in its built-in corruption, so thoroughly established, like the old Chinese 'squeeze,' that one doesn't know whether to groan or admire."[47] Others claiming to sympathize with Nigeria denigrated it in the same breath. Drew Pearson, writing for the *Post*, characterized Nigeria as "a federation kept together by hairpins, chewing-gum, the red tape of British-trained civil servants, and American aid." Pearson lamented poor "Nigerian manners," citing several examples of tardiness of certain officials invited to attend dinner with the American ambassador, and the excessive "red tape" with which American visitors were greeted. These shortcomings he deemed even more serious than "side-of-the-road urinals" or "the fact that human meat is sometimes sold surreptitiously in the Lagos market to satisfy certain pagan rituals."[48]

That Nigerian development and the American aid program had yet to pick up steam became painfully obvious quite early. In February 1963, the affable Mennen Williams visited each of the three major regions in Nigeria in a major tour of USAID projects.[49] Ambassador Joseph Palmer hailed Williams's visit as a "conspicuous success," citing very positive Nigerian press coverage. However, Palmer acknowledged that Nigerians repeatedly asked tough questions about aid implementation, revealing "major governmental and public dissatisfaction" with the pace of the American effort.[50] In the Eastern Region, the premier, Dr. Michael Okpara, acknowledged that Nigerians had "much to learn" about how to correctly apply for loans, but he pleaded with Williams for additional U.S. aid. Pointing out that a lack of U.S. aid implementation had made the first year of the Six-Year Plan more expensive for Nigeria than expected, he warned that if more aid did not arrive in 1963, the plan's scope might be reduced by half. The Eastern Region needed "concrete, viable projects," particularly in education and farm settlements. Williams commented that farm settlements and related agricultural schemes might not "fit into AID programs," and Ambassador Palmer, present at the meeting, drew the conclusion that Okpara realized he had "bitten off more than he can chew" and simply wanted "loans to help bail him out." In the Western Region, the site of recent political turmoil, Williams noted that the regional premier, S. I. Akintola, "bluntly asked for more American aid and expressed [the] hope [that] my visit would be followed by [a] rain of 'American dollars.'" Though he expressed gratitude for past U.S. aid, Akintola declared the United States "fabulously wealthy," and therefore, capable of doing more. In response to Akintola, Williams argued, according to Palmer, that "part of the reason projects were not being implemented faster was their own fault."[51]

Explaining that U.S. legislation required loans and grants to go to specific development projects, Williams suggested that Nigerians prepare a "shelf of projects" they could act on when ready, so that U.S. aid would flow more rapidly.[52] This Nigerian reaction is all the more telling given that the U.S. Information Service devoted 95 percent of its resources in Nigeria to efforts "to derive maximum psychological effect from the AID program," according to a top administrator.[53]

Williams concluded from his visit that the plan had "run out of gas." The problem, he noted, was that Nigeria had paid nearly all of the program's costs from its own budget, as only a small slice of the $225 million promised by Washington had actually been received. No American loan money had been spent yet, and the State Department and USAID still struggled "to get implementation rolling." Despite the difficulties revealed by the Williams visit, Ambassador Palmer reported himself "more convinced than ever" that the successful implementation of the plan "is central to our efforts to build [an] exemplary relationship [with] this key African country."[54] However, warnings grew more frequent and pointed. In a 1964 CIA report, worried analysts attributed the slower than anticipated growth of the Nigerian economy to the fact that "private foreign investment has dropped off sharply since 1961" while "widespread corruption at all levels of both federal and regional governments" and the "blatantly ostentatious living standards" of officials had distorted the economy, leaving Nigeria more susceptible to radical internal agitation.[55]

At the Lagos embassy, Palmer suggested that Washington "may be counting too heavily on Nigeria," a newly independent nation beset by a number of problems. Though critical of USAID's shortcomings, Palmer placed more blame on the Nigerian government, citing their inability to grasp the legal requirements for receiving assistance under the new American law. As for USAID, Palmer noted that it already had 227 personnel working in the country, with another 140 scheduled to enter during the next fiscal year. To send more would create a "'presence' problem" that could undermine USAID's effectiveness and the American embassy's influence in the country.[56]

Nigerian frustration with the slow pace of U.S. aid and the cumbersome red tape in which it was ensnared raised the image of an America that did not truly care about Nigerian development. Official documents reveal the repeated Nigerian complaints, from federal, regional, and even university officials, about USAID's "detailed demands" to inspect facilities, audit budgets, conduct feasibility studies, gather statistics, and more. The vice-chancellor of the University of Nigeria, an institution largely paid for by the Nigerians but assisted by Michigan State University and the U.S. government, told Dean Rusk that "AID pushed too hard," and that Nigerians likened the situation to one in which in-laws move into a young married couple's bedroom during their first year of matrimony.[57] USAID would, he lamented, often "get in our way," adding, "Americans are used to red tape but Nigerians are not." More important, "they feel so much supervision reflects a lack of confidence in their ability and responsibleness." A representative of USAID could only reply that Congress required the agency to collect the extensive information as a prerequisite for each project. Edmond Hutchinson, head of USAID's African program, complained that he experienced difficulty implementing the funding for the "well-planned projects in Nigeria."[58]

Even before it became clear that the Americans would struggle to implement the aid they had promised, Nigerians had reservations about the close relationship so quickly achieved between Washington and Lagos. For Nigerians seeking development, nation building, and a leadership role in Africa, the United States was a crucial model. As the Nigerian Speaker of the House told Kennedy, his country hoped to "some day reach the stage of development the United States had attained." Like Washington, Lagos strongly disliked the model offered by Kwame Nkrumah.[59] Yet a widespread desire to keep Nigeria out of the Cold War naturally made the country receptive to aid and examples from all quarters.[60]

Nigerian perceptions of the American model also suffered from the overriding issue of race. As U.S. officials knew painfully well, Nigerians, like other Africans, avidly followed the news of racial conflict and discrimination in American society, often with rising indignation. The legislative achievements of 1964–65 critically boosted American prestige, though they did not erase painful memories. The U.S. Embassy understood this, reporting "overwhelmingly favorable" Nigerian press reaction to the Civil Rights Act, though many Nigerians felt the law overdue and that "much will depend upon enforcement of [the] law and its acceptance in [the] South."[61] Carl Rowan, director of USIA, reported in 1964 that Nigerian radio, "ordinarily quite friendly to the U.S.," argued that if Johnson failed to enforce the Civil Rights Act and end the violence in the South, "the new law can from the beginning be dismissed as a dead letter." Rowan noted that Nigerians seemed "dismayed by the recent outbreak of violence in the U.S. and what they see as Federal inaction," as well as an ominous "white backlash" that had resulted in the Republican nomination of Barry Goldwater for president. "We can expect the Harlem riots to be given massive coverage," warned Rowan, "and to set in motion a severe adverse reaction that will erode much of the benefit that we had hoped we would achieve with the civil rights legislation."[62]

Nigerian diplomats, like other Africans visiting the United States, suffered racial discrimination from Americans unaware of (and usually unconcerned by) their status in the eyes of Washington. One incident in 1962 briefly threatened to take its toll on Nigerian affinity for the United States. Chukwuma Azikiwe, son of Nigerian President Nnamdi Azikiwe and a student at Harvard, complained that Cambridge police "used abusive language and violence" while arresting him for loitering during a late-night incident. Ambassador Joseph Palmer warned the State Department, "These incidents [are] hard enough [to] explain when [they] occur in [the] South and on Route 40," but this incident had the potential to greatly strain U.S.–Nigerian relations if it became public. The Nigerian student threatened to file suit against the Cambridge police, prompting a sarcastic rejoinder from Harvard alumnus McGeorge Bundy, the president's National Security Advisor. Police harassment of Harvard students was "an ancient and honorable tradition" and had "nothing to do with race, creed or color on either side," insisted Bundy. He acerbically added, "As a taxpayer in the city of Cambridge, I feel reasonably confident that we neither could nor would pay Azikiwe a million dollars because our police were rude to him."[63]

The State Department learned that the Cambridge police had stopped young Azikiwe while searching for an alleged black rapist reportedly walking along the street at 2 A.M. Naturally, Harvard was "anxious to keep [the] situation quiet" and warned that a suit would be "useless and ill-advised." Nevertheless, in Lagos, Palmer's anxiety mounted. He sought a meeting with President Azikiwe and asked the Department for a "confidential, personalized Presidential message expressing regret and putting [the] case in [the] context [of the] administration's efforts" to end racism.[64]

Meanwhile, Harvard officials told the State Department that the police had told Azikiwe, "Come here, you prick," and "Get in the car, you son of a bitch," but did not use racial epitaphs, though the Nigerian inferred a racial undertone. The Nigerian embassy in Washington conducted its own inquiries, but it shared Harvard's desire to suppress news of the incident so that it would not harm the young man's future political career. By the end of June, the matter had been essentially resolved. President Azikiwe told Palmer that he appreciated the U.S. government's efforts to obtain an apology to his son, or at least to ensure that he did not have a police record, and that he had admonished his son to remember his status as a guest in America. Reporting this to Washington, a relieved Palmer thanked all American officials involved "for timely and skillful handling" of the potential crisis. While the Azikiwe incident did not explode as Palmer had feared, it nonetheless revealed that race constituted a soft underbelly of the U.S.–Nigerian partnership.[65]

While Nigerians complained of racial insults, Jim Crow, and sloppy aid implementation, Americans bemoaned Nigerian corruption incessantly and powerfully. Corruption took on a life of its own in the American imagination. An upbeat survey of Nigeria's economic potential often included some acknowledgment that "There is a certain amount of bribery and corruption which must be dealt with and which is taken for granted in the Nigerian scheme of things." American business and government officials generally believed "dash" a minor irritant and not a real roadblock to either Nigerian development or American profits, at least during the early 1960s.[66] A Time magazine report on Nigerian politics briskly noted, "'Dash,' as Nigerians cheerfully call their ritualistic system of payoffs, is so universal that many traffic cops have a fixed bribe price for every violation (running a red light costs 28c), and hospital nurses sometimes demand a penny for bringing a patient a bedpan." The corruption of political officials "whose Cadillacs and Mercedeses help make Lagos traffic jams among the worst in Africa" joined that of Nigerian businessmen, described by "a European banker in Lagos" as "the biggest bunch of con men I've ever seen."[67] Though corruption figured in American accounts of other areas of Africa, Nigeria appeared a singular example, the land of "dash," a term Westerners and Nigerians alike repeatedly invoked to convey the sense of pervading greed in matters large and small, official and unofficial, involving payments in return for favors or services. Visitors to Nigeria were told to expect, almost immediately, to encounter "dash." "One 'dashes' the boy who insists on washing your car," according to one report in the *Christian Science Monitor*, "just as one 'dashes' a government official who may be able to veto an application to build a gasoline filling station."[68] "Dash" perturbed American travelers and officials engaged in sightseeing.[69]

Corruption became a basic trope in official discourse as well. In February 1962, Stolper made the connection between corruption and stalled development clearest when he confided to his diary, "It isn't the stealing itself so much as the effect it has on priorities, on costs, and on the morale of the people who know." As a result, "This makes the problem of enforcing the Plan priorities so important, fascinating, and probably impossible," a fatalistic statement that illustrates Stolper's sense of irony, and also accounts for the American desire to closely monitor how Nigeria used its foreign aid. In 1965 the CIA, in a National Intelligence Estimate, reported that Nigerian "development is hampered by regional and tribal parochialism, the dearth of essential skills, and a high incidence of corruption." Americans seldom explored the roots of Nigerian corruption in the colonial era. This failure contributed to their own unrealistic expectations for rapid development, and reflected their inability to think of Nigeria as a concrete historical entity rather than a cultural essence.[70]

Political scientist Bassey E. Ate highlights the pernicious impact on Nigerian autonomy of the tying of U.S. aid to the implementation of the plan. He documents Nigerian frustration with sluggish implementation of aid in the early years of the plan, and perceptively suggests that Washington secured its influence in the country even as the First Republic crumbled. To get American aid and private investment, Lagos had to meet exacting, even unreasonable U.S. technical requirements to fund projects. As Nigeria strained to navigate the convoluted loan application process and draft acceptable feasibility studies, it gave Washington "effective control over the processes of implementing the public expenditure aspects of the Nigerian plan" and a growing demand for U.S. exports and technical expertise. All of this produced a profound "conditioning effect" on Nigerian officials, as Lagos found itself ensnared in "an interlocking of obligations, responsibilities, and expectations" in the bilateral relationship. One might add that the Americans wielded the greatest influence within the Washington-based World Bank, and Rivkin's career transition to the Bank neatly illustrates how the multilateral development his writings advocated extended the U.S. reach into Nigeria. In the 1980s, the Bank became clearly dominant in its impact in Nigeria and nearly all of Africa.[71]

Losing Nigeria

The flawed assumptions of the secular missionaries have drawn stinging criticisms from the very beginning. As early as 1962, Wallerstein acerbically commented: "There is a widespread belief that of all the newly independent African nations Nigeria is the outstanding example of a fairly stable, relatively pro-Western, liberal democracy. This belief is largely an illusion, nourished on superficial analysis and self-deception." Already, as Stolper's diary demonstrates, the problem of Nigerian corruption threatened to roar into the headlines. Journalistic and academic accounts, even those sharing the "illusion" decried by Wallerstein, frequently referred to the rise of a "political class" or "new class" of political and business leaders who benefited far more than ordinary Nigerians from the nation's close ties to the West and the growth of the export-oriented market economy. Though corruption's roots lay in the colonial era, independence brought an explosion of jobs, contracts, tax incentives, licenses, and other enticements that made the First Republic a bulwark, not of the "stability" admired by Rivkin and other Americans, but of an increasingly cynical, conservative, chronically partisan, parasitic class. The postcolonial "gatekeeper state" evident in other African nations had an American imprint in Nigeria, as Ate notes that politicians "benefited personally from contract negotiations on development-related projects sponsored through U. S. and other foreign loans and grants."[72]

Despite numerous complaints about the sluggishness of their mission in Nigeria, and evidence that Nigerian development had not unfolded as planned, officials of USAID continued to call Nigeria a "perfect test case" for planned development in the mid-1960s. As the *Washington Post*'s Donald H. Louchheim put it in a glowing dispatch on USAID's Nigerian program, "Nigeria remains a country that gives an overpowering sense of bustle, energy, enthusiasm and constructive concern."[73] Even on the eve of the collapse of the First Republic, the Johnson administration noted with satisfaction that Nigeria had "systematically taken" a lead as a moderate state in Africa, one whose democracy meant it could "lead others in Africa to move towards serious modern democracy."[74]

In January 1966, after many months of mounting tension in Nigeria, a coup ended the First Republic. An Igbo-led military regime came to power in Lagos after the assassination of Balewa and key members of his government. In retaliation, northern Nigerians killed thousands of Igbo living in northern cities, and in July another military coup brought northerners back to power. All of this caught American intelligence off guard. When Balewa was ousted, a CIA operative admitted "the chief problem at the moment was the absence of adequate information on what was happening in Nigeria, the identities behind the coup, and what the significance was." Williams's deputy, Wayne Fredericks, seemed shaken. "Should Nigeria go over to the radical coup the loss to the US would be most serious," he warned, and he dwelled "upon the stake the US had in Nigeria, the biggest in Africa." Fredericks wondered, "If Nigeria could fall victim to military takeover, then it could happen anywhere in Africa. The stage was set. What sort of advice could we give the remaining civilian regimes?"[75]

After the Igbo suffered atrocities during the northern riots, their leaders threatened to secede from Nigeria and make Biafra an independent nation. To deter them, the Lagos embassy urged the Secretary of State to allow it to warn the Igbo that secession would not be met not with U.S. recognition but with the evacuation of Americans and the end of U.S. aid programs in Eastern Nigeria. Dean Rusk flatly rejected the proposal. "I think we should be very careful about nominating ourselves as the supervisor of Nigerian federal unity," he declared. Rusk conflated Nigerian unity with larger federations in other areas. "The proposed West Indian Federation and East African Federation did not come off. French-speaking Africa broke up into far more units than we expected or hoped for. Singapore broke away from Malaysia." Americans might "regret all such divisiveness but it is not up to us to go around telling people how they should solve such problems under pressure of US sanctions." If any external force should be applied to Nigeria, he argued, it should come mainly from the former metropolitan power, Great Britain. The State Department thus abandoned its commitments to a country it had hoped to see as a catalyst for Africa. That Rusk's logic—and political geography—was confused or careless illustrates how little depth Washington had attained in its understanding of Africa.[76]

In 1967, on the eve of the devastating civil war, the African specialist on the National Security Council staff, Edward Hamilton, grimly predicted Nigeria's dissolution. Hamilton advised the White House to limit its goals to an attempt to "salvage the most useful tokens of unity—a common currency, a single representative at the UN" while trying to avert an all-out war and harm to U.S. citizens in the country. Hamilton believed the United States must remain neutral, calling the crisis "an internal problem—very different from the Congo." Anything that forced Washington to choose sides "threatens our ability to do anything for anybody in Nigeria—our aid programs are an immediate case at point." The United States could not bring the conflict to an end without sending many American troops, "if then." Why? "This is an ancient, bitter, tribal dispute to which there is probably no entirely satisfactory solution."[77]

Hamilton was not alone. During an NSC meeting, the Undersecretary of

State blandly insisted that in Nigeria, "The trouble arises primarily out of tribal differences. Our AID programs have not been a failure."[78] Thus the same U.S. government that had essentially drafted Nigeria's development plan, begun a major aid program, and touted Nigeria as a regional model, now prepared to cut its losses. It contemplated writing off Nigeria, not merely as a power, but as a unified nation, seeing a hopelessly "tribal" Nigeria whose nation building had malfunctioned where once it had imagined an ideal modernizing society.[79] Even African Americans who had celebrated Nigeria's independence and advocated more American aid did little to arrest the momentum of fatalism. African American civil rights leaders expressed caution in response to the war. Nigerian unity was a symbol of pride for them, yet they could not feel enthusiasm for the kind of hard war Lagos intended to wage against the rebels. African Americans, by adopting a neutral stance, could therefore have no role in influencing American policy.[80]

Rather than focusing on prying Nigeria and the rest of Africa loose from the grip of neocolonial trade, investment, and security ties, American aid strengthened Nigeria's dependence on the world market for cocoa, and later, oil. Rather than striving for social justice and greater equality among Nigerian citizens, and seeking reconciliation and adjustment among the various competing peoples of the country, the would-be allies pursued the chimera of Kennedy's "Decade of Development." Failing to address these structural weaknesses inherited from the colonial regime, Nigeria collapsed into a nightmarish civil war. While its outcome did not produce the permanent rupture American officials had feared, the postwar elite used the hectic oil boom to entrench their class, and corruption dramatically increased. With Africa's "model" of development and democracy revealed as anything but, the region experienced countless coups, ethnic and state-to-state conflicts, and the economic collapse that has shocked the world's conscience in the past quarter-century of unbridled poverty and pandemics.

By 1967, Africanists could only rue their early naïve optimism. As one put it, it had been "fashionable" for scholars and others interested in Africa to go to Nigeria "as if in pilgrimage" to an ideal country.[81] Political scientist George Jenkins had been among them, conducting research at the University of Ibadan. His 1967 review of recent scholarship on Nigeria noted the publication of over two hundred books on the country since independence. Major funding from sources such as the Social Science Research Council had flowed disproportionately to Americans working in Nigeria. Much of the resulting work, Jenkins argued, had been narrowly conceived and altogether opportunistic. Little of the Western outpouring on Nigerian law, governance, and economics had much value for Nigerians, and most of it had been written, Jenkins suspected, because American researchers had been attracted to the relative safety and convenience of working in the stable, English-speaking country. In their zeal for career advancement and the performance of a liberal mediating role between Lagos and Washington, many scholars had missed an opportunity to question American premises about Nigeria as a "unique nation." They had therefore contributed nothing to restrain Washington from its oscillating between naïve optimism and self-serving fatalism.[82]

Despite problems of planning and implementing foreign aid, and the myopia of visiting scholars, Nigeria's economy could have boomed by the end of the decade, had war not intervened. Economic growth had been slower than expected, until 1966, when oil revenues increased substantially. Like other African nations, Nigeria suffered from the decline in commodity prices, especially for cocoa, the nation's second leading export. While the nation suffered from continued poverty, illness, and illiteracy, the terms of its foreign trade worsened, with its foreign reserves down from $737 million in 1960 to $294 million in 1963, a result of massive imports and falling cocoa prices.[83] Despite oil, Nigeria proved less than unique. Rivkin had expected Nigeria to provide the "historical demonstration" that Africans could, through modernization, create stability, enlarge justice, and preserve peace. It provided a very different kind of example, one today's neo-liberal, globalization enthusiasts would do well to consider, as a new democratic regime confronts corruption while religious and ethnic conflict threatens again to rend Nigerian unity.[84]

Six

"Decade of Disillusionment"

Mennen Williams, as if in conscious reaction to *Ugly American* stereotypes, applied to his African travels the folksy informality that had won Chester Bowles respect in India. His tours of the continent, though somewhat less frenetic than Lyndon Johnson's, proved theatric, and they generated an eva-nescent goodwill. His three-day visit to Guinea in 1962, at a key moment in the rapprochement between the United States and Sékou Touré, seemed a major success to the embassy, which credited Williams's "warmth, sincerity, and command of French." The Guineans "seemed react with pleasure to Wil-liams's informality with crowds at markets spontaneously singing and cheer-ing" and engaging three Guinean officials in the Charleston and the Twist. The Minister of Information paid Williams the highest compliment, "calling him 'un vrai politician.'"[1]

Such performances, however, while effective short-term public diplomacy, had no more connection to the implementation of aid than LBJ's Senegalese sojourn. More important, Williams's constant complaints within the Ken-nedy and Johnson administrations about limited aid to small African nations contributed to his eventual decline in influence. By 1965, his travels in Africa were contemptuously dismissed by the National Security staff as pure public relations. Ulric Haynes, called by McGeorge Bundy "the ablest young Negro I have met in ten years of fairly constant looking," summed up the widespread contempt for Williams within the Johnson administration. Haynes tartly concluded after Williams's thirteenth trip produced no major policy recommendations but evident goodwill, "The Governor likes Africans and Africans like him."[2]

The decline of Williams's influence during the Johnson administration both reflected and reinforced a retreat from the kind of African aid program launched under Kennedy. The change in presidents, however, had far less to do with this basic shift in American policy than the wearing succession of failures American officials encountered. By the middle of the Decade of Development, American policymakers began to distance themselves from the burden they had assumed in Africa, not by renouncing their interest in aiding development, but by changing the method of doing so. Confronting Africa's cascading economic and political failure, Washington replaced its strategy of entering into many bilateral aid programs to support countries with promising plans (and others valued for their bases or historic ties, such as Ethiopia and Liberia, or their symbolic importance in the Cold War, such as the Congo) with multilateral aid for regional projects, with a less visible American label in an Africa largely left to the devices of European neocolonialism.

"The Second Phase of Modern African History"

In just a few years, optimism dissolved into despair. Chester Bowles, after an official visit in 1962, concluded that his travels in Africa "have increased my feeling that with luck and courage we have possibility of a brilliant success in Africa." That such a conclusion seemed to ratify his earlier predictions of African success did not detract from its summation of the zeitgeist of the period.[3] By the mid-sixties, however, Americans had become disillusioned with foreign aid, and USAID felt increasing pressure from Congress to justify its budget. Beyond Washington, conferences and meetings staged by the Council on Foreign Relations, the World Bank, and the UN, among others, addressed what they perceived as "an emergency" in an era of increasing uncertainty about development and aid. As David Ekbladh notes, "There was broad agreement that assistance efforts were suffering from a 'paralysis of leadership,' which fed a belief that 'at present everything is going wrong.'"[4] In the West and Africa, the failure of African development and nation building became widely recognized, discussed, and debated. Economic growth faltered due to problems of foreign aid implementation, as the cases of the Sudan, Ethiopia, and the Congo illustrate, problems on both the Western and African side. Lack of skilled manpower and technical expertise combined with corruption—both legacies of European colonialism—left newly independent states ill prepared to use Western aid to design and implement development plans. National unity proved fleeting, as politicians mobilized ethnic identities in ways that quickly destabilized African politics. Meanwhile, the overall economic context of African independence shifted quickly. The terms of trade, already worsening at the start of the decade, reached dangerous levels. The growing volume of Western economic aid, investment, and technical assistance could not match the transfer of wealth out of Africa, as the value of primary commodities continued to fall. At the very moment when Africans sought to import more Western manufactured goods and machinery to stimulate growth and satisfy pent-up acquisitive aspirations, they found their cocoa, groundnuts, coffee, and other food crops bought less and less. By 1965 the problem of the terms of trade had become so manifest that Immanuel Wallerstein could label it "virtually universally recognized."[5]

Against that economic and political backdrop erupted the era of African coups. The shift from charismatic nationalist politicians to the banality of military rule and single-party dictatorships did not meet the expectations that democracy and development would rise together. It did, however, fit in with the views of those analysts of political development who saw strong men as the key to stability, and stability as the key to consolidating nations (and preserving Western economic and strategic interests). What the derailing of development and democracy also did, however, was to generate a mixture of bewilderment, disillusionment, and recriminations from Western analysts, travelers, and officials. The changing representations of Africa went hand in hand with new American policies, and the confidence in bilateral U.S. aid to support development plans yielded first to an incoherent American strategy, and then to a long-term reliance on regional aid and the growing influence of the World Bank.

Williams, more than anyone else, repeatedly argued for aid programs in even the smallest countries at a time when a consensus had formed that aid should be concentrated in a few promising states. From the beginning of his tenure at the State Department, he protested against the concentration of money "in a few countries to the neglect of a great many," calling it "a perhaps unfortunate fact of political life that we must have some program—usually a very modest one—in virtually every country in Africa." "We simply cannot," he insisted, "at the beginning of the highly publicized Decade of Development, tell these badly underdeveloped countries that we are not interested in assisting them." Williams's complaint illustrated a key ambiguity at the heart of a U.S. aid policy ostensibly based on such "hard" criteria as planning and absorptive capacity, but also influenced by "soft" diplomatic concerns about American influence across the continent.[6]

In one instance, Williams urged USAID to recognize the political value of "a token development grant aid program in Mauritania this fiscal year." He argued, "I do not believe we can remain unresponsive to this pro-Western Government's repeated requests for aid when we have programs under way in every other West African country," including states with declared radical ideologies such as Ghana, Guinea, and Mali. Refusing to aid Mauritania would, he warned, give credence to the notion that America mainly aided countries that flirted with the Communist Bloc. "Mauritania," Williams noted, "is perhaps the poorest country in Africa and very badly needs help of all kinds."[7] He returned from his third trip to Africa convinced that more needed to be done to "meet reasonable expectations of support in nation-building and prevent the Decade of Disillusionment." Since most African nations could not meet the new U.S. aid criteria, Washington must apply a "liberal interpretation," since virtually all African nations needed aid. The overall amount of aid for Africa must also increase, he argued. In an annex to his report on the trip, Williams attached a memo, "Problems in Implementing U.S. Aid Policy in Africa." USAID, he argued, should not strictly apply its planning and "economic growth prerequisites" to African countries that could not meet them. Nor should Washington be content to supplement British or French aid, a strategy which left it "limited leverage" in a number of African countries. Warning that USAID moved too slowly and with too small a budget for Africa, he proclaimed, "there is an overriding need for a banner year of AID assistance to Africa in FY 1962."[8] By 1963, however, Williams's travels in Africa revealed USAID's continued sluggishness in beginning "actual work on the spot," and its difficulty convincing Africans to do "thorough and coordinated planning." The United States had attempted "to stretch a far too modest amount of AID money over a continent which is bursting at the seams with a vastly increased capacity for effectively using assistance in economic development."[9]

Though he mocked Williams's politics of empathy, Haynes shared his unease with the lack of boldness and clarity in American policy in Africa. The administration, he argued, needed "a dramatic, impact demonstration of the President's personal interest, something that can be labeled a 'Johnson Plan for Africa' and which will have an immediate identifiable effect on the lives of all Africans." Satellite technology to improve communications or a program of medical vaccinations, by contrast, could yield such benefits.[10] President Johnson, harboring his own dreams of modernizing Africa, once told Rostow that he wanted "as soon as possible a design for an African Alliance for Progress, perhaps including the expenditure of several hundred million dollars over some years."[11] That Vietnam and other problems distracted the president is less important than his instinctive impulse, when contemplating Africa, to think in such grandiose terms. Like Haynes, Johnson hoped American technology and capital could, in a bold stroke, cut through the kinds of dilemmas that had beset the aid program in Africa since Kennedy's promise of a Decade of Development.

Courage to try any such bold measure proved elusive, however, as Africa's mounting economic woes became manifest. By 1965, a National Intelligence Estimate concluded that African growth would remain slow and the region would continue to experience "setbacks" due to "a desperate shortage of virtually all kinds of technical and managerial skills; indeed, the basic institutions and staff for economic development are often inadequate or absent." Aid and foreign investment simply could not materialize "on anything approaching the scale required for sustained economic development." With the CIA all but burying hopes of a Decade of Development, it warned that "African relations with the U.S. will remain ambivalent and difficult." Analysts took solace, however, in the knowledge that the region possessed no resources "essential to U.S. security," and thus America's "material interests" would escape serious damage.[12] Internal hand-wringing escalated. By 1967 the State Department lamented, "Our AID and other economic programs for Africa are running into heavy weather both in Congress and in Africa." While Congress was "disillusioned" by the failure of Africans to live up to the excessive expectations earlier in the decade, a feeling aggravated by the crises in the Congo and Nigeria, Africans were "dismayed by our phasing out of bilateral assistance from some twenty-five countries." In response, the Department recognized that it had to obtain more aid for Africa "or suffer a serious psychological blow in Africa as to the validity of our interest in the continent, to say nothing of the loss of influence."[13]

The bad news had the effect, for many American officials, of inducing fatalism and indifference, and with Vietnam demanding more American resources, the search was on for an African economic exit strategy. Robert Komer, an NSC staffer often involved in African issues and eventually engrossed by Vietnam, argued, "The new African countries are mostly in such a primitive state of development, and are so hipped on internecine quarrels that I doubt whether even a massive U.S. investment over a long period would show a commensurate political result."[14] Even those still committed to the secular missionary's article of faith in the inevitable progression through stages of growth agreed that the sense of urgency to aid Africa had ebbed, Williams notwithstanding.

Johnson appointed the American ambassador to Ethiopia, Edward Korry, to head an inquiry into the effectiveness of foreign aid and to recommend more sustainable approaches. Years of exposure to venality at the court of Haile Selassie did nothing to predispose the ambassador to adopt an outlook like that of Williams. In 1966 Korry submitted his report, and upon its adoption, the United States shifted the focus of its aid away from mostly small bilateral programs with many nations to a more intense concentration on a few programs that operated across an entire African region. The Korry Report endorsed greater reliance on the World Bank. Insisting that "the fact that an eloquent case can be made setting forth a need does not mean that it is the responsibility of the United States to satisfy that need," the report called for an increase in total USAID appropriations, but a less direct strategy for promoting development. In fact, by urging the administration to work through the World Bank and regional institutions, "the report separated the economic aspects of development from political considerations and thereby risked undermining the rationale for assistance."[15]

Elements within the Kennedy administration had always resisted major U.S. aid commitments to Africa. At the State Department, George Ball wrote a paper critical of America's aid to Africa that, as he put it, caused "a lot of broken heads around the Department." Of its critics he said, "They are holding some tribal dances down in the African Bureau," and "this is the kind of issue that creates that kind of anguish, particularly among the African missionaries."[16] The shift to regionalism represented a return to the attitude of the Eisenhower years. Eisenhower's Secretary of the Treasury, Robert B. Anderson, frequently expressed concern about the expense the United States faced in trying to respond to African aid requests from "a lot of little, newly independent countries." He argued the administration should increase its support for the World Bank and redirect African requests there, noting, "The World Bank was a stable institution and the Russians were not in it." As early as 1960, the State Department lamented the need to satisfy the urgency of African aid requests, and officials already recognized the problem of aid implementation. "The Africans complain that we study everything to death," a tendency that had to change because of "the need for quick action" to prevent countries from becoming dependent on Communist aid.[17] Yet regionalism as a doctrine of foreign aid could never be fully implemented. In response to the threat to U.S. interests caused by escalating racial conflict in Southern Africa, the Policy Planning Council proposed "restoration of U.S. bilateral aid programs (primarily technical assistance) in Zambia and Malawi, where these programs are currently being phased-out; and the establishment of similar bilateral aid programs in Botswana, Lesotho and Swaziland."[18]

As the United States relieved itself of some of its responsibility to aid Africa, it also adjusted the concept of political development to account for, and come to terms with, the retreat of African democracy. Americans largely accepted one-party rule and eventually coups as events that seemed appropriate to African culture, conditions, and stage of development. By early 1963, Williams noted the view of U.S. ambassadors in Africa that the rise of one-party states was "inevitable rather than all bad." Their interpretation reflected a premise: that African nationalist leaders sought, above all else—even formal democracy—to achieve development and national unity. In Tanganyika, for example, the consolidation of political power seemed intended to "harness all of their energy for the task of building their nation."[19] Not all agreed. In an incisive contribution to those debates, W. Arthur Lewis noted the premise about African culture that underpinned claims of "inevitable" one-party rule. "One can only be amused," remarked Lewis, "by people, including African politicians, who present the single-party state to us as a specifically African creation, emerging out of the African personality and the African social system—as if the single-party state were not one of the commonplaces of the twentieth century, to be found in nearly every continent."[20] While astutely noting the cultural premise of the argument, Lewis's dissent did little to alter Washington's tacit abandonment of Kennedy's original goal of demonstrating the compatibility of liberal economics with liberal politics.

Perhaps no African did more to prepare Americans to take such a step than Nkrumah. When the Ghanaian leader, an acute thorn in Washington's side, published *Neo-Colonialism*, U.S. officials were stunned by its "scathing, sweeping denunciation" of American agencies as well as the World Bank and International Monetary Fund. Responding to its allegation that all American officials and Peace Corps volunteers were "agents of an international monopoly capitalist plot to exploit the underdeveloped world," Haynes concluded, "His line is definitely Marxist." In response, Williams provided the Ghanaian ambassador a formal note of protest while USAID rejected the country's most recent requests for aid.[21] While eager to refute Nkrumah's claims and highlight his book's use of Communist sources, the State Department's African Bureau believed the Peace Corps and USAID's technical assistance program in agriculture were the key to pro-American sentiment in Ghana. By contrast, Haynes argued that U.S. prestige in Africa would improve rather than diminish with the expulsion of USAID and the Peace Corps from Ghana. Keeping them in the country in the face of Nkrumah's insults "baffles friendly African governments," he argued, while "a strong U.S. response might also chasten" the egotistical Nkrumah.[22] For some time, Washington had hoped for an alternative to Nkrumah, and in 1965–66 it anticipated a military coup against him, learning about the plotters and their plans. Though not caused by the United States, the coup that drove Nkrumah from power shortly after the opening of the Volta dam in 1966 certainly received an unequivocal American blessing.[23]

Nkrumah's downfall brought temporary relief to Washington, for his successors proved far more pliant and altogether less charismatic. No longer would Ghana undermine Nigeria or other moderate African states trying to set the tone for the region. Though spectacular, the Ghanaian coup was not unique. After a series of coups, Komer explained their significance to President Johnson. "Telescoping the historical experience of the older nations of the world, the new nations of Africa are ending the first phase of their modern history," according to Komer. "It was one of great popular euphoria—sparked by the end of colonialism and the beginning of independence. Hopes and aspirations were high." The coups "signal the beginning of the second phase of modern African history. This latest phase is born of frustrated hopes and aspirations, and disappointment with the performance of the independence leaders." From the American perspective, "this new phase in Africa is a healthy one, because the dreams and myths which accompanied independence are being replaced by the realization that austerity and hard work are required for survival." What mattered now was how "to get this notion across to the masses of African people without dashing their faith in their new leadership."[24]

The coups led U.S. intelligence analysts to claim that American predictions had been vindicated. "Ghana's virtual bankruptcy has been revealed after Nkrumah's overthrow," while the "radical" regimes of Guinea and Mali "have severely strained their economies by mismanagement."[25] The American commitment to modernization provided a motive and means to embrace military and authoritarian regimes in spite of the previous denunciations of the authoritarianism of Nkrumah and others. Having failed to predict and shape Africa's future in the Decade of Development, Americans could, from their position of relative power, rewrite history and attempt anew the forecasting of Africa's future. The post–Korry Report World Bank would bulk large in that endeavor, to the material benefit of the United States and other wealthy industrial powers.

Africans' Changing Plans

While observers in Washington and American academe reevaluated the wisdom of aid to prime the pump of economic planning, African leaders had reasons of their own for thinking anew. African complaints about the details of U.S. aid implementation—frequently enumerated and reiterated to American officials—revealed a deepening disconnect between the American and African conceptions. While many analysts have focused on the dramatic confrontation between Ghana and the United States over the fate of the Volta project, some of the minor disagreements illustrate the broader problem more clearly.[26] Few American aid commitments were as large as Volta, and most African leaders attracted less worldwide interest than Nkrumah. One of the numerous minor rows happened in Uganda. Milton Obote, prime minister of the small East African nation, clashed with American officials over USAID's decision to delay a loan that had been granted to open new schools in the country. While expressing his acceptance of the USAID criteria of prepared projects, the Ugandan complained that neighboring Tanganyika received American aid "without having to go through the projects procedure." Obote also argued that USAID's project procedure proved costly and time-consuming "without firm assurance that USAID would ultimately finance a project," and thus disrupted Ugandan planning. In a meeting with Williams, the frustrated prime minister asked whether Uganda had been "written off" by Washington "because we don't count for much" in America's view of Africa. Williams replied that funds for Tanganyika, as for Uganda, would be disbursed only "on the basis of approved projects." This answer could hardly have consoled Obote, as it reiterated America's policy of reserving the right to withhold funds on a case-by-case basis, which could only slow the aid process and impose additional costs, and possible loss of political control over Uganda's development planning. Nor could the Ugandan have been consoled when Williams "assured" him that Tanganyikan and Nigerian leaders had "complained . . . about delays and apparent inequities in U.S. assistance to their countries." Apparently, Williams believed that in Africa, misery loved company.[27]

Ugandan and Tanganyikan complaints echoed elsewhere in Africa. According to Robert Komer, when the prime minister of Somalia visited Washington seeking military and economic aid, he "let his hair down on the US aid program." The Somali leader alleged U.S. "procedures are too slow, conditions too restrictive, and that we often fail to consult the Somalis." USAID's retort, that the problem lay in "poor Somali planning and lack of coordination within the Somali government," prompted Komer to suggest the president take the opportunity to "deliver a little lecture on the need for sound planning and self-help. Our projects take time because we, unlike the Soviets, are more interested in making a well-planned economic contribution than a political splash." While Washington sought to improve its performance, Komer argued, "Somalis need to jack up their planning and improve coordination within their own house. We're serious about self-help."[28] Nevertheless, the Somalis claimed U.S. aid "is not having the desired effect," due to poor coordination between U.S. and Somali officials, the "extreme slowness" of American implementation, and the "high administrative costs of U.S. aid not justified by results." Projects such as work on Mogadishu's port were "begun and then abandoned." USAID, while acknowledging that the agency "had a long way to go in our implementation procedures," noted that American and Somali officials often failed to agree on which projects were "economically and technically sound." The president, while reciting the usual litany of constraints—congressional cuts in foreign aid, stringent congressional requirements, the balance of payments deficit—could do little more than express sympathy, commenting that "Somalia had a staggering problem, consider the $45 average income of its people."[29]

Senegal, where Johnson's romp had expressed optimism at the start of the decade, never fully grasped the requirements of USAID, nor did the Americans appreciate the Senegalese way of development planning. In 1961 Washington believed "Senegal's development plans are sober and realistic," with an appropriate focus on education, vocational training, and agriculture, and "not on economically wasteful prestige projects."[30] Mennen Williams called it a nation engaged in "serious development planning and adopting a moderate, Western-oriented foreign policy." In a flourish of overstatement, he claimed, "It would seem that almost no African country is better qualified for help under the new criteria."[31] By the following year, however, Ambassador Philip M. Kaiser told the Foreign Minister that Senegal was "not using aid already provided by U.S. as expeditiously as possible." Kaiser informed Washington that the Senegalese were "threshing about to find some Deus Ex Machina to bail them out of dilemma." They suffered, he believed, "wounded pride in face of hard fact that clearly not up to carrying out program of this magnitude and complexity," a failure that implied a greater dependence on French aid. Kaiser vowed to "hold GOS [Government of Senegal] nose firmly to grindstone of economic reality and urge it reduce expectations to level of its capacities." While it "rationally recognizes" the truth, it lacked the "psychological" willingness to accept it. He told the Senegalese the United States would "under no circumstance" replace France as the principal donor and provide "direct budgetary aid." Senegal, he reported, had begun to recognize that it had "over-extended itself" by launching "new and costly ministries as Foreign Affairs and Defense" along with the Four-Year Plan. The country lacked the "talent and money" to do both at the same time.[32] Things did not improve. In 1966 Rostow noted the persistence of Senegal's complaints that USAID's "administrative procedures are more complex and time-consuming than those of other donors."[33] As Edward Hamilton, Africa specialist of the NSC staff put it, "AID has a long history of bickering with the Senegalese over the paperwork required for AID projects. We maintain that they are slow, incompetent, and unwilling, they say we are niggling and bureaucratic."[34] The weary, accepting tone of Rostow and Hamilton reflects the normalization of disagreement. Ideological differences and a failure to communicate about the processes of development planning and aid implementation became predictable.

Kennedy's energetic ambassador to Guinea, another small former French colony in West Africa, William Attwood, illustrated the tension in a characteristically folksy anecdote. "You couldn't blame the Guineans for being confused by our procedures; we had trouble understanding some of them ourselves," he recalled. American officials taught a Guinean government minister to memorize "a chart with thirty-four boxes, each describing a different administrative action that had to be taken between the receipt of a request for assistance" and American implementation. "The Guinean minister who memorized the chart," according to Attwood, "confessed later that it dispelled his last suspicions about American intentions in Africa; any people who tied themselves up in knots the way we did could not be all that eager to muscle in." Whether or not Attwood's interlocutor thus captured a typical African response (which is doubtful), it scarcely constituted a ringing endorsement of U.S. competence and the American model of planning and implementing development. This is not what American professions of innocence had meant to imply.[35]

Disappointment of African expectations of generous American aid concerned Washington, if not as urgently as it did Williams. Having raised expectations with talk of a "Decade of Development" U.S. officials attempted to publicize the extent and results of the aid program as an aspect of cultural diplomacy. According to a memo from the U.S. Information Agency, "directly or indirectly, support of AID consumes much more than one-half of total USIA resources in the underdeveloped world." USIA's efforts reflected Washington's desire "to derive maximum psychological effect from its AID program," as in the case of Nigeria, where 95 percent of information efforts went to support AID.[36] However, where Africans initially imagined America limitlessly wealthy and capable of Marshall Plan–type assistance, the limited funding and poor implementation of USAID led to charges of American negligence and an image of selfishness. This dashed African hopes for reduced dependence on the former colonial powers and shaped African perceptions of the United States. Washington never reached its original stated goal of devoting 1 percent of its GDP to aid and private foreign investment in the developing world. Peaking at 0.8 percent in 1962, the percentage fell to 0.57 percent five years later.[37]

The official African pronunciation of a "Decade of Discouragement" came in 1967 from Robert K. Gardiner, the Ghanaian Executive Secretary of the UN Economic Commission for Africa (ECA). Though high hopes had greeted the creation of the ECA almost a decade earlier, it failed to inscribe its approach to development in Africa, and became something of a bystander to the region's decline. Described as "a big, quiet man" whose work ethic led him to try "to fit more than 24 hours into a day," Gardiner had impeccable credentials. Educated at Cambridge and the London School of Economics, he worked for Ralph Bunche in New York at the United Nations Secretariat. During the 1950s Nkrumah appointed him to organize the Ghanaian civil service, and shortly after joining the ECA, Gardiner oversaw the training of a civil service in the Congo. Gardiner and the ECA worked for the UN in New York, and like Western economists, he evaluated African plans according to what the ECA's African critics considered a "strictly economic criteria." The ECA did not follow the Organization of African Unity, also based in Addis Ababa, in combining development with political and cultural agendas. As a result, the two organizations found cooperation difficult throughout the 1960s and '70s. For his part, Gardiner believed the failure of development owed less to a lack of available knowledge than to failure of will. The conventional doctrines of development were right, and only the decision-making and implementation had failed. Africa's largest problems, he concluded, lay in "the difficulties inherent in the transition of African society from the traditional to the modern."[38]

While some Africans complained of diminishing or inefficient Western aid, others saw the aid process itself as a political and economic cul-de-sac. This had always been true, and became more common from the mid-sixties onward. The evolution of American aid policy and the decline of African democracy and development, two related phenomena, created more space for a radical African critique of American motives and methods. A contributor to *Transition* astringently noted the African dependence on imported personnel and ideas. "Foreign 'experts' and peace corps swarm the country like white ants," he lamented. "Every week planes leave Entebbe, Nairobi, or Dar-es-Salaam with returning 'experts' and foreign ministers to negotiate foreign aid and more 'experts,' and because we believe in 'positive neutrality,' we seek aid from both East and West." From this perspective, Western and Communist aid shared a fundamentally alien essence, offering little more than deepened African dependence.[39] Americans had, of course, launched their African Decade of Development in hopes of securing the region from Communist influence, but they noticed the persistence and growth of radical sentiment in Africa. President Kennedy, in a White House meeting with Julius Nyerere, asked if "much of the hostility" expressed by African youths toward America meant they were "Marxist" or that they "might be needlessly concerned that we were cool to their approach to economic development." In reply, Nyerere observed slyly that "many Africans thought that Communism had been helpful to their countries, since if it were not for Communism, the United States would not be interested in providing assistance." The father of Tanzanian independence, one of Kennedy's favorite Africans, evolved later in the decade into a serious proponent of African socialism, declaring a Tanzanian path to socialism that involved self-reliance and a highly skeptical attitude toward American assistance and American foreign policy.[40]

By the 1970s, a school of interpretation influential in academe and beyond known as dependency theory offered one of the most bracing challenges to American development doctrines. Walter Rodney's *How Europe Underdeveloped Africa* (1972) became the best-known attack.[41] Long before such writing became common, African and American officials understood the importance of international trade as a problem for African development. The terms of trade eventually overshadowed the evanescent appeal of planning, as Africans realized the futility of seeking development through aid-financed exports while the value of African products steadily diminished. When Senghor met President Johnson in the White House, he acknowledged American generosity, but noted "it was unfortunately more than canceled" out by Africa's falling commodity prices.[42]

Washington made its contribution to the mounting problem. American trade policies particularly compounded the plight of Nigerian and Ghanaian cocoa producers. From the early days of the American aid efforts in Africa, many grasped the reality that loans, grants, and other forms of assistance mattered less than the international terms of trade. In 1963 Mennen Williams, though an ardent advocate of bilateral programs in virtually every African country, showed his interest in the larger trade issue by lobbying the State Department to take a "positive" position at the conference to negotiate an international cocoa agreement, calling it "essential" for U.S.–African relations. Nigeria and other cocoa producers would be aggrieved by a "negative position" because Washington "favors 'trade over aid'" while those nations "feel" they suffer from unstable world prices more than they benefited from aid.[43]

African economies, as American scholars often noted at the time, depended heavily on the export of one or two commodities, usually unrefined agricultural crops or minerals. African governments needed strong export earnings to finance their development plans, but the world market for many African goods turned volatile during the late 1950s and 1960s, and in some cases the prices remained low for decades. Washington had foreseen this possibility, and the State Department Policy Planning Council recommended that the United States and its Western allies make "significant one-way trade concessions" to help African exports. "This," according to one memo, "will help demonstrate that the West is not trying to perpetuate the old colonial system through imperial preferences and like arrangements," and trade concessions would also "help keep the newly independent African countries in the Western system." This kind of help would particularly benefit former British colonies, as they lacked eligibility to receive the kinds of trade advantages made available by the European Economic Community to former French colonies. The African Bureau predicted that a fall in export earnings would "more than cancel out external economic assistance" for many nations, thus necessitating an international "commodity price stabilization" plan to cushion them from fluctuations in the world market. The State Department set up a task force to study how to help poor nations find more export markets, and the president expressed his commitment to help them expand the export earnings of nations that pursued development through self-help. The problem, however, as George Ball, Undersecretary of State for Economic Affairs, put it, lay in the protection industrialized nations routinely afforded their own farmers and producers of raw materials. Until America and Western Europe made the political commitment to lower farm subsidies and other trade barriers, African exports would continue to have limited markets. Worse, despite decades of African diplomatic efforts, no sat-isfactory international price support plan took hold for most of Africa's critical export commodities, the prices and distribution of which largely remained under the control of a small number of firms. Africa's "colonial" status in the world economy would change little in the 1960s or for the remainder of the twentieth century, and this condition, perhaps more than any other, ensured the ultimate failure of most large-scale development efforts.[44]

In 1962 an international Cocoa Study Group prepared a draft agreement that met African demands for increasing the price of cocoa on the global market. However, the following year a United Nations negotiating conference collapsed after several weeks when the United States led cocoa-consuming nations in rejecting the producers' demands for an increase from the then-current price of 25 cents to somewhere between 31 and 43 cents. The United States demanded the lowest price of any nation, refusing to accept any guar-antee of prices above 21 cents. The State Department's rationale was that Amer-ican "cocoa merchants, chocolate manufacturers, and confectionary industry" had always "strongly opposed an international cocoa agreement as an unwar-ranted restriction on free trade." These interests even hired Washington insider Clark Clifford, former advisor to President Harry Truman, to lobby the gov-ernment against any agreement. Cocoa prices continued to plummet, reaching a low of 12 cents in 1964–65. By that time, Nigerians had joined Ghana and other producers in blaming Washington for blocking another cocoa agree-ment after the Americans "took positions which proved to be at the farthest remove from the African producers and Brazil," as a State Department official acknowledged.[45] By 1965, the State Department watched nervously as prices hit 17 cents, the lowest in two decades, which it attributed to a lack of demand to match the 70 percent increase in cocoa production since the mid-1950s. The economies of cocoa producers like Nigeria, Ghana, the Ivory Coast, and Cameroon were "bad, and likely to get worse."[46] Cocoa prices, which had crested above 30 cents in the late days of colonialism, had fallen to 12 cents before rebounding to 23–24 cents in 1966, when another conference failed to reach an agreement. Ghana and Nigeria led a chorus of African complaints that placed the blame squarely on Washington and the cocoa-consuming American industry, which the State Department proved unable to persuade to accept anything higher than 18 cents.

Chocolate merchants alone did not cause this estrangement between the United States and cocoa producers. The larger problem lay in policymakers' perception that American interests in the world economy could not be recon-

ciled with the kinds of altered terms of trade necessary for African development. In November 1963 George Ball, a critic of American aid to Africa, submitted a memo to President Kennedy urging a hard line on trade negotiations
with African and other poor nations. He noted that U.S. officials had resigned
themselves to the "inevitable" creation of the United Nations Conference on
Trade and Development (UNCTAD), which poor nations demanded. Ball
warned the president that "considerable mischief" might occur during the
UNCTAD meeting in Geneva schedule for March 1964, as the poor nations
had come to regard GATT as "an institution run by and for the benefit of
the great trading nations." He derided their interest in reaching commodity
price agreements as a means to increase their export earnings, as well as the
demand for preferential treatment of their manufactured goods imported by
wealthy nations as "the newest steed in the LDC stable of hobby horses," one
that "could turn out to be a particularly fractious beast." What producer
nations wanted, he alleged, was to use agreements to artificially inflate prices
"well above existing levels" and make them into "a subsidy" to "finance their
development requirements." Ball warned that pressure from the cocoa industry and Congress would force the administration to oppose the kind of prices
the producer nations like Ghana would likely demand, a refusal that could
become an "embarrassment for us."[47] In 1967 Ball told a congressional committee that if the Europeans continued to develop their preferential trade
agreements with Africa, the United States should willingly accept the codifi-
cation of a "closed system" between those two regions, and the economic
pattern should even be elaborated into a "geographical division of responsibilities." This would free America of African obligations at last.[48]

In that same year, Vice President Hubert Humphrey toured Africa. Far more
sympathetic than Ball, the presidential aspirant reported, "African nations live
at the mercy of commodity prices," and U.S. renegotiation of the international
coffee agreement and completion of a cocoa agreement would help Africa "far
more" that USAID programs. While Humphrey's assessment certainly reflected
the input of African leaders, there is an irony to his "trade, not aid" argument.
It did nothing to stem the shift to regionalism that empowered the World Bank
at Africa's expense. Nor did the attention to commodity prices support any
argument for reversing the decline in overall American aid to Africa that had
begun during the Johnson-Humphrey administration. Until Bono, no one in
the West figured out how to make a plea for fairer trade with Africa match the
excitement of Kennedy's Decade of Development or the various mantras of
the Peace Corps.[49]

One of the African retorts to the "gospel of modernization" came in the form of "African Socialism." Most African states in the 1960s espoused some degree of commitment to a mild form of socialism, usually calling for a strong governmental role in economic planning, though many leaders seemed content to remain vague about what socialism meant to them, or how it would work. Some Americans found professions of socialism alarming, others were dismissive, while still others embraced them as necessary, at least during Africa's "transitional" period. In 1963 *Africa Report* ran a special issue on African Socialism with sympathetic articles by influential Africanists, including Ruth Schachter Morgenthau, who argued that the phenomenon simply reflected Africans' determination to achieve development on their own terms, avoiding the excesses of capitalism and the Western historical experience of industrialization.[50] African leaders could espouse socialism and, in effect, pursue whatever specific policies they wished, rationalizing them after the fact as socialist. Socialism implied no commitment to an anti-Western political program.

By contrast, accusations that the West sought to maintain dominance in Africa in the guise of neocolonialism were more charged. They were also, ironically, more widespread than self-declared socialist rhetoric, for accusing the West of perfidy did not necessarily imply a preference for socialism or political alignment with the Communist Bloc. As early as 1961, the term and concept of neocolonialism became common in African discussions of the continent's relationship with the West. At the All-African Peoples' Conference in Cairo in March 1961, a "Resolution on Neo-Colonialism" defined the concept, identified specific instances of its occurrence in Africa and OK means of resistance, and named as neocolonial powers the United States, the West European nations, Israel, and South Africa.[51] In his book *Neo-Colonialism: The Last Stage of Imperialism*, Kwame Nkrumah anticipated one of the key features of contemporary Western commentary on African poverty, debt, and political conflict when he defined neocolonialism as "power without responsibility." Unlike the former colonial powers, the new kind of imperial power practicing neocolonialism did not assume the paternalistic obligations of protection. Working through the IMF, World Bank, and other multilateral organizations and forums, the United States in particular has enjoyed economic, diplomatic, and strategic advantages in Africa without assuming the burden of a traditional empire or even a donor committed to implementing a Marshall Plan for Africa.[52] By 1963, the term *neocolonialism* had been so frequently used in African criticisms of Western economic aid that the government of France issued a report on aid that acknowledged that the complaint "cannot be neglected." In general, many African intellectuals and some officials had always questioned the motives and methods of American and European aid. Their critique of Western concepts of planning included the fear that the "swarm" of expats helping to draft African plans would focus so narrowly on investment in agriculture and increased production of exports valued by the West that Africans would remain locked in dependence on fluctuating world prices and Western demand. Industrialization and diversification of the economy and patterns of international trade, they argued, were more economically efficient and politically necessary approaches to African development. Africans urged the West to make concessions on the price of their commodities, and many leaders shared with Nkrumah the desire to build organizational expressions of African unity to reduce their nations' vulnerability to Western economic advice or manipulation. However, as Wallerstein observed, no African state proved willing, "however committed to a revolutionary ideology," to sever its economic and political ties to the West as had China. Moreover, the Organization of African Unity, preoccupied with political crises in the Congo and the campaign to liberate Southern Africa from white rule, "expended relatively little time on economic projects." Criticisms of the West, therefore, yielded no decisive resistance to Western-defined and -controlled development agendas.[53]

The weakness of African resistance notwithstanding, Americans had little cause for celebration. Ambassador Attwood, following his stints representing the United States in Guinea and Kenya, opened his memoirs with the declaration, "We must dismantle the Agency for International Development if we are to save and strengthen our vitally important foreign assistance program." Such a proposal reinforced the lesson many took from the weakness of USAID's African programs: foreign aid had been sabotaged by bureaucratic ineptitude. However, as David C. Engerman and others have argued, such conclusions ignored the more fundamental problem of how planning was conceived. Faith in planning, whether American or Africa, rested on the premise that it was an economic activity, when in reality, "economics *was* politics." Experts did not offer purely technical, politically neutral advice, for "decisions about resources are inherently political." When African planners and heads of state had essential political interests and ideological commitments to build certain kinds of projects or to pursue industrialization first, or to spend their state's revenues at a certain pace, they could hardly be swayed by American experts or officials who proposed a more technically correct interpretation, any more than India's planners could be persuaded to change their development plans to reflect new data from CIS computers that undermined their approach.[54] Adebayo Adedeji has dismissed the African plans of the early postindependence years because they "were more often than not prepared by foreigners with relatively little experience of the countries concerned," and thus lacked a political basis for legitimacy and implementation. African states employed Western expatriates to fill the gaps in their own planning personnel, while the political leadership set its own economic agendas and freely departed from the plan at their convenience.[55]

While African leaders pursued alternative visions of development and nation building, a much wider array of Africans began resisting the untrammeled authority of Africanist researchers. Those who encountered American researchers gained a reputation for hospitality. However, many came to feel their generosity had been abused. By 1965 the pages of *African Studies Bulletin* warned of evidence that, in the words of a State Department official, "Africans are disturbed at being regarded as guinea pigs and their countries as laboratories to test scientific hypotheses." The flurry of American researchers had left many African hosts feeling put upon, fielding the same questions over and over "with very little, Africans feel, being received in return for what some of them consider exploitation." When some of the CIA's role in financing African Studies became public knowledge, the ASA became sensitive to the issue of African antipathy. By 1968 a revolt brewed within ASA, as a black caucus formed. Black Africanists advocated an increased presence and role in the ASA and a dismantling of the conceptual wall Africanists had erected between sub-Saharan Africa and the diaspora as subjects. Following their takeover of the ASA's annual meeting in Montreal in October 1969, change could no longer be postponed. The black activists accused the ASA of contributing to "colonialism and neocolonialism through the 'educational' institutions and the mass media" and insisted that African Studies required "a pan-Africanist perspective" making the subject inclusive of all black peoples. In the wake of the black revolt that led to a splintering of ASA, a caucus of radical whites formed and sent out so-called research guerillas to demonstrate African Studies' dependence on the national security state. Africa Research Group, as they were known, skewered "America's tribe of Africa experts" as servants of the same American "Empire" responsible for the war in Vietnam. Africanists in the United States, they charged, working in conjunction with the CIA and the big foundations, were "men preoccupied with understanding the process of change so that it might be better controlled."[56]

The revolt within African Studies, though profoundly important to academics and their foundation and government partners, had little effect on prevailing American understandings of Africa. At the close of the Decade of Disillusionment, few advocated ambitious American programs to modernize Africa, and African leaders, for their part, chastened by the frustrating experience with American aid and their myriad internal problems, advanced no great platform either. Americans pointed to many economic, technical, and political problems that had bedeviled African development and nation building. However, without seeing any contradiction, many also believed Africa's economic and political woes had been, in essence, not merely economic or political, but also *cultural*. Departing from the universalism of modernization theory and the liberal optimism of the secular missionary, they questioned whether Africans, while sharing the blame for poor implementation, had ever been bona fide candidates for rapid modernization. Doubts about African planning reflected and reinforced broader and deeper misgivings about Africa's rendezvous with modernity. Out of the brief but intense American experience in Africa during the sixties emerged resurgent colonial representations of Africa, updated and transformed, and destined to shape America's Africa of the mind—as well as America's African policy—for decades to come.

Seven
"Just Not a Rational Being"

In 1966 the U.S. Ambassador to the Ivory Coast took the unusual step of recommending a new point of emphasis for U.S. policy throughout Africa by writing directly to the White House. He suggested to National Security Advisor Walt Rostow that the Johnson administration publicly defend its foreign aid program against conservative critics by emphasizing that its "real aim should be to inject the American ingredient that is qualitatively essential to the particular country's best development." That American ingredient: "our practical faith that what must be done can be done." He added, "We have demonstrated that we are a 'can do' people," an attribute vital to progress. What the ambassador had experienced convinced him that Africans "need it deeply."[1]

American ambassadors in Africa frequently expressed such sentiments, obviously influenced by The Ugly American. However, as the previous chapter indicated, the "can do" optimism of the New Frontier, with its emphasis on economic aid tied to development planning, dissipated in an Africa beset by slow growth, political turmoil, and uneven American influence. Nevertheless, Americans still hoped to change Africa in the way the ambassador and the novelists envisaged, by sending good Americans abroad to "stimulate dormant communities to undertake self-help programs" and to "awaken people to the possibilities of progress." They turned to culture for explanations of African failure, and for possible solutions. That Americans believed Africans needed such a psychological revolution reflected the influence of an evolving repertory of images, stereotypes, and fears about African culture. They brought to life cultural material that is being recycled and adapted in the twenty-first century to explain the even greater sense of African failure rooted in difference.[2]

"That Amiable Irrationality"

Despite the early optimism about African development and nation building, American commentary always included a less sanguine emphasis on African difference. Insisting that Africans lacked an impulse to take initiative (and that it must be supplied by Americans), Americans expressed frustration and impatience with African progress in areas considered vital to modernization. African corruption, inefficiency, and irrationality (both inside Africa and in African diplomacy) received lavish attention from the same array of Americans who constructed an innocent, modernizing Africa. Despite an explosion of scholarship, journalism, travel writing, and diplomatic attention, Africa remained, for Americans, a bewildering cultural essence. This entailed more than just factual ignorance or inadequate attention; Americans imagined Africa in ways that made possible the displacement of U.S. and Western responsibility and that depoliticized African economic, social, and political problems. Alan McPherson has shown that, in the case of Latin America, American officials have tended to ascribe problems, including persistent anti-Americanism, to "unchanging cultural differences." Such a blithe assumption enabled Washington to push ahead with its assertive policies in the region, uninhibited by the need to question the causes of Latin American resistance.[3] While Americans in the 1960s believed Africans were modernizing, they fretted over the extent and pace of the process, and quickly connected African policies, statements, behavior, or beliefs they found incomprehensible to the cultural essence of Africa. What is unique about American representations of Africa as a region allegedly possessing a cultural unity and essence is that, unlike other world regions, this cultural work has not been merely to legitimate intervention. Instead, in Africa, it facilitated an American denial of responsibility.

Writing for the Times, Paul Hofmann wryly described unceasing "red tape" encountered by foreign travelers in Nigeria and elsewhere in Africa, commenting, "The weary African traveler cannot help thinking that [explorer Henry Morton] Stanley at least did not have to fill in so many forms."[4] Hofmann's cheeky complaint—complete with a wistful colonial reference—

neatly illustrates the trope of ineptitude found in the vast majority of news articles about Africa. That he wrote it in 1960 reminds us that the story of American disenchantment with African culture is not a tale of declension. Martin Staniland and others have argued that the optimism ebbed by the mid-1960s, and there is much to commend in that assessment; coups and civil wars and faltering economies certainly registered with American observers. However, those unfolding events made sense to Americans in the context of longer traditions of representations of African culture that echoed, recycled, or otherwise adapted elements of colonial-era Africanist discourse. Americans were therefore primed to respond to any evidence of African failure by arranging a post-mortem narrowly focused on African corruption, inefficiency, and irrationality. African American and African representations of African culture challenged this prevailing association of Africa with failure or incompetence, though in an indirect fashion. Renewed interest in Pan-African cultural politics and a celebration of black art certainly substituted pride and assertiveness for the docile, defensive role white narratives cast for blacks. Yet no coherent counter-narrative effectively contested the cultural interpretation whites advanced in the face of mounting evidence of real problems in African governance and economies.[5]

Inefficiencies in Africa, many travelers concluded, reflected fundamental failures of rationality. After difficulties with his appointments and reservations in Bamako, Mali, one traveler noted that the experience illustrated "that amiable irrationality which seems to be characteristic of Africa." Such nations displayed "the cheerful coexistence of incompatible ideas," making it harder for "the handful of trained men trying to bridge the gap between tribal Africa and western technology."[6] "For whites who have just arrived in Nigeria," explained one news account, "two big irritants are the slip-shod standards of many Africans and the widespread corruption and graft."[7]

Frequent use of the expression, "the African," implied that all Africans shared the same traits, and often writers seemed inclined to feel that the African landscape, climate, and cultural traditions explained almost everything about individual Africans' behavior. Ambassador Darlington in Gabon wrote, "African thought processes differ from ours in subtle ways. . . . Because most Africans appear open, it is easy to delude yourself that you understand them, but underneath their surface there is another plane of consciousness where you cannot enter." To illustrate this claim, Darlington cited his principal interlocutor in Gabon, President Léon Mba, a man fluent in French and agreeable in the company of Americans. "But," Darlington recalled, "as time went on I began to see beneath his urbane manner, and what lay hidden was less attractive. He was suspicious, domineering and ruthless."[8] By implication, Mba's negative attributes reflected African (not even Gabonese) culture, rather than those of his political class or his own personality. Such associations easily led to the assumption of African irrationality. Before deciding to remove him from power via assassination, Eisenhower and his advisors concluded that Lumumba was "just not a rational being," a drug-addicted man with "messianic" impulses.[9] As Undersecretary Douglas Dillon had it, Lumumba was "irrational, almost 'psychotic'" during their meeting in Washington in August.[10] Not that Washington felt much better about his Congolese successor. During the Adoula regime, U.S. officials understood, as one put it at an NSC meeting, the regime to be "obscurantist, arbitrary, primitive, totalitarian, willful and irresponsible."[11]

Wolfgang Stolper warned his wife not to circulate his letters—the basis for his Nigerian diary—because they so often made disparaging references to individuals and Nigerian society. "Africans," he explained, "are incredibly sensitive." It was widely assumed that Africans were, as Bowles put it, "pathologically determined to assert their independence," and that they would want aid from Washington in order to lessen their dependence on the former metropolitan state, without developing a new dependence on America. Some Foreign Service officials believed that African diplomats and government officials nursed "feelings of deep personal insecurity." This had been caused by "their rapid transformation from men living a tribal life in the bush to officials with responsibility for deciding highly complex questions on which they have very inadequate background." As a result, their "insecurity" might lead to a striving for "reassurance" and prestige, or "violent, highly emotional behavior of the kind we associate with Lumumba." Even Williams worried about Africans' volatile yet malleable personalities. Africans, according to Williams, had long been accustomed to "communal ways of living." In a country like Mali, where the government had a leftist orientation, he was "struck by the ease with which a few determined men" had the opportunity to "lead their uncomprehending populations down the path of totalitarianism." Only rapid American aid could prevent a slide toward Communism, and even that might not be enough.[12] Americans were cosmopolitan, Africans provincial; this conceit infused policymakers' response to African political requests or criticisms of American policy. A White House aide cheered when Ambassador Edward Korry had a "forthright" talk with Haile Selassie. The United States, he believed, should be less "defensive about our policies and about the way we see the world—which is certainly a more sophisticated view than these little countries can command." Feeling put upon by African critics, Americans could fall back on a presumed epistemological superiority. This is something missionaries and European explorers of an earlier era could have identified with.[13]

When Lyndon Johnson ordered a U.S. airlift to rescue Belgian paratroopers from Kisangani in November 1964, he privately explained, "We just couldn't let the cannibals kill a lot of people."[14] Instead, the CIA sponsored mass violence over the next year as Mobutu regained the city and other rebel areas, resulting in numerous atrocities. If "cannibals" must not rampage, South African mercenaries could.[15] In late 1965 the U.S. Ambassador, G. McMurtrie Godley II, remarked, "Congolese individual is not good insurgent or counterinsurgent. He does not have the moral or physical fiber or courage to sustain protracted guerilla actions or countermeasures." This, he explained, is why "Non-Africans have been required despite obvious political drawbacks," and why mercenaries would remain necessary until full stability had been achieved. The mercenaries contributed to "nation building," as they helped eliminate "seeds of future insurgency." Avatars of apartheid thus seemed better for Congolese unity than Congolese fighters.[16] Time informed readers that one of its reporters covering the violence in the Congo enjoyed working in Africa because, as he said, "I am interested in abnormal psychology." The Congolese, not the South African or American whites, were the abnormal one.[17]

Though Americans questioned African rationality and held aloft the United States as a model of rationality and modernity, nonrational, even physical, factors shaped American constructions of Africa. As Mark M. Smith has argued, how people perceive the sight, sound, smell, taste, and touch of another society potentially contributes to "the construction of the other." Sensory experience gave immediacy to subjective impressions of Africa. Travelers were fascinated by Africa's allegedly primal smells, sights, and sounds. As Staniland notes, travel descriptions frequently featured "how forcefully the continent attacked all the senses," and their initial encounters with African airports, hotels, or cars—"not only vivid" but also "quickly loaded with immense significance and portentous symbolism"—typically shaped subsequent judgments about Africans.[18] The senses provided Americans with certain associations that proved resistant to change. Sensory perception added fuel to Americans' preconception of African exoticism, and sometimes to its poverty and perhaps hopelessness. Travel accounts used sensory descriptions with such frequency and intensity because they offered more than colorful anecdotes or fulfillment of the conventions of a literary genre. The sensory experience of Africa provided intuitive, nonrational, yet powerful impressions and forms of knowledge about a region that Americans routinely complained was too complex to truly understand. According to the *U.S. News and World Report*, "A riot of smells, none of them pleasant, greets the visitor on his arrival in Lagos. It's a city, he finds, of slums and filth."[19] Thus, even in the late 1960s, as one *Washington Post* reporter put it, Americans continued to "think of Africa in terms of noisy animals, strange languages and dark jungles."[20] Chester Bowles, also invoking sensory perceptions in the American imagination, lamented, "we have a stereotype view of Africa which includes predominately witch doctors and shouting politicians at the UN."[21]

The senses, including smell—frequently described in the modern world as less rational and, hence, less important than sight and sound—could influence even social scientists' impressions of the Third World. Modernization theorist Daniel Lerner, writing in the late sixties of the dangers of excessive growth in the largest cities of "the transitional world," illustrated his concern about "overurbanization" (a problem, he insisted, "modern" societies had learned to avoid) with a reference to typical sensory experience. "No traveler in Cairo and Calcutta," he wrote, "will forget the sights, sounds, and smells of debilitated peoples who perform no productive functions for themselves or their environment." Lerner regarded "these millions of hapless people" as "the psychic displaced persons of modernization," individuals who no longer believed they could achieve "anything beyond survival and reproduction." They therefore inhibited their "transitional societies" from successful modernization.[22] Smell, as geographer J. Douglas Porteous argues, has powerful associations with place. Just as novels on India invariably dwell on its "peculiar smell," summarized as "a mixture of dung, sweat, heat, dust, rotting vegetation and spices," so, too, writers have emphasized African smell. White visitors "associate certain smells with the continent," some quite specific, as when novelist Graham Greene recalled the smoke emitted by Freetown, Sierra Leone as what "will always be to me the smell of Africa." More commonly, Robert Ruark's *Uhuru* (1964) invoked a range of smells associated with black Africans—a "native slum" reeking of "urine and dung and rotting meat"— while, as Porteous notes, he "never conjures up the smell of white Africa, and rarely goes beyond sound and visual impressions when dealing with blacks."[23] Nigerian novelist Chinua Achebe points out that Elspeth Huxley, a prolific midcentury British author of fiction and nonfiction and spokesperson for white settlers in Africa, claimed that her expertise on Africans extended to her capacity to distinguish African peoples by scent. Her *Flame Trees of Thika* expresses her preference for what she described as the "dry, peppery, yet rich and deep" smell of the Gikukyu of Kenya, a vegetarian smell that many Europeans loathed. The "sometimes cannibals," the peoples of the Victoria Nyanza basin, had a less agreeable "much stronger and more musky, almost acrid smell."[24]

The tenacity of such literary images also owed much to the American press, whether the stories came from British or American reporters. Huxley, for instance, contributed many condescending portrayals of African reality to such outlets as the *New York Times*. Expatriate views were in vogue, despite their contradiction of the prevailing American narrative of innocence. Whiteness, after all, conveyed expertise. According to a critical *Washington Post* correspondent, little had changed in U.S. press methods of covering the continent since H. M. Stanley had been sent to Africa by a New York editor. U.S. editors in the 1960s still sent journalists with little or no African experience, asking them to cover tremendous areas of the continent, rarely letting them stay long enough in one place "to look at Africa from the inside" As a British critic noted, American writing on Africa tended to "emphasize the bizarre,'" use little up-to-date African history, overdraw the differences between "good guys" and "bad guys" among African political leaders, "and throw in evocative remarks about the landscape, wisecracks about African habits and customs, large generalizations about African politics, and light relief about the hardships of the trip." African leaders charged that "the most distorted American press coverage of Africa is found in the weekly news magazines." *Time's* coverage of the Addis Ababa conference in 1963 that founded OAU comprised "a few supercilious paragraphs devoted mostly to the dancing girls in Ethiopian night clubs." The New York–based men who slashed most of the material provided by the *Time* correspondents and who highlighted the juicy stuff on girls did it to sell more magazines, and the resulting article "caused the subsequent issue to be banned in Ethiopia."[25]

Journalistic whiteness reigned. One survey showed that "of the 59 correspondents reporting for the American media from Africa, only 20 were of U.S. citizenship, including stringers; the majority were British." Africa received too little attention from the U.S. press, and "When an African story does make the grade, it tends either to be very brief, and therefore incomprehensible to the average reader without background, or tailored to American preconceptions."[26] Americans' sweeping generalizations about African geography, landscape, and climate "created an intimidating, even mystical idea of the continent as a place possessed by forces beyond the mastery and even the understanding of human beings." One writer concluded that, in much of Africa, "the only dependable constants seem to be that Africa's peoples are mostly dark-skinned and have problems."[27]

African critics of the U.S. press argued that it, "more so than any other foreign news media, castigates the efforts" of African leaders. As the Liberian ambassador to Washington put it, "What the American press does to damage the influence of the United States abroad cannot be undone by foreign aid or by sending emissaries of the same racial or religious background to these foreign lands." Added Tom Mboya, "The American press is America's worst enemy."[28] An editor at Lagos's *Daily Times* complained about "the unjust coverage of Africa by the expatriate press. Some sections of the foreign press have treated Africa with levity and cynicism, warping the news to give gloomy and ridiculous pictures to the European reading public."[29] Even staunch American ally (and American-educated) Nnamdi Azikiwe, governor general of Nigeria, lamented that "regular tendentious references to African political leaders . . . is becoming one fashionable feature of Anglo-Saxon journalism, on both sides of the Atlantic. . . . The simple reason is their congenital racial snobbery." He warned that he and others of the "older generation in Nigeria" had remained steadfast in their ties to the West and faith in democracy, "in spite of regular doses of insults and gibes from the Anglo-Saxon press; but I cannot guarantee that our children will stomach your continued irreverent attitude toward Africans and their political leaders."[30]

African travelers commented on the gap between image and reality of Africa in American press coverage, and also in popular culture. Visiting the United States, a group of African women educators lamented, "In Africa, we picture Americans as people who carry guns and shoot whenever it is necessary. . . . But in America we Africans are pictured as people who are as wild as the lions and crocodiles in the national parks."[31] An African newspaper editor from Southern Rhodesia who traveled in the United States for three months in 1957 on a State Department grant reported intense feelings about the country, whose "way of life" he considered "the greatest phenomenon in the present century, representing as it does supreme human achievement in democracy and creativeness." Yet he found that, as "delightful" as Americans were individually, everywhere he went. he met with "pretty dismal" ignorance about Africa. "The average educated American knew next to nothing about us except Ghana perhaps or what he had seen in Hollywood spectacles—dancing elephants and unclad black men and women."[32] Writing from a more pointedly skeptical political perspective, Alioune Diop, the editor of the French periodical *Presénce Africaine*, spent two months touring the United States and concluded that "American culture is still in the process of creating itself." Relying on contributions from many ethnic groups, "unlike the French national culture, it does not have a soul." He found ignorance of foreign affairs in general. "As for Africa, Americans seem to consider it a phantom continent which it is better not to mention in the press." Among those who did know something of Africa—"Africanist milieus"—he found "authentic colonialist tendencies" inherited from the Europeans which marred American attempts to fashion an Africa policy.[33]

Nkrumah saw "the cinema stories of fabulous Hollywood" as one of the cultural "mechanisms of neo-colonialism." Violence against Native Americans and Asians in American Westerns and other films, their "incessant barrage of anti-socialist propaganda" and glorification of policemen, FBI agents, and "the CIA-type spy" comprised "the ideological under-belly" of American covert intervention abroad.[34] However, in Africa, movie-goers and consumers of American music and magazines sometimes embraced such images. An American Peace Corps volunteer found young Nigerians believed "'America' is a John Wayne with six-guns flaming in Technicolor, an Elvis with 'geetah' twanging, a tanned Kennedy with hair blowing in the wind"—a glamorous if fanciful "America" Henry Luce would have been proud of.[35] If this frustrated Peace Corps idealists ambivalent about aspects of American culture, U.S. officials had the opposite concern. When such American TV programs as *Naked City*, *Tombstone Territory*, and *Highway Patrol* aired in Africa, their depiction of U.S. culture was taken seriously by many viewers. According to one survey of in a village north of Lagos, "After a week of TV-watching, the majority of villagers said that they believed that most Americans carried guns for self-defense, and that many rode to work every morning on horseback." A dismayed U.S. information official lamented that USIA sought "to project an image of America, and behind our backs American films on TV here create an entirely different impression."[36]

Emotional and Immature

Africa, for many Americans who discovered it during the years of decolonization, seemed full of promise in an essentially feminine way. Congresswoman Frances P. Bolton returned from Africa convinced that "Africa is so vital" and "There are moments when one says 'she' unhesitatingly, so great is the sense of maternity, of the creative, passive, waiting forces " inherent in the place. Yet, the region's gender role could reverse: at times "Africa is all male—aggressive, powerful, ruthless, invincible."[37] Of Africa's "awakening," she said: "It is as if a great giant stirred for the first time in many centuries, stretching himself, opening his gentle eyes upon an unknown and very disturbing world."[38] Similarly, Ambassador Darlington in Gabon expressed the urgency of his work in a gendered idiom, one that implied expansive opportunities for American power. The United States must act quickly, for "other countries would not be slow to work such virgin soil could they get the chance." America had a small window of "opportunity to win the minds and hearts of the whole people."[39]

Such effusive gendered rhetoric belies the more meaningful roles gender played in making America's "Africa." Rather than signaling promise and opportunities for American influence, cultural constructions of feminine African men undermined American confidence in African reliability. American officials tended to evaluate African governments by assessing their emotional stability and evidence of political and cultural maturity. Jennifer Walton has argued persuasively that the Kennedy administration's ideological fixation with the politics of masculinity shaped its foreign policies, and in the Congo, "a discourse of maturity and modernity" shaped its "perceptions of Congolese abilities," as well as "its choice of leaders for the Congo." For Kennedy and his advisors, "maturity was a key characteristic of moral masculinity," and it entailed cultural and well as material attributes. Washington therefore sought to find in the Congo "men who were rational, intelligent, and mature" and who could stabilize the country and prepare it for modernization.[40] In fact, some American officials wondered all along whether such men existed in the Congo. When the Congo crisis erupted in 1960, "reports of the rape of white women were widely featured in the American press" and became a "'continuing pre-occupation' of the White House and the State Department." As the Belgians passed on "detailed and lurid 'first-hand' accounts of rape," these "became items of such passionate discussion in the State Department that one Foreign Service Officer felt obliged to remind his superior in writing that 'The UN did not go into the Congo to save white women from being raped.'" The association of forceful, irrational Congolese men coveting white women was reinforced when a visiting Patrice Lumumba reportedly asked a State Department official to provide him with a white woman for the night, a request the CIA attempted to fulfill.[41] Fowler Hamilton, commiserating with an embattled George Ball about the "explosive" meetings within the Kennedy administration over the Congo crisis, "said they are just savages." Hamilton's reference, by implication, applied to all Congolese factions.[42]

Americans worried about the immaturity of Africans produced by their recent emergence from antiquity. African political leaders were often "first-generation literates," noted one foreign policy analyst, "who are proud of having spanned the gulf between their tribal illiterate society and the responsible posts they occupy as administrators and diplomats, but have not had the opportunity to acquire the experience in public affairs which Western democracies have accumulated over centuries."[43] This perception shaped American reactions to African diplomacy. Ambassador Attwood claimed that in Guinea, where Foreign Ministry officials "needed considerable coaching on world affairs," during the 1962 Chinese invasion of India he had to explain to one particularly befuddled official "that the Indians were not American Indians, and that the invading Chinese were not Nationalists from Formosa but Communists from Peking."[44] U.S. officials, bemused with African behavior at the UN, interpreted it as evidence of immaturity. Attwood, in a speech in Washington, urged "patience and understanding as well as firmness" toward Africans. "For we are dealing with the teenagers of the family of nations," the ambassador declared, "and, like most teenagers, these young nations are sometimes high-strung, unpredictable and exasperating." Officials took wry satisfaction at African diplomatic difficulties. "For the new nations and their even newer representatives," wrote Harlan Cleveland, "the discussions in the General Assembly and the smaller United Nations Councils and Commissions, including the regional commissions and the Specialized Agencies, have a very important role to play as a global training ground for responsibility." When, during a debate over Cuba, "the Nigerian delegate proposed to amend the Latin American resolution in an unfriendly way, he was brought to his senses by a Latin American threat to prevent a two-thirds majority for a resolution on the Cameroun issue that was favorable to the Nigerian point of view." Cleveland concluded, "The immersion of excitable diplomats in practical politics of this kind has its educational value."[45] Africans, it seemed, had in store further training in the art of diplomacy. American officials, whether patient or not, would watch with bemusement. Though deeply condescending, this American belief that African officials were undergoing a linear process of maturation replicated the faith in African modernization, and it proved as illusory.

If African leaders and officials struck Americans as excessively emotional—

feminine—they seemed less reliable as diplomatic or economic collaborators. Rostow described Ghanaian Finance Minister K. A. Gbedemah, a pro-U.S. political leader deeply involved in the negotiations over the Volta project and increasingly hostile to Nkrumah, as "apparently, subject to emotional phases" after seeing Gbedemah depressed.[46] Even pro-U.S. African leaders failed to measure up. Mennen Williams, after meeting with Kenyan leaders and witnessing that nation's independence celebrations, reported to Washington that Tom Mboya, praised by many Americans as the embodiment of African modernization, was "essentially Western oriented but arrogant and foolhardy." Leaders in Nairobi, though generally pro-Western, exhibited naïve indifference to growing Communist influence in Kenya, Williams believed. The Kenyans were "determined to ride tigers back convinced they are smarter than communists or anyone else," a conceit for which they "will probably get mauled a little before its over." He concluded, "With enlightened British and American tolerance and concern, [I] believe Kenya can develop usefully."[47] Nor did Williams's paternalism extend only to East Africa. New nations in West Africa, he insisted, could be expected to oscillate between the Eastern bloc and the West, though "as their maturity develops," the leaders would discover that the United States shared their goals. In what he intended as a compliment, Williams's memoirs expressed "great respect for the innate good sense of Africans and their institutions, primitive or exotic as some of these are."[48] African politicians and leaders confident that they could work with Communists without the latter attempting to dominate were not just wrong; "African emotions," American officials believed, caused such a "naïve and dangerous point of view." As an American representative at the UN Security Council commented, "Africa is much more emotional and unsophisticated than Europe and Asia and the game must be played there in a different way."[49]

African opposition in the UN to U.S. handling of the Cuban missile crisis struck Stevenson as merely a reflection of African delegates' weakness. "A growing desire 'to get away from it all,'" dismay at the American refusal to consult them at the UN, "and a feeling that they were caught in something 'too big for them'" kept Africans from performing effectively under pressure. In New York, "most Africans seemed unable to grasp the idea that US moves in Cuba were made in self-defense." That Africans must have been "confused" rather than merely in disagreement with Washington resulted from the fundamental attributes Stevenson had come to associate with his UN counterparts. Most notoriously, Stevenson fumed to a reporter his desire for a time ahead, "when the last black-faced comedian has quit preaching about colonialism so the UN could move on to the more crucial issues like disarmament." Beleaguered by vociferous African criticism of the American airlift in the Congo, Stevenson declared, "never have I heard such irrational, irresponsible, insulting and repugnant language in these chambers." Chester Bowles, Kennedy's Special Advisor on African, Asian, and Latin American Affairs, has been characterized as "the strongest advocate of a verbal offensive against apartheid." Yet he opined that African leaders had a "mercurial quality" that led to their "often irritating" pronouncements on Cold War issues on which they suffered from a "lack of background." These men were widely considered among the most sympathetic to African aspirations within the Kennedy administration, yet they, like many less charitable officials, shared the belief in African irrationality and volatility.[50]

If Africans lacked emotional stability and maturity, their passionate attachment to novel concepts and ideologies, or political causes such as the liberation of Southern Africa from colonialism and apartheid, need not be seriously engaged at an intellectual level. One scholar noted that "the emergence of African states has not been universally received with respect for the integrity of Africans," as Westerners at times dismiss African nationalism "as little more than a grotesque comedy."[51] U.S. intelligence analysts considered Pan-Africanism "a mystical concept, glorifying racial kinship and the African personality and culture" whose "chief target is 'neo-colonialism.'"[52] Seeking to channel African passion, Dean Rusk asked Wayne Fredericks for a list of "intra-African problems to which we might direct the African enthusiasms which are at present expended in some more unhelpful directions." His subordinate expressed sympathy, but noted that Africans really did care more about colonialism and apartheid than border disputes between Ethiopia and Somalia, for instance.[53] When asked by President Kennedy if Nkrumah was a "Marxist," Ambassador William Mahoney declared Ghana's leader "a badly confused and immature person who is not quite sure of what he wants except that he wants to lead all of Africa."[54] African critics, too, questioned Nkrumah's sanity, often to flatter Americans. Senghor told Kennedy that the Ghanaian leader "required the attentions of a psychiatrist" to cure him of his stupendous dreams of leading Africa and his absence of principles.[55] As for Guinea's nationalist leader, Sékou Touré, American observers repeatedly belittled his economic decisions, and a Central Intelligence Agency report insisted he lacked "any clear grasp of the economy and how it functions, even less of development and how it is achieved." While his long rule over Guinea cer-

tainly failed to produce great economic growth, Touré did devote three books
of over 1,000 pages to discussion of socialism and development. The main
American concerns seemed to have less to do with the credentials of the African leaders than the ideology they espoused or specific policy disagreements.[56] U.S. officials believed it would be difficult to speak with Touré about
details of the aid he had received from the Communist Bloc not only because
of his secretiveness but also because, as a White House aide put it, "Apparently Touré himself is totally ignorant about foreign assistance to Guinea,
whether it be Bloc or non-Bloc—he simply does not and will not understand
it."[57] Attwood's successor in Conakry reported "Touré's unhappiness over the
US aid program in Guinea," though he claimed "that the issue is being
resolved" and that "the major problem . . . is educating Touré" on how U.S.
aid works.[58]

Julius Nyerere, according to an American diplomat in Tanganyika, though
a good political leader, had proven a "poor administrator" who "has no head
for complex economic development programs."[59] By the mid-1960s the CIA
regarded him as "enigmatic." At a time when Tanzania courted Communist
China's support for the construction of a railroad that would permit Zambia
to transport goods without going through white-ruled Rhodesia, Nyerere
became increasingly less identified with the West. CIA analysts sneered at his
"newly-found mission as the prime mover in the 'liberation' of southern
Africa," as well as his efforts to help Congolese rebels gain access to "Communist arms" in their struggle against the American-backed regime. The
United States provided a small $6 million annual aid program, and "the Peace
Corps largely staffs Tanganyikan secondary schools," yet Nyerere complained
the volunteers spread anti-government propaganda. Speculating that he now
believed the Americans would not help him fight colonialism and apartheid,
"and that Communist China represents the wave of the future," CIA analysts
predicted that, under his "weak and ineffectual leadership," radicals and
Communists would grow increasingly influential. Rather than stop there and
chalk up Nyerere's views and behavior to a political or ideological conflict,
the CIA report groped for ways to naturalize his intransigence. Nyerere's
statements they deemed difficult to classify, and "many even defy rational
analysis." At times, the Tanganyikan leader wept and became distraught during meetings with diplomats. With such an unmanly leader, the CIA offered
the cynical conclusion that, if he continued to lean to the left, it would not
mean that he would do much. Nyerere had "ambitions rather than plans" and
lacked "courage" to accomplish much.[60] When Nyerere responded to the U.S.

airlift in the Congo by writing to President Johnson, the U.S. Ambassador called the letter a product of "emotionalism, suspicions, and fear," rather than the understandable concerned reaction of an African nationalist. Unable to understand him as anything other than a typically emotional African, the United States came to hold the view that "under the mercurial and fiercely independent leadership of Nyerere, Tanzania is the bastion of radicalism in East Africa."[61]

U.S. concern over corruption and the irrationality from which it purportedly sprang led Washington to view with equanimity the series of coups across Africa in 1965–66 in such countries as Ghana, Nigeria, and the Congo. All along, some American observers within and beyond the Beltway had insisted that Africans needed political stability more than democracy. Immanuel Wallerstein himself had justified the prevalence of one-party states during the early 1960s, believing Africans required "the iron hoop of a strong state."[62] The State Department noted that "In almost every case the younger officers have joined with experienced officials to eliminate a layer of politicians who were either corrupt or ineffective." The new leaders were more focused on internal development and less on "foreign adventures, especially extra-African issues." They would bring "honesty in government, and a corresponding lower tolerance of corruption," and emphasize "competence" in government while guarding against Communist influence. The coups yielded "less emotional atmosphere in some cases, permitting more practical cooperation with the former metropoles and the United States." U.S. interests would benefit, as the new leaders exhibited "greater realism in facing up to economic difficulties. These leaders are instinctively more open to sound advice from Western governments or international organizations, such as the IBRD and the Fund. Although continuing to be thoroughly African in their world outlook, they are more prepared to minimize or cut ties with Communist countries." The coups therefore did not mean an end to African development or the removal of the rationale for the U.S. aid program.[63] As Komer wrote Johnson, "Military coups like those in Ghana and Nigeria are not really a matter of civilians vs. military, but of a dynamic educated element of the new African societies getting fed up with the ineptitude or posturing (or both) of the original leaders of these young countries."[64] Thus, Americans' only real regret about the wave of African coups was that Sékou Touré and Julius Nyerere were not among its victims.

While Americans decried African corruption, a State Department review of CIA activities noted that, in the Congo, the agency had covertly helped Adoula and Tshombe "to buy the support of political and military leaders." This activity prompted the question of "whether the wholesale buying" of a country's leaders "is a sound basis for establishing a stable government," though "in the Congo there appears to have been no feasible alternative."[65] In reaching such conclusions, Washington moved along a logical chain some academics had begun to explore. Samuel Huntington's *Political Order in Changing Societies* argued that the African coups of the 1960s were part of a larger global pattern, and that coups were "an inseparable part of political modernization."[66]

Some American scholars, however, recognized the irony. Wallerstein, in a 1968 book review of an anthology featuring major ASA scholars entitled *African Diplomacy*, noted the consensus that African denunciations of neocolonialism and the spread of radicalism in Africa reflected an "irrational" African impulse. "The aggressively declared African hostility to neocolonialism symbolized the continued existence of a high degree of frustration," insisted one contributor. Another, economist Andrew Kamarck, blamed Africans for being "not yet conscious of the costs that must be paid" to achieve development. Wallerstein demurred. For "if one is weak, and oppressed, there is nothing irrational about either aggressiveness or radicalism. Indeed what is unreasonable and irrational is to accept the existing system that perpetuates, if not causes, the weakness." That the liberal mediators had failed to arrange a meeting of the minds between Americans and Africans now seemed undeniable. As Wallerstein understood, Americans expressed their incomprehension of African leaders through representations of irrational, effeminate, and unsound Africans. This is how Americans coped with the awkward reality that, despite their initial optimism about African leaders, African goals and methods seemed increasingly incompatible with the American "can do" mission.[67]

Eight
"Fetish Nation"

Tribes and Juju

When Eric Sevareid published a profile of Nigeria on the eve of independence entitled, "Nigeria: Black Monolith . . . or Triptych?" the CBS news analyst included photos depicting "the ancient and the modern in Nigeria." Photos juxtaposed "barbarically" attired Hausa "tribesmen" and Nigerians working in a college laboratory to illustrate the contrasts in a transitional new nation. Yet greater weight went to the "ancient" Africa, highlighted by a photo of a traditional dancing ceremony. Its caption read: "Like most of Africa, Nigeria is attempting to leap a millennium in a generation. But even as the new encroaches, the old persists. Above, Jeba dancers perform in weird and colorful costumes." Prurient interest aside, Sevareid's fixation with such simplistic impressions of African difference yielded an upbeat, if self-serving, conclusion. "We may as well face it," he wrote. "Culturally, for good or ill, the West has won the world. Is it bad that peoples everywhere are giving up their native clothing, music and customs for those of the modern West?" Modernization was inevitable. "Nigeria," he argued, "is going Western, and American to boot."[1]

Americans easily saw African "tribesmen" and imagined them either a relic, as Sevareid did, or an obstacle to development and nation building. Sevareid's was an early statement, and its optimism proved difficult to sustain in the years ahead. Of course, as his article's title indicated, Nigeria was to him not merely a land of tribesmen, but specifically of black tribesmen. Race, never absent in the American-African encounter, received ample commentary. As previous chapters have shown, whiteness made some African cities more attractive to Americans and symbolized modernity. Racism in the United States, a prime concern of Africans, became more than theoretical when African visitors, including diplomats, experienced it first-hand. Responding to Western racism, some African intellectuals and leaders espoused such concepts as negritude and the African Personality, while African states forged basic ties of unity in the OAU.

Race, however, became even more complicated as Americans came to recognize African ethnic diversity. Americans knew African ethnicity as "tribalism," something different from the bands of culture, memory, and identity found in Western societies. To be African meant to belong to a tribe, and tribes were primordial, isolated, self-contained, and antagonistic to other tribes. Africanist scholarship on ethnicity had yet to cashier, even among the educated, American tropes of tribe.[2] Americans did not understand the history of African ethnic identities. Before colonialism, Africa comprised thousands of distinct societies, organized politically in large and small kingdoms, chiefdoms, city-states and "stateless societies." Cultural and social cohesion—shared language, kinship ties, communal land and labor, common customs and values—depended on social units that could preserve traditions while adapting to new circumstances while trading and co-existing with other peoples. Consolidating Africa into a few dozen colonies, the Europeans had reified differences between peoples with overlapping cultural traits and histories of cooperation. Missionaries taught Africans to see themselves as Igbo or Yoruba, Zulu or Xhosa, Hutu or Tutsi, while the colonial state, governing through a variety of indirect means, entrenched division and rivalries. This is the Africa that Americans before 1960 knew, the one featured in *National Geographic* that few African Americans could identify with.

Because tribe, unlike race, seemed to evoke specific kinds of institutions and customs—most of which Americans judged incompatible with modernity—its presence troubled Americans in profound ways. American officials worried about the untidiness of African "detribalization." As an NSC report put it, "The tribal and family traditions of the people in question are such that they remain, despite the many advances that are currently being made, extremely primitive in many of their social outlooks. These traditions, while breaking up at an accelerated pace, remain strong, and even the urban African looks for a source of authority to replace the head of the tribe or family." Such transitional, detribalized Africans seemed

"an easy target" for opportunists and subversives who could offer leadership during a time of uncertainty and change.[3] Transitional tribes would
face daunting problems with democracy and development, according to
American officials. During a 1960 NSC meeting, Maurice Stans, Eisenhower's Budget Director, declared, "The Africans do not understand Western-
style ballot box democracy," and a diverse country like the Congo should
be politically reorganized along more suitable "tribal" lines. Africans there
should form "tribal federations like those formed by the American Indians." Amplifying this bizarre comparison, he explained that Africans did
not care for democracy "beyond the village," as they instead "look to the
chief of the tribe who is a kind of dictator." To illustrate this parochial
African perspective, he described the "Basonge tribe in the Congo." When
it had "become conscious of a world larger than that of the tribe itself,"
its members decided to assess each one a dollar per year for an economic
improvement fund. They planned to seek American advice about what
crops to grow and where to find markets for them. "The idea was excellent
in concept," said Stans, "but not being successful in finding a way to use
the funds collected, the chiefs of the tribe used them to buy fourteen Ford
cars."[4]

Staniland notes that many Americans found African "parochialism"
troubling, fearing African suspicions of foreigners betrayed their lack of
the rationality and capacity for innovation essential to development. In
this context, most American observers deplored Africa's allegedly "tribal"
ethos. "Tribalism" struck Americans as retrograde and a remnant of the
colonial era. American scholars described African "tribes" as without
value, an obstacle to progress, and a source of disunity for new African
nation-states. Colonialism, many feared, "has inevitably caused Africans
to view all change as being motivated by selfish interests; the security of
tribal society and the power of familiar magic has been weakened or
destroyed."[5] Edward Korry, as an editor for Look, produced a cover story
on Africa in transition. Employing the trope of tribe as a catchy advertisement, the article was billed as "a moving, eye-opening story of progress
stymied by tribalism, of violence tempered by patience, of the ultra-prim-
itive in daily contact with the ultra-modern."[6]

Look found plenty of company in the American press. Life ran a long and
lurid description of the influence "witchcraft and sorcery" continued to
play even in the thoughts and deeds of educated African leaders. In fact,
"magic, far from being on the way out in Africa, seems on the way to a

vigorous resurgence." With the white man leaving the continent, his laws no longer restrained it, while African proponents of "the African Personality" or the concept of negritude approved "almost any traditional African practice," according to a *Life* correspondent in Uganda. "In Lagos," according to Elspeth Huxley's article on tribes in the *New York Times Magazine*, "there are glass-fronted stores that sell anything from Cadillacs to Paris hats; just a few paces away, in the market, you may buy a withered monkey's skull, dried bats' wings and nameless claws to make you a potion as eerie as anything cooked up by Macbeth's witches." She described the unrest in Belgian-ruled Rwanda as "the outcome of an age-old enmity between two tribes: the Watusi, a race of aristocrats who grow seven feet tall, and the Bahutu, four million Africans who were once their slaves." The riots in Rwanda thus illustrated "what is probably Africa's greatest danger today—a revival of tribalism once white rule is withdrawn." The end of colonialism might mean a return to "precolonial days," when "the normal condition was one of intertribal war."[7]

Most African American observers preferred the evident modernization associated with middle-class and educated Africans to an association with "tribal" Africa. Richard Wright, in *Black Power*, concluded that Nkrumah should accelerate modernization in the Gold Coast to "atomize the fetish-ridden past, abolish the mystical and nonsensical family relations that freeze the African in his static degradation," and to eliminate "parasitic chiefs" in order to "project Africa immediately into the twentieth century!" Writing as a social scientist with greater familiarity with African societies, St. Clair Drake displayed a more nuanced understanding. He argued that "the very tribalism that makes the achievement of national unity difficult also hampers the organization of unified opposition; the emotion of respect and habits of loyalty to traditional rulers carries over in some measure to the new educated African heads of state." Drake, however, while seeming to suggest that ethnicity impeded democracy, also contended that strong communal bonds and communal land, rather than "a 'drag' on development," actually helped modernization. Such social units absorbed "poverty" and unemployment through networks of kinship and affiliation.[8]

American fixation with African tribalism began, of course, before most African nations became independent. Indeed, the examples discussed above are from the late 1950s and the early '60s. Chronologically, one might wonder why we should consider such representations of tribe at this point, having surveyed the rise and fall of Americans' optimism about modernization and nation building. As noted in the Introduction, however, this volume does not strictly follow a chronological order. Moreover, it is fitting that we consider American interest in "tribe" now because, I argue, it illustrates how American thinking about Africa came full circle by the end of the sixties. What was old was new again, as Americans witnessed the coups, civil wars, and economic false starts of mid-decade Africa. Colonial tropes of tribalism, savagery, and superstition, never entirely displaced by development discourse and expressions of American support for nation building, resurfaced with a vengeance when things fell apart. As liberal expectations for African progress melted, many erstwhile advocates of aid to Africa and prognosticators who had forecast sunny days ahead for the African nation-state now relapsed, recycling cultural arguments to account for African failure. These explanations for disturbing events stressed African difference or otherness. Many of the images that attained purchase in the late sixties accomplished more than the exculpation of American policies, for they remain potent even in early twenty-first-century American news accounts and political discourse.

What exactly was at stake in American belief in African tribalism as an element and disturbing force? First, American plans for African development seemed threatened. A 1964 presidential task force reported that, whereas South Asia had "at least a part of the apparatus of a modern society," improved living standards remained a distant goal for "African countries where the majority of the population is still organized in the institutions of tribal agriculture."[9] Edmond C. Hutchinson, declaring "the tribe is still a social, spiritual, and economic reality," approvingly cited Waldemar Nielsen's argument that tribalism "is the embodiment and the fortress of primitivism and the past. To modernize and stabilize the new states, means will have to be found to reconcile tradition and change, to shift loyalties from the tribes into building blocks rather than road blocks to progress."[10] Hutchinson argued that "absorptive capacity" in Africa included a "cultural dimension" that "takes the form of resistance to change. This has been an immemorial roadblock in the way of development and growth." It thus contributed to the economic aspects of "absorptive capacity" that justified limitations on the size of USAID commitments in Africa.[11] Tropes of tribe also offered ready-made explanations for African violence. During the Congo crisis, a *Wall Street Journal* account of cultural and material regression used an anecdote from an expatriate cleric whose mission no longer received eggs daily. The boy who used to bring the eggs had been killed by a "Baluba war party" that also "cut him up, and fed him to his chickens." This story—with its invocation of the tropes of tribe and mutilation—"illustrates," according to the *Journal*, how the country had begun "regressing to the jungle." No longer protected from vengeful, primitive tribal enemies by "a firm Belgian hand," Congolese like the slain "egg boy" became victims of a conflict Americans could imagine as a primordial one with "its roots in dim history which far predates European rule." The more recent Belgian colonial exploitation and American covert intervention against Lumumba seemed less salient. Beyond the Congo, in 1964 one observer noted, "The American press has carried extensive accounts of the slaughter—sometimes described as systematic genocide—of thousands of Batutsi tribesmen in the Republic of Rwanda since the turn of the new year. There has been remarkably little effort, however, to examine the underlying causes of this bloody chapter of Central African history."[12] Thirty years later, the Rwandan genocide exposed the horrifying consequences of that failure to seek context.[13]

Assuming that Africans were tribal—bound by immemorial rites and mutual antagonism, isolated from one another and from the world—fit awkwardly with the ebullience of narratives of innocence. To approach tribes was to approach the many local African religions associated with them, as well as the Africanized Islam and Christianity that bore marked traces of indigenous beliefs, symbols, and practices. In 1960, readers of the *New York Times* learned of a dark side to the "Year of Africa." As the editors put it, the newly independent nations had begun "a relapse into ancient and even barbaric customs that include witchcraft, mass poisonings and public executions."[14] Thereafter, news accounts continued to stress the persistence of "traditional" African religion (often called "pagan" or "animist" by Christian and Muslim alike), with its allegedly superstitious array of "witch doctors" and strange rituals. Identified by historians Andrew Rotter and Seth Jacobs, among others, as frequently a key factor in American foreign relations, religion struck many Americans as relevant to African difference and development. The "literary" colonial Africa dissected by Dorothy Hammond and Alta Jablow had dismissed African religions as "merely a mass of superstitions and weird rituals." Travelers in the centuries before European conquest, according to historian Philip D. Curtin, exhibited little interest in local religious beliefs. They did, however, seize on "spectacular festivals, human sacrifice, judicial ordeals, and polygyny" as vignettes with which to entertain readers back home, and they lavished detail in accounts that "often stressed precisely those aspects of African life that were most repellent to the West and tended to submerge the indications of a common humanity." In the nineteenth century, "All travelers, and especially the missionaries, were opposed to 'paganism,' but few understood it." While Europeans alleged Africans either lacked religion or worshipped the devil, they were preoccupied with "the 'fetish,' a material object endowed with certain spiritual powers" they believed Africans worshipped, a practice thought to encapsulate the essence of their "superstition." Most believed this barbarous set of beliefs (or their absence) and the ubiquity of the "fetish" constituted "a positive evil depressing society below the moral level attainable by unaided natural reason."[15]

Like their colonial forbears, Americans, in their preoccupation with tales of African "juju," breathlessly recounted every minor anecdote about rain making, superstition, and cannibalism. After reading Clarence B. Randall's report on his 1958 tour of Africa, Eisenhower said in an NSC meeting that "he was so impressed with the work of the missionaries . . . that he proposed to increase his contributions." At another NSC meeting, the president, responding to a discussion about economic aid and African education, remarked that he was "reminded of a recent movie which had stressed the theme that the black man, under the influence of religion, was taking a more realistic view of his problems." Randall agreed, noting "a great reservoir of good will for the United States was being created by the missionary movement in Africa."[16] Planners, Michael Adas reminds us, typically dismissed "nonwestern epistemologies—including religious and philosophical systems"—as barriers to modernization and having no useful knowledge about local conditions. All customs associated with the older ways of farming and working had to be replaced with Western technology and knowledge.[17] Development would have to work miracles epistemological, spiritual, material, and political, and Americans would have to drag Africans into the salvation of the space age. If not, military planners would manipulate African religious beliefs to better wage counter-insurgency warfare. In 1964 the Army commissioned a study from American University of "Witchcraft, Sorcery, Magic, and other Psychological Phenomena and their implications on Military and Paramilitary Operations in the Congo."[18]

The fodder thus provided to American reporters and editors proved ample. The Associated Press reported from South Africa, "Witch doctors are doing a roaring trade in Johannesburg." Mixing potions with the same ingredients as "his jungle predecessor," the modern "mutiman" used "bats' wings, bark, tree roots, hippopotamus fat and ostrich eggs" and did business at a counter with "a window display of monkey skins." One potion of "hippo fat and snake fat" sold heavily to "job-seeking Africans." "After smearing this evil-smelling grease on his body," the African "steps out confidently to meet a prospective employer." Stories of witchcraft and strange juju rites appeared in many accounts. In Nigeria, insisted one report, "from time to time, you get evidence that things have not changed too greatly, deep in the gloom of the forests." When a plane crashed near Calabar, before police could get there, "local tribesmen" had come and "made off with six heads for use in juju—black magic—ceremonies."[19] One *Wall Street Journal* reporter related an incident in which police in Lagos found a suitcase in the railroad station containing "the body of a small boy who had been missing for some days. The body was being transported to the hinterlands for a cannibalistic ritual feast of a witchcraft cult."[20]

Such speculation was not limited to middlebrow journalists. American and other expatriate advisors to the government of Nigeria speculated, during discussions of economic development, about such exotic cultural and social phenomena as cannibalism, slave-raiding, and belief in the efficacy of juju. According to American economist Wolfgang Stolper, principal author of the country's development plan, "if you read the papers, you will see a column about jujus, with some people expressing strong belief in it." After visiting a Yoruba shrine in Ibadan, where he found "the whole atmosphere oppressive," Stolper remarked, "I was glad I saw it, and glad I got out. There was something dirty about it, and my respect for missionaries went up." This revulsion gained strength as he toured the "part of the market given to medicines . . . or the juju market as it is usually called, where traditional medicines and charms are on sale." He recalled, "I didn't see any dried monkey heads, but there were dried bats' wings, dried skins of various sorts, and miscellaneous things which were simultaneously revolting and picturesque." The following year Stolper disappointed traders when he declined to purchase a monkey's head at an Ibadan market, despite its reputation as a "very powerful" juju.[21]

American concerns were shared, in part, by Nigerians eager for modernization. In 1960, a page-one story in the *New York Times* quoted a Nigerian newspaper's indignant complaint that the country could "become a fetish nation" if such traditional beliefs and practices were sanctioned by traditional rulers like the Oba of Lagos. The Oba, "a well-educated former civil servant," hired "juju rainmakers to make sure that Nigeria's independence celebrations would not be marred by seasonal downpours." The *Times* reporter warned, "Witchcraft, known as juju in this part of West Africa, is still a problem, even in coastal provinces where Nigerians work in factories and offices." The "problem" was illustrated with such examples as the following: "no one has difficulty there in buying ground monkey heads, serpent fangs and even weirder ingredients of black magic." Articles like this seldom conceded any possible value or positive aspect of indigenous beliefs, and sought instead to warn Americans and "educated Nigerians" not to underestimate "juju," and "that combating superstition is a prime cultural task" for the new nation. That the Americans' inordinate fixation on "juju" might appear irrational and too much like the old concerns of missionaries was seldom discussed.[22]

The rain-making incident that prompted local fears of Nigeria's relapse presaged continued American preoccupation with the country's "exotic" customs and beliefs. During a visit to the Oba of Benin, Stolper found the monarch curious about "why people wanted to go to the moon, whether I thought there were spirits there, whether I believed in good and evil spirits . . . I told him that our business was not to worry about things we could not know anything about, but to do God's will here and now, for example by developing the Second Five Year Plan." Unimpressed by Stolper's business-like American cosmology of development, "The Oba didn't bite," insisting there must be many good and evil spirits, some of which must also be on the moon. The Oba insisted that when humans landed on the moon "we would meet spirits more powerful and intelligent than we are. He always came back to this point." The American economist believed his hour-long encounter with the traditional ruler of Benin "interesting for a number of reasons." Recognizing the Oba's wealth and political influence, Stolper was struck by the monarch's cultural conservatism; "he believes in the traditional religion with all its superstition as well as good things—and no matter what present-day anthropology says, there is a lot of superstition based on fear—and he showed no interest in development or anything of the kind." If Stolper thus explicitly dismissed the cultural relativism of Melville Herskovits and his disciples, he did not even allude to the alternative source of knowledge about African religion that lay beyond the Western academy, such as the novels of authors like Nigeria's Chinua Achebe. That the Oba had a reputation for being "too progressive by many Binis" left Stolper further alarmed.[23]

Traditional religion clashed with the space age in a more direct fashion five years later. American newspapers reported a public meeting of the Oba of Benin with an American astronaut—ironically named Conrad—touring Africa after orbiting the earth aboard Gemini 5. Clad in an "Ivy League suit," Navy Lt. Commander Charles Conrad called on the sixty-seven-year-old monarch adorned in a "flowing white robe and settled back in his red leatherette throne." To one American journalist, "Between the two lay a gap on this planet as wide as any that may exist in space." The Oba allegedly embodied "ancient Africa," and his references to "the space" seemed a sharp contrast to Conrad's "photographs and clinical verbal descriptions of his voyage." Despite the conceptual and cultural gulf, and Conrad's inability to impress the Oba with his two-foot-long model of Gemini 5, "the once notorious City of Blood proved a friendly and understanding port of call." The correspondent for the *New York Times* noted the Oba's reference to "'the space' as if it were a total entity," and his question to Conrad as to whether "'the space' was covered by a spiritual 'canopy,' as foretold by the gods of Benin." A NASA physician replied, "Well, nobody has seen any canopy, but it might still be there," an answer that seemed to satisfy the Oba. This exchange symbolized, for American observers, the persistence of a traditional African culture quite incompatible with modernity. Citing a number of allegedly naïve questions posed to the astronauts, Lloyd Garrison, the *Times* reporter, speculated that "the tour's impact on the 'average' African seemed little more than skin deep." Nigerian journalists covering the American tour were described as bewildered by the astronauts' technical terminology. "For Nigerians," wrote Garrison, "terms like 'booster' and 'space flight environment' have no meaning, and no definitions were given. Furthermore, many Africans still cling to traditional notions about the universe." That "booster" and "space flight environment" are abstract, even opaque words to most Americans mattered as little to the American reporter as the inaccuracy of his sweeping characterization of Africans as too "traditional" or superstitious to grasp the meaning of space exploration.[24]

If, however, African rulers could not combine spirituality with modernity, Americans would have to do it for them. Ambassador Darlington argued, "our most effective tool is the spirit that an ambassador is able to communicate. This is something that Africans are quick to grasp. Because few can read, and perhaps because animist beliefs are widespread among them, they are extremely sensitive to spiritual forces." Proper "demeanor and conduct" by an ambassador and his wife could "exemplify our country and our people," and thereby influence Africans. "The American ambassador must, it seems to me, regard it as a principal part of his job to help these people, by spiritual as well as material aid, to use their freedom creatively . . . To help them to find the resources within themselves to build their nation must surely be one of the purposes of our relationship with them."[25]

While few Americans shared Darlington's literal missionary zeal, contempt for African religion and political concepts that invoked religious traditions remained widespread. "It would be one thing," scoffed a report in the *Wall Street Journal*, "if the African could boast a spirituality superior to the West's 'sordid materialism.' But he cannot. His spirituality is a dungeon of terrors, revealed in its most extreme form in the savage bestiality of Mau Mau. Rejection of the white man and all his works, return to barbaric, terroristic Africa—this is indeed Mau Mau leader Jomo Kenyatta's attractive formula for 'projecting the African personality.'" Such references to the freedom movement in Kenya reflected the American fear that, lurking beneath the surface of cultivation, even African leaders remained prisoners of superstition and harbored hearts of darkness.[26]

Romance and "Culture Shock"

If any secular missionaries could transcend, if not combat, representations of African tribalism and juju, it seemed a job for the Peace Corps. No one more enthusiastically exemplified optimism and a desire to effect change in Africa than young American volunteers who heeded Kennedy's call to service. Uniquely idealistic while also expressive of Cold War priorities, the Peace Corps was a natural tool for Washington's African agenda. Created in 1961, the agency found Africa receptive to young American volunteers, despite concerns about its alleged ties to the darker side of American influence, the CIA. As Michael Latham has demonstrated, Washington (if not the volunteers) viewed the Peace Corps as a potential catalyst for poor countries to create "viable nation-states." Building schools, teaching students, and engaging in community development projects, volunteers "could promote nation building by encouraging provincial peoples to conceive of themselves as part of a larger national body, a society organized along the same lines as their village." In Africa, the Peace Corps was also an effort to apply more fully the "can do" American values celebrated in *The Ugly American* that could change the cultural context of economic develop-ment and democracy in newly independent nations. Ghana received the first volunteers dispatched anywhere in the world. Yet those young Ameri-cans, like other American visitors to Africa, found many aspects of their encounter with local cultures disquieting.[27]

Under the direction of the president's brother-in-law, Sargent Shriver, the Peace Corps had, within two years, over 4,300 volunteers, of whom 1,148 worked in Africa. The considerable presence of Peace Corps volun-teers in Ethiopia, Nigeria, Ghana, and Liberia made a favorable impression on Africans. Bowles described the volunteers as a "brilliant, outstanding success," and Williams reported that all over Africa, he heard nothing but praise for them. They had demonstrated, he declared with satisfaction, "that a few dedicated, sensitive, hard-working, friendly Americans can make an indelible impact on peoples abroad." Volunteers were "some of the most effective salesmen we have," he added, partly because of their willingness to live "under extremely Spartan conditions" in Africa.[28] The Peace Corps' success seemed evident in spite of attacks by African critics such as Nkrumah, whose suspicions about its motives mounted until, in *Neo-Colonialism*, he attacked it as one part of the myriad American cultural, economic, and political means of dominating the Third World. Nkrumah made much of the long ties between Shriver—"a millionaire who made his pile in land speculation in Chicago"—and Allen Dulles, thus making him and his Peace Corps a collaborator with the CIA.[29]

Rostow believed the Peace Corps, "while separate in important ways, should be linked to Education and Human Resources development," so it could enhance "a nation's capacity to absorb capital productively." Peace Corps teachers could assist "underdeveloped" countries in coping with their acute shortage of skilled personnel. Shriver, eager to preserve the image of the Peace Corps as altruistic and clearly distinct from Cold War politics, displayed his own opportunism. The first Peace Corps volunteers went to Ghana, and Ethiopia received another of the first major overseas missions. Shriver justified this allocation of so many volunteers to Africa by citing Ethiopia's desperate need of teachers to help cope with a 95 per-cent illiteracy rate. Moreover, noting the importance of Ethiopia in Africa, he quoted an USAID education expert who effusively declared, "this may have a more lasting impact than Cleopatra's visit to the Conquering Lion of Judah 1500 years ago." The allusion to ancient Ethiopian history may have mattered less to Kennedy than Shriver's point that Ethiopia and Nigeria were major African nations that wanted Peace Corps volunteers and needed English-language teachers. Though the president wanted a rapid dispatch of volunteers to Latin America to have priority, Shriver pointed out that fewer volunteers spoke Spanish well and Latin American governments had shown less immediate enthusiasm for American teachers than the Africans.[30] Nevertheless, references to Cleopatra illustrate the American conception of an innocent, if ancient, Africa awakened by the arrival of idealistic young Americans. Their presumed catalytic power would turn the fiction of *The Ugly American* into reality.

Harris Wofford, a white civil rights advocate who played a major role as a liaison to African American activists during the early Kennedy administration, made three trips to Africa to supervise Peace Corps work before requesting appointment as director of the mission in Ethiopia. Writing to the president, Wofford confided, "Africa is in my blood." He wanted to work in Ethiopia because a successful American aid effort there could ensure "stability and democratic change in all of East Africa—and a vital center of friendly power." He persuaded Kennedy to make the Ethiopian appointment so that Wofford could work on "the international side" of what he considered the major issue in the world. This he defined dramatically as "the Big Integration of us less-colored Westerners into a largely colored world." He felt that working in Africa could make a bigger contribution to this historic goal than continuing to serve Kennedy in civil rights politics.[31] Wofford, "a student World Federalist in the 1940s" and an early proponent of a Peace Corps-type organization, had been "thrilled" by its creation.[32]

In April 1962 Wofford and the Ethiopians reached agreement on the establishment of the Peace Corps mission, and he became Country Director. As he told volunteers, "The New Frontiers are not in Washington" but rather "they are out where you are going." Planning to double the number of Ethiopians enrolled in secondary school, the Peace Corps trained volunteers at Georgetown University where, it later admitted, instruction in the Amharic language had been "inadequate." Nevertheless, Wofford, who wanted to "move into Africa on a big scale" with New Frontier élan, remained undaunted. The volunteers endured training that included intensive exercise and physical fitness activities, and frightening health presentations that had them convinced, as one recalled, "that schistosomiasis, elephantitis, and leprosy were just around the corner." While reproducing old stereotypes about the dangers of Africa, the Peace Corps also encouraged volunteers to consciously form their own representations. Wofford told them of Ethiopia, "It's all so wide open," a place "limited by your imagination." Wofford insisted that "Africans are a young people, making history" and the "Peace Corps want[s] to encourage the African countries to think even bigger." According to Gary May, "Wofford cast a spell that only the most cynical could reject. Tall, lean, handsome, and eloquent, he seemed the very personification of the New Frontier. Friends and critics alike called him the 'Philosopher King' of the Peace Corps."[33]

Wofford's inspirational rhetoric reflected the resonance of old American myths associated with expansions that Michael Latham has detected in modernization and nation-building discourse. "We are a pioneering people," Wofford declared, "with the frontier still in our blood." Peace Corps volunteers were called upon to embrace the total ethos of the New Frontier. "We do not want to stay at home in our safe suburbs while the city is burning and being rebuilt . . . It is truly our need and our desire . . . to participate in the great adventure of world development." Volunteers recalled Wofford's relentless optimism and his vision of "sending people to bring the message of democracy and individual initiative . . . It was all very romantic and we believed it." However, as the volunteers—including Paul Tsongas, future U.S. senator and presidential candidate—rode a bus from the airport in Addis Ababa to the University College to begin a two-week orientation, they experienced "culture shock," gazing at "all the huts, the mud, the masses of people, donkeys, sheep, cattle and cars crowding the airport road. We had traveled back hundreds of years when we dropped out of the sky." The volunteers wanted to "fulfill their mission—to bring Ethiopia into the twentieth century." They would do so by making their schools modern, eliminating the rote learning methods of the Indian and Ethiopian teachers. "We were hell-bent on teaching them to think," one recalled.[34]

Despite developing rapport with their students and remaining committed to their educational goals, many volunteers felt disillusioned. As they prepared to depart in 1964, one summarized the mood: "Generally we are cynical and disillusioned about the Ethiopians and their values, but we remain idealistic and enthusiastic about the Peace Corps and the importance of our work here." Many volunteers concluded that Ethiopians were "passive, apathetic, hostile and suspicious of all foreigners, . . . and new ideas. They are not interested in working to help themselves, or in any work at all, but only in how much other countries will give them. This is not an underdeveloped country, it is an underdeveloping country!" One volunteer declared Ethiopians "a lazy, seemingly useless people." The Americans admitted their failure to master Amharic and that they had fallen short of making "the 'supreme' effort to overcome the cultural barrier between themselves and the Ethiopians."[35] They shared this with their colleagues working around the world, who by the middle of the decade "were more likely to plead guilty than innocent" to charges of "cultural imperialism." Jonathan Zimmerman's sympathetic discussion of the volunteers' struggle to transcend cultural barriers and prejudice concludes that these secular missionaries shared with their Christian predecessors key premises or "imperialistic assumptions." As American volunteers tried to encourage their students to preserve local cultural traditions—such as crafts and songs—they seldom realized that they had assumed a cultural prerogative "to determine what was 'authentically' African." Like their colonial forebears, the volunteer teachers "assumed a basic, essential difference between their students and themselves." Accepting that premise compromised their goals for changing difference (the official Peace Corps commitment to modernization) or preserving a healthy cultural diversity by encouraging tradition, as many volunteers preferred.[36]

Wofford spoke expansively even as his Ethiopian volunteers struggled, describing the Peace Corps as "an invitation to the imagination, an invitation to large action, to moving fast, to thinking big, an invitation to its volunteers and to all Americans . . . to extend themselves," not merely "for our survival but for our salvation." He reported that Ethiopians, under the influence of the Peace Corps, were "learning that all things are possible in time." However, one volunteer wrote home lamenting the Peace Corps' narrow emphasis on education. He suspected "that we are educating these people for nothing," as the Ethiopian students would find it difficult to get a job. The mission of educating students could end up producing a "dissatisfied minority" that could become a revolutionary force undermining Ethiopia. Yet Washington continued sending volunteers throughout the decade as teachers. By 1967, there were 434 volunteers in the country. "When a student-led revolution finally toppled Selassie's government in 1974," writes May, "and a Marxist regime sympathetic to the Soviet Union took power, many volunteers wondered if the Peace Corps by commission or omission had contributed to the outcome."[37]

Similar problems plagued the mission in Nigeria, which for a time,

hosted the largest contingent of American volunteers. An incident in 1961
illustrated the difficulties volunteers faced when confronted with economic and cultural difference. Arnold Rivkin had been "skeptical" about
a Peace Corps mission in Nigeria, fearing "the problems it might raise"
and "the possibilities of it backfiring on the US." While the State Department believed the Peace Corps mission would "definitely accelerate Nigeria's capacity to absorb and utilize external assistance," some Nigerians
loudly criticized the Peace Corps as an "agency of neo-colonialism." Meanwhile, the government in Lagos insisted on having a voice in the selection
of volunteers, specifically insisting on a higher percentage of African
American volunteers. As the minister of economic development told the
U.S. Ambassador, such demands "are as much in the interests and protection of the United States as they are of the government of Nigeria."[38]

In 1961 an incident did materialize. Twenty-three-year-old Margery
Michelmore, writing a private note to a friend back home, described Nigeria in provocatively derogatory terms while preparing a postcard in Ibadan.
The postcard, which the Nigerian press described in detail after it was
found, apparently misplaced, on the street, caused a firestorm of contro-
versy. She had found "squalor and absolutely primitive living conditions
rampant both in the city and the Bush." Dismayed by public urination on
the streets of Ibadan, Michelmore concluded, "We had no idea about what
'underdeveloped' meant." Michelmore, who worked with other volunteers
at University College, Ibadan (UCI), apologized for her remarks and offered
to resign from the Peace Corps. Although the incident led the Nigerian press
to question the motives of the American volunteers, the U.S. Embassy and
State Department defused the crisis by transferring Michelmore to a Peace
Corps training center in Puerto Rico.[39] Ambassador Joe Palmer suggested
the Peace Corps not return Michelmore to Ibadan, though he claimed she
had "handled herself admirably since her initial thoughtless act," and "has
been most cooperative in efforts to minimize damage which has resulted."
During a long meeting with Azikiwe, Palmer, convinced that much of the
public furor had been manufactured by leftist elements, urged him not to
allow militant youths at UCI to use the incident as a pretext for anti-Peace
Corps, anti-American propaganda. Azikiwe, himself a longtime newspaper
editor, sympathized, and "felt incident had been exaggerated by students,"
and at the ambassador's suggestion, he agreed to meet Michelmore, whom
Palmer described as an "unusually intelligent girl with good intentions and

high ideals who had come Nigeria in a real spirit of service." The Nigerian leader met Michelmore and offered consolation. Palmer met with Balewa to discuss the Michelmore incident after the prime minister issued statements critical of her actions. The ambassador reported to Washington that he had convinced Balewa not to turn against the Peace Corps, though "despite my best explanations," the prime minister remained sharply critical of Michelmore.[40] Political scientist Harvey Glickman interpreted the Michelmore incident as evidence of "more than the brittle sensitivity of many Africans to all but the most innocuous reactions to African conditions and interests. It indicates also that 'culture shock' is probably unavoidable for most Americans upon their first contact with Africa outside the plush hotels."[41] However, Léopold Sédar Senghor, father of Senegalese independence, assured Kennedy the Peace Corps had "won our astonished admiration" and that the Michelmore incident was "not important," having been caused by "a few communist sympathizers among the Nigerian students." In his country, by contrast, "we merely laughed about it."[42]

The achievements of the Peace Corps, however small compared to the outsized ambitions of Wofford, gave Washington rare good news from Africa. A State Department report noted, "Somalia has not been an easy place for Volunteers to work. Somalis are traditionally suspicious of foreigners," though U.S. preference for Somalia's hostile neighbor, Ethiopia, did not help. However, the sixty-seven volunteers then teaching and the twenty building schools had become "vital to Somalia's educational system."[43] One political scientist, writing in the *Journal of Modern African Studies*, praised the Peace Corps as "revolutionary." He argued that "the revolution is indirect. By speaking honestly to the tribal element, by planting the seeds of thought and knowledge, ideas come into being that at a future time may alter the economy and polity of any given state."[44] In other ways Africa influenced America through the Peace Corps. One study of former Peace Corps volunteers from the 1960s and '70s, including a number who worked in Africa and later became anthropologists, found that the experience led many of them to stress applied anthropology and what is called the "anthropology of development" in the American academy. A number of Africanists in other disciplines also spent part of their youth serving with the Peace Corps in Africa.[45]

Whiteness, however, did not lose its salience in the Peace Corps. The Michelmore incident and the complaints of volunteers in Ethiopia about local laziness and apathy evoked American racial stereotypes. White volunteers also identified with other whites in Africa more than Wofford would have liked. One volunteer recalled that in Addis Ababa, they went "to parties every weekend with all the degenerate expatriates in Ethiopia and spend their money like any group of rich foreign plutocrats."[46] When a white volunteer teaching in Tanzania visited South Africa—a violation of Peace Corps policy that cost him six months pay—he found ample compensation. Enjoying the company of friendly white South Africans, beer, and a week of "surfing and swimming and genuine hospitality," he silently endured their tirades about the mental inferiority of Africans, choosing not to counter their claims by citing his own experience of bright, inquisitive African children.[47] In some measure, the Peace Corps itself advertised the whiteness of "America" internationally. Some African Americans held important administrative posts within the organization, and individuals like St. Clair Drake trained volunteers for Ghana in 1961–62.[48] However, African American targets of Peace Corps recruitment faced the dilemma of whether to apply their idealism and courage to the American freedom movement or to a Washington-sponsored overseas mission. Though blacks served in the Peace Corps from its onset, the numbers remained smaller than the agency had hoped, reflecting both the pull of the Civil Rights Revolution and Black Power and, with the Vietnam War, a growing black distrust of American foreign policy.[49]

The Peace Corps yielded mixed results from the perspective of Africans, U.S. officials, and volunteers. Education received a modest but symbolic boost from American teachers. Volunteers found a meaningful outlet for their surging idealism and energy. Washington polished an image increasingly tainted by charges of neocolonialism. Yet, like foreign aid and development plans, the Peace Corps could not match the vast ambitions of its creators. Julius A. Amin concludes that volunteers in Guinea—who were eventually expelled—"were in the wrong place at the wrong time with the wrong education." Their training had not equipped them to do the kind of community development, agricultural reform, and teaching expected by the Peace Corps in Washington. The volunteers could not transform Africa, or avoid having their self-understanding complicated, often in painful ways. As a tool of cultural communication, the large Peace Corps missions in Nigeria, Ghana, and Ethiopia proved capable, but not dynamic. The New Frontier in Africa dreamed of by Wofford remained elusive. As one observer wrote in 1964, though the Peace Corps did admirable work overseas, "they are not exactly revolutionizing four dozen nations." Several thousand volunteers, "thinly scattered among scores of millions of humans held in bondage by ignorance, feudalism, superstition, ancient mores and tribal customs, can't be expected to spread American progress like a giant wave over millions of square miles of mountains and jungles and deserts, over huge cities blemished by the worst slums on earth."[50] In America, the Peace Corps was unable to transform the Africa of the mind that singled out African culture as the source of African difference and, to Americans, failure.

"Not All Barbarians Here"

As for Africa's "America," Americans feared the political impact of African stereotypes about Americans. Vernon McKay, sounding like the authors of *The Ugly American*, believed in educational exchange programs, arguing, "Even if economic aid backfires, the more Africans there are who know Americans as personal friends, the more difficult it will be to build up a stereotype of the United States as a money-grubbing giant with no appreciation of esthetic and spiritual values." He identified the key group needing persuasion: "It is essential to win the confidence of African intellectuals. . . It is they who set the patterns for Africans to follow."[51] U.S. intelligence analysts worried that Africans saw the United States as a nation "which does not fully understand Africa's problems or fully support African aspirations." This, they believed, lay behind the African states' willingness to take aid from the Communist Bloc.[52]

When, during a meeting in the White House, Kennedy asked Senghor to explain the concept of negritude, the Senegalese poet-statesman characterized it as the positive "contribution Africa could make to the civilization of the universal" in the arts, based on independence for all Africans. Kennedy also asked why African youth had a "Marxist outlook" and "seemed anti-Western, anti-American and attracted to the Soviet bloc and Communist China," citing the University of Dakar as an example. The United States, he claimed, had never had African colonies and still had no economic presence on the continent comparable to that of the Europeans. Why, he asked, "was it so hard to attract a sympathetic cultural and intellectual interest in the U.S.?" In reply, Senghor assured him that Communists remained a small if vocal minority at Dakar and in colleges across Africa. Nationalism and negritude, not Communism, were "attractive to us culturally," he explained. Moreover, religion and the Western cultural heritage bequeathed by colonialism also operated as cultural forces against Communism in Africa. As for Senegal, it sought "to use socialist methods—planning, cooperatives and the like—and keep spiritual values and Western political values at the same time." Socialism, for Senegal, did not entail a rejection of "the 'American Way of Life,'" it merely fit the different circumstances of Senegal. Kennedy, at the end of the wide-ranging conversation, urged Senghor "jocularly to go back to Senegal and tell his people we are not all barbarians here, even if we do not have French culture."[53]

Kennedy's witty remark revealed Americans' barely concealed lack of confidence; they worried about the comparison Africans would make between themselves and the Communists—the central theme of *The Ugly American*—and also with the British and the French. Given African irritation with unreliable American economic aid, postcards from Ibadan, violent news from Birmingham and Selma, and insulting American stories and films, this unease seems well founded. Washington struggled to find a gesture or strategy of cultural diplomacy appropriate to countering the kind of suspicions Kennedy feared. Ulric Haynes could only reply with a playful "Wild!" in the margins when he received a report that the U.S. Ambassador in Burundi had suggested that the "US should distribute the National Geographic magazine throughout Africa as it does an excellent job of presenting 'the US image.'"[54]

While white Americans strove to demonstrate their cultural sophistication, artists, intellectuals, and activists of African descent from both sides of the "Black Atlantic" countered with an affirmation of black culture. Malcolm X made solidarity between African Americans and continental Africans a key part of his evolving strategy for a global black liberation even as he pioneered an influential cultural nationalism that expressed pride in African identity. Even African Americans who worked in the U. S. government or served in Africa evolved such a cultural politics. Mercer Cook, a Ph.D. from Brown University, taught French at Atlanta University and published books in French and English during the 1930s and '40s before becoming one of Kennedy's African ambassadors. After his stint in the Dakar embassy, Cook co-authored a volume entitled *The Militant Black Writer in Africa and the United States* (1969). In 1974, he made a major contribution to this Pan-Africanism in editing and translating the pioneering work of Senegalese scholar Cheikh A. Diop, *The African Origins of Civilization*. Thus, one of Kennedy's African ambassadors, far from reproducing the "can do" style of neoimperialism that went hand in hand with the narrowly conceived civil rights of Cold War liberalism, helped popularize a powerful African argument for Africa's seminal contribution to the world.[55] Meanwhile, AMSAC had for years "played a leading role in exposing African culture to the United States, arranging tours and academic exchanges," as Plummer notes. The climax of these endeavors may have been in 1966 when Dakar hosted the World Festival of Negro Arts. A celebration of Pan-African identities and cultural politics, it confounded the neat demarcations white American Cold Warriors had erected. Washington, hoping to distract attention from its unpopular Congo policies and the overthrow of Nkrumah, expressed support for the festival by sending First Lady Lady Bird Johnson and sponsoring the participation of African American artists. The State Department viewed Dakar as another opportunity to promote a brand of cultural diplomacy it had employed for several years, as Penny Von Eschen has demonstrated. Emphasizing the achievements of African Americans burnished Washington's claims of American "colorblind universalism." Black artists, however, expressed their own opinions about what their work meant with "unprecedented assertions of black cultural solidarity that far exceeded the cultural politics and vision of American officialdom." Rather than an homage to America, artists like Duke Ellington used their opportunities in Africa to express their consciousness of an identity and culture of the African diaspora. Others such as James Baldwin and Harry Belafonte boycotted the festival in protest of Senegal's close ties to Washington.[56]

In the years ahead, both the conventional American denigration of African culture and the black solidarity displayed at Dakar continued to evolve and gain strength. Lyndon Johnson had wanted to avoid a segregated foreign policy, he said, when he blocked the consolidation of a black lobby on Africa. Ironically, America since the 1960s has had, if not a segregated African policy, a bifurcated relationship with African culture. Assigning Africans the blame for their misfortunes has freed Western governments and the World Bank from shouldering responsibility, which is one reason why representations of African barbarism persist in popular culture, the media, and officialdom. Yet the delayed black lobby on Africa did emerge. More important, the blossoming of African American engagement with African culture has provided a vital counterpoint to the hegemonic representations. Though Africa lost its hold on most Americans' attention after the initial euphoria of independence, the United States continued to exert a major influence, directly and through the Bank and other multilateral organizations and non-governmental organizations. The Decade of Disillusionment ended, but not the American Century, and it remained only a matter of time before America rediscovered Africa as a major challenge.

Conclusion

Long before presidential tours of Africa became de rigueur, Lyndon Johnson planned to make the first such pilgrimage. Five years after LBJ's Senegalese expedition, presidential aide and confidant Bill Moyers reported that "the President feels that of all the places he would like to visit abroad, perhaps an African visit would pose the least problems and get the greatest return," though Moyers admitted the idea "was still very much in the 'thinking stage.'"[1] By the final year of his presidency, Johnson hoped, much like George W. Bush forty years later, to polish the badly tarnished image of his war-scarred presidency by highlighting U.S.-aided African success stories. In June 1968, Rusk, who had yet to make the trip himself in nearly eight years as Secretary of State, had "cleared off on the proposed African itinerary." The president wanted to visit Ghana, in particular. The post-Nkrumah regime, staunchly pro-American, seemed a safe choice, and LBJ could visit the Volta Dam and other USAID-financed projects, to "see progress made in Ghana economic development, rather than attend meetings." The planned nine-day trip scheduled for mid-August would give the president "a firsthand view of Africa's diversity and potential." By the time that month arrived, however, it became clear that the trip had fallen through, though the State Department had to infer this from a White House press announcement that Johnson intended to spend August at home in Texas. LBJ, perhaps influenced by his dour Secretary of State, or simply exhausted at the end of a failed presidency, pocket-vetoed a historic opportunity.[2] As America descended further into the abyss of Vietnam and social upheaval, African crises spiraled beyond anyone's control. The president now merely sought the comforts of a private sanctuary.

The president's instincts may have been sound. As previous African tours by Mennen Williams and other Americans had revealed, Africans were increasingly bitter about the gap between the rhetoric of American aid and the reality of red tape. Their commodities had fallen sharply in value while the cost of importing goods had soared. Their development plans, despite the best technical advice America could offer, lay in tatters. That the Peace Corps had successfully projected American goodwill and educated a number of African students had not erased memories of the American airlift of mercenaries into the Congo or the overthrow of Nkrumah. Nor could positive press coverage of a presidential visit have changed the relentlessly negative stereotypes about African culture common in American representations of corruption, irrationality, emotionalism, tribalism, and "juju."

LBJ's retreat from Africa was a metaphor for the withdrawal of the United States. In his 1969 book, Waldemar Nielsen ruefully referred to "Africa, that habitual afterthought of American foreign policy. . . ." By then, he expressed little hope that Washington would revive its interest in the region, unless a domestic constituency for it gained a foothold in Congress. Nielsen proved prescient in his anticipation that African American voices would eventually influence at least some elements of American policy, such as the movement for divestment and sanctions against South Africa. Striking, too, is the indignation of a key figure within the Africanist community; Nielsen's African-American Institute had been very much a part of the collaborative relationship among the federal government, foundations, and academe in making Africa a Cold War area.[3] Though Americans had seen an opportunity to modernize Africa, the aid levels had remained modest when compared with such undertakings as the Alliance for Progress and assistance to such allies as Israel. Even during the middle of the Kennedy presidency, the United States provided only a little over $200 million a year in bilateral aid to African nations, much of it plunged into the bottomless pit of the Congo. Cold War priorities in Ghana and Ethiopia absorbed aid even as Rostow and State Department officials insisted that aid should primarily flow to states serious about planning for development. Overall, American aid during the Cold War largely bypassed Africa, as the continent received less money than any other world region, and only a third of the largesse devoted to East Asia.[4]

However, although the United States did not match the expectations it raised in Africa, a commitment was made. Development remained a powerful discourse that Africans could appropriate. Even as U.S. officials scaled back the Decade of Development, some understood that "U.S. relations with Africa are distinctly different from those with other regions of the world. The ties that link us are many and significant; they will grow in the future." Americans would continue to "hear the voice of Africa in world affairs, a voice with increasing insistence and power in the United Nations. . . . We hear it amplifying via such organizations of poor-nation protest as UNCTAD, through the International Coffee Agreement and similar channels. We hear it within the context of race differences in our own society."[5]

Indeed, African Americans did not withdraw from Africa. To the contrary, in the 1980s they spearheaded the imposition of United States economic sanctions on South Africa. Attachments to African culture influenced African American life in many different ways, from Black Power champion Stokely Carmichael's self-transformation into Kwame Touré (honoring the fiery nationalists of Ghana and Guinea) to the mainstream acceptance of the holiday Kwanzaa. Even if few other Americans in the era from 1968 to 2000 reflected much on Africa as a political and economic subject, they, too, were influenced by the globalization of African culture. Derided by Americans even now as a space signifying difference and inferiority, Africa has confounded Henry Luce's prophecy. "Zanzibar" has not been Americanized. True, American products and culture have an influence on the island of Zanzibar—now part of the nation of Tanzania—and throughout Africa. However, cultures of the Islamic world, Europe, and South Asia possess even more. African music's global popularity and the growing success of African soccer, symbolized by South Africa's hosting of the 2010 World Cup, and the scholarship and creative genius of African academics, artists, and writers— many of whom have lived and worked in the United States—all testify to Africa's importance in the world, even as its political and economic crises continue to define the world's impressions.

Nevertheless, despite the deepening engagement of African Americans and of the growing popularity of "things African" around the world, the U.S. relationship with Africa since 1968 has yielded few achievements, particularly when judged against the expectations of the Decade of Development. With American bilateral aid diminishing throughout the late twentieth century, Africa's picture became bleaker decade by decade. The era of coups did not, as Americans hoped, produce stable, pro-American governments enjoying popular legitimacy and possessing the competence that had eluded the civilian regimes. Instead, nations such as Nigeria swung violently from one regime to another, with the military's involvement in politics bringing neither stability nor development. Nigeria's civil war did not end Nigerian unity, as the federal government's triumph ended Igbo secession. However, ethnic and religious rivalries have multiplied since the 1980s, while the stakes rose along with Nigerian oil profits. Americans today know Nigeria mainly for its beleaguered Niger Delta, where soaring violence and resentment of multinational oil firms contributes to the rising price at the American gas pump. In the 1990s, Somalia and Rwanda became global cautionary tales, prime examples of a "failed state" and ethnic cleansing/genocide, respectively. Any mention of African politics, governance, or identities evoked shudders of horror.

The only thing more disturbing than the explosion of violence producing Idi Amin's atrocities, the dismemberment of civilians in Sierra Leone, and other crimes against humanity was the misery and death imposed by economic catastrophe. Ethiopian famine in the 1980s did more than a thousand years' worth of copies of National Geographic to cement the image of Africa as a land stalked by hunger. Though less visceral, the statistics associated with African decline acquired their own paralyzing power. By the late 1990s, African countries carried an unimaginable external debt worth well over $200 billion. Individually these nations faced debts larger than their Gross Domestic Product and spent more money on interest payments ("servicing the debt") than on education and health care combined. Wealth was being transferred from Africa to the West, just as in colonial times, as most Africans remained trapped by an export-only, monoculture economy in a world whose economic giants had already moved from industrialization to the information economy. The staggering scope of Africa's economic needs vastly outstripped those of the 1960s, as Africa slid inexorably into the status of the world's "poorest of the poor." The new needs also outstripped what the industrialized world was willing to offer as aid or trade concessions, and the vastness of African distress seemed to provide more support for those who argued the futility of aiding Africa. What good would a few billion dollars in loans or grants do? Johnson's aborted Africa trip would not be reattempted for thirty years. Although Jimmy Carter briefly stopped in Nigeria in recognition of American dependence on its oil, the first real presidential tour would be Bill Clinton's. Real American interest in African problems as political problems, and not irresistible forces of nature or inevitable by-products of African culture, began only in the twenty-first century.

Such a record of manifest failure begs the question of motives: Did the United States policymakers of the 1960s show such fervent (if short-lived) interest in Africa because they wished to exert imperialist control? Too vexed a question for this book to determine definitively, it cannot be sidestepped. Readers by now should see that I do not ascribe to American officials or others engaged in Africa during the period a completely selfish motivation. Americans within the mainstream, Cold War liberalism of the age of JFK and LBJ who visited Africa, studied Africa, made policy toward Africa, or engaged with Africans via diplomacy, technical assistance, or volunteering certainly wished to see Africa develop. The problem lay less in their wishes than in their definitions of what African development meant, how it could be achieved, and who should direct the process.

Like their colonial predecessors, American scholars, experts, commentators, and officials succumbed to the hubris that promised complete knowledge and freedom of action. Despite Wolfgang Stolper's admission to the contrary in *Planning without Facts*, before the Nigerian civil war the American consensus held that enough information, analysis, and calculations could be arrayed to study and solve many African barriers to development. Where colonial anthropologists, missionaries, and District Commissioners had failed during the era of European rule, Americans, endowed with the genius of postwar social science and the experience of life in the wealthiest and evidently freest nation in the world, could guide newly independent African leaders through their "transition" to modernity. Epistemology, therefore, furnishes part of the explanation for the failure of the U.S.–African endeavor of the sixties.

Despite the boldness and self-confidence of secular missionaries in the New Frontier and LBJ's expansive era of combining guns with butter at home and abroad, something else lay just beneath the surface of the American experiment in Africa: ambivalence. The Cold War rivalry of the superpowers bore many of the marks of a classic imperial rivalry, and in spite of Washington's professed tolerance of African neutrality, any expansion of U.S. power (political, military, economic, or cultural) in newly independent Africa implied at least neoimperialism. However, as the Europeans had demonstrated generations earlier during their conquest and colonization of Africa, an imperial power can pursue large aims without conceding its goal of keeping down costs. Much of the history of European colonialism in Africa was shaped by the reluctance of the first-generation colonial offices to spend significant money on anything in the newly won territories beyond what was needed to service European exploitation of local resources. Railroads were built, but only toward the coast to facilitate the export economy, not to promote future

African development in the interior, for example. In the 1960s, secular missionaries, too, attempted to penetrate vast areas of Africa largely untouched by American influence during the colonial era, in what can be regarded as a kind of informal, Cold War scramble for Africa. Like their European forebears, the Americans were cost-conscious. With imperial obligations across the globe and growing strains on the American economy, Washington would not commit the resources to fully fund its own vision of planned development in Africa.

If the Americans failed to transform Africa into a continent of largely peaceful, modernizing nation-states, the United States has, nonetheless, benefited from the relationship forged during the sixties. In Cold War terms, Washington avoided direct involvement in African wars or wars with Communist armies from Cuba, China, or the Soviet Union. It also "lost" few countries to Communism in the Ethiopian fashion, though the cost of keeping Africa in the "free world" orbit was the generation-long subsidizing of Mobutu and other dictators. As the post–Cold War world has revealed most clearly, the American insistence on African adherence to a neocolonial pattern of world trade and investment that keeps Africa locked into dependence on the West and such Western-dominated multinational institutions as the IMF and World Bank has meant, in effect, American hegemony in Africa. Without launching its own costly development projects, the United States could, directly or indirectly, deter African governments from abandoning Western-oriented market economies. The "Washington Consensus" of the 1990s fixed economic liberalization in Africa as solidly as anywhere in the world, at the expense of the state in Africa. If this produced a debt crisis that has forced the United States, the multinational organizations, and an ever-growing array of NGOs to try new means of aiding Africa, it has also tightened American influence, or control, over much of the continent. Only in this decade, with the rise of a new imperial rival—China—is this arrangement in question. In short, if the United States failed to bring the New Frontier and the Great Society to Africa, it did not suffer, as Africans have, from that failure, and its leverage has actually grown over time.

Their moment over, had the secular missionaries gone forever? Could not Africa still play a role in a bid for a new American Century? Hollywood and novels have renewed American interest, not so much in concrete African problems (to say nothing of African aspirations), but in Africa as a site confirming the benevolence and inevitability of American hegemony. Surveying the spate of Africa-related films, nonfiction narratives, and novels appearing in this decade, Harilaos Stecopoulos has concluded that "cultural producers have invited Americans to put an old Africa on their map." Drawing on the Africa represented by white British explorers and colonialists over a century ago, American and other white Western filmmakers and writers have found in "Victorian Africa" images and stories for our post-9/11 times that "offer a historical justification for US geopolitical power" and use Africa as "an exemplary signifier for Western intervention." Americans and others have learned to fear an Africa capable of nurturing and perhaps exporting HIV/AIDS and Ebola, to say nothing of terrorism (or uranium for Saddam Hussein, in the case of George W. Bush's infamous claims about Niger). "Fear-inspiring Africa might not warrant a major US intervention in and of itself," writes Stecopoulos, "but tales of the heart of darkness help dramatize the need to combat evil in the world."[6] This Victorian Africa reproduces much of American narratives of innocence and images of colonial modernity, as discussed in chapter 1, as well as representations of African cultural darkness explored in chapters 7 and 8.

Culture continues to haunt American discussions of African development. American scholars, officials, journalists, travelers, and activists all invoke alleged cultural differences as explanations for Africa's deviance from Western norms and its failure to replicate Western achievements. Evidence that the *Heart of Darkness* trope retains its influence in contemporary discourses about Africa is abundant, as demonstrated by even a cursory search of books and articles about Africa. In his searing indictment of the failure of Western aid to Africa (primarily Somalia), journalist Michael Maren finds it fitting to introduce his book with an epigrammatic quotation from Conrad's novella.[7] Another author at the beginning of this decade felt compelled to account for African violence with a book entitled *The Graves Are Not Yet Full: Race, Tribe, and Power in the Heart of Africa* (2002). Americans continue to ascribe political and economic conditions to unchanging cultural attributes. "During the Cold War," notes Mahmood Mamdani, "Africans were stigmatized as the prime example of peoples not capable of modernity," and now "Africa is seen as *incapable* of modernity." In some basic sense, African cultures are still imagined in opposition to progress, now understood in terms of neoliberalism.[8]

As at the dawn of African independence, current Western discussions of African economic and political crises are burdened by what James Ferguson labels "Africa Talk." This urgent discourse speaks of "Africa" as a collective entity sharing essential problems. "It is never just Africa, but always the crisis in Africa, the problems of Africa, the failure of Africa, the moral challenge of Africa to 'the international community,'" writes Ferguson. If in the colonial era Africa signified "a radical other," a "dark continent" for Westerners, even now, "for all that has changed, 'Africa' continues to be described through a series of lacks and absences, failings and problems, plagues and catastrophes." In this "Africa Talk," tropes of "corruption" are inseparable from "development," shaping how governments, investors, and aid planners imagine and intervene in Africa.[9] "Corruption" does yeoman work. It explains for the successors of Wolfgang Stolper why foreign aid does not work the way experts at the World Bank expect. It explains African poverty. It relieves the West of moral responsibility beyond that of humanitarianism. It saves analysts from having to complicate their theories of the state in Africa; everything is reduced to endemic corruption. Why and how corruption came to exist and flourish in Africa, how multinational corporations and Western governments are implicated, need not be asked, let alone answered.

While insisting that Africa's problems as aid recipient are rooted in a culture of corruption, American experts in the field of U.S. foreign aid see America's shortcomings as a donor in more narrowly technical terms. All that is really wrong, they suggest, is the insufficient amount of aid and a few bureaucratic inefficiencies, problems that certainly can be fixed. Carol Lancaster and others in the field continue to focus on streamlining the aid bureaucracy and getting more aid implemented on the ground, not changing the basic concepts of development. This is a message post-9/11 Washington was ready to hear. Development became a priority for the Bush administration with the release of the National Security Strategy a year after the terrorist attacks. Earlier in 2002 Bush expanded the existing aid bureaucracy by creating the Millennium Challenge Account, administered by the Millennium Challenge Corporation. In January 2003, as he prepared to invade Iraq, Bush announced a commitment of $10 billion over five years to fight HIV/AIDS, and the administration's FY 2006 request for a 15 percent increase in foreign operations budget showed that development in this decade has enjoyed a degree of attention "not seen since the early years of the Kennedy administration." Bush, in two visits to Africa, exemplified the easy compatibility of American aid for African development with militarism, as the U.S. presence in Djibouti and the intervention in Somalia brought Africa into the global "War on Terror."[10]

Recent enthusiasm for new means of aid to Africa, such as the U.S. African Growth and Opportunity Act and the New Economic Partnership for African Development, share basic premises of the earlier development decade. Aiming at saving Africa through bold aid packages directed by the West, these initiatives do nothing to reverse a generation of decline and weakening of the

African state. This decline, usually associated with the structural adjustment programs of the 1980s and '90s, began, as demonstrated in chapters 5 and 6, in the mid-1960s, when the United States countenanced a spate of coups, a retreat from democracy, and a shift in aid to the World Bank. As William G. Martin has recently pointed out, the new initiatives raise false hopes in Africa of a return to the strong, developmentalist state of the early postcolonial years, while in fact they deepen African dependence. Martin sees greater reason for hope in the efforts of Africans to work with others beyond national borders to fight for improved international terms of trade, though one should recall that Africans have been fighting this battle since the sixties.[11]

Frederick Cooper, discussing debates over where the blame for African decline and debt lies, advances a historical answer that requires a longer time frame. He argues that the period 1940–73 was a distinct "development era" in African history. The late-colonial (European) and early postcolonial (African) regimes successfully generated some economic growth and built schools, hospitals, roads, and dams, but they failed in their larger endeavors, such as industrialization, diversification of the economy, and, above all, economic independence (a goal of African leaders). Two basic schools of thought offer explanations for what went wrong. One argues that the developmental state—and its foreign donors—"did too much." Reliance on technology transfer, big prestige projects like the Volta dam, and loans that had eventually to be repaid resulted. Governments, according to this view, were too ambitious, spent too much, left too little to free markets. Others argue that not enough development was attempted, as donors like the United States pulled back too quickly, while failing to negotiate with Africans fairer terms of trade. African states such as Nigeria and Ethiopia failed because they were never serious about development and broad-based social justice. Cooper, responding to these arguments, points out, "These are counter-factual propositions, and one must ask what the imagined alternative was." No easy answer exists. In fact, as this study suggests, it would be worthwhile to synthesize the arguments of the two schools. African states, paradoxically, probably did do too much and too little all at once. They sought rapid development—symbolized by big projects, plans, and big aid packages— but feared the political and social consequences of empowering (economically and politically) ordinary farmers, workers, and women. However one assigns the blame within Africa, it ought to be possible to categorically dismiss the self-serving professions of American and Western innocence one commonly reads in publications such as the *Wall Street Journal* and the *Economist*, among many others. American experts and officials helped write African plans, funded

African projects that produced mixed results and substantial debt, and—in a move abetted by middlebrow representations—blamed African culture for the failures that ensued.

Washington's amnesia about the American experience in Africa's "development era" enables the United States to approach African development now with naïve confidence and a clear conscience, much as it did over four decades ago. Once again, Americans can congratulate themselves and insist on African gratitude for aid, the value of which is, we are led to believe, self-evident. In 2005 Madagascar, the country where Arnold Rivkin first glimpsed a vision of "transitional" Africa ripe for change, became the first to sign an agreement with the United States for $110 million as part of the Bush administration's Millennium Challenge Corporation (MCC). The MCC channels U.S. aid to poor nations "with a demonstrated commitment to democracy, free markets, and investment in people," and develops "clear and measurable goals and performance commitments for each party." As with the planning criteria of the development era, the MCC provides another lever for American intervention in Africa and, if (when?) things fall apart, a ready-made excuse for withdrawal.[12]

That it is up to African leaders to do what the West considers self-evidently necessary is the theme of countless statements. Consider the following example from the magazine *Foreign Policy*: "Some African countries will certainly master engagement with the international economy. But accepting globalization is not merely a conclusion to be reached after studying economics; it's a revolution in attitude that forces leaders to confront and overcome a brutal past."[13]

This recent quotation from a noted political scientist of Africa could have been written in 1960, with "modernization" replacing "globalization." African leaders are enjoined to "accept" a Western definition of the world economy and the policy prescriptions that flow from it. Moreover, they must do so not merely because the economic wisdom of the West is manifest; they are (or should be) caught up in a beneficent "revolution in attitude" that brings their feelings into conformity with reigning theory and practice. Those African leaders—and the African and international observers who share their skepticism—who resist this historical inevitability doom their peoples to poverty. They do so not as a result of their convictions, or the existence of political conflict between North and South. Rather, they commit the historical sin as a manifestation of a psychological or emotional immaturity, an evasion of responsibility to play their appointed role in the world.

Again, this is not a new idea. During the Decade of Development, an official of the Rockefeller Foundation, in a presentation to the ASA, admitted that foreign aid alone could not solve African economic problems. However, he assured his listeners, "its greatest value can be in forcing governments to face realities and make the necessary hard decisions concerning economic growth and welfare—decisions such as the priorities to be given to education vs. roads, or the issue of subsidization of urban vs. agricultural sectors, and so forth." This emphasis on forcing Africans to make decisions on matters important from a Western perspective—evident in Stolper's private assessment of how the Nigerian plan would work—anticipated the eras of structural adjustment and today's schemes for African aid.[14] It may well be, in fact, impossible for American leaders to imagine, let alone attempt, an aid program for Africa that does not seek to control African thought and undermine African sovereignty.

Bush's six-day visit to Africa in February 2008, a transparent attempt to distract attention from his Iraqi quagmire and to burnish his credentials as a "compassionate conservative," explicitly cast the United States as benevolent benefactor of a disease-ridden, impoverished Africa. The president himself declared upon arrival in Benin that Africa featured "a lot of great success stories, and the United States is pleased to be involved with those success stories." More important than Bush's political motivation was the form in which he expressed American interest in Africa. The centerpiece of his trip—a $700 million commitment from the Millennium Challenge Corporation to Tanzania—exemplified the new American approach to consolidating influence and control in Africa.[15] Visiting "success stories" in countries such as Ghana and expanding aid to Tanzania demonstrated Bush's confidence that U.S. aid to countries following American-defined political and economic rules of conduct produced "measurable results." Arguing that development and democracy went together, he declared that "people who live in societies based on freedom and justice are more likely to reject the false promise of the extremist ideology." Like his predecessors, Bush fashioned aid policies and public diplomacy to highlight their selective "results" as part of a project to use Africa as a proving ground, a laboratory for American political and economic ideas. Africa's value—aside from providing a beleaguered president brief respite from nearly ceaseless criticism in the United States and the rest of the world—lay in its potential to justify broad axioms upon which rested the essentials of American foreign policy.[16]

"Africa is dying . . . there seems to us no future in the future." These words, shouted by Edem Kodjo of Togo, carried extra weight. Making the proclamation in 1980 during a historic meeting of African heads of state in Lagos,

Kodjo was the Secretary-General of the Organization of African Unity. Kodjo's words and the conference's adoption of the Lagos Plan of Action, a blueprint for economic development and a rebuttal to the notorious World Bank report of the previous year, marked a new phase in the African struggle to redefine the terms of global economic change. Alas, that phase yielded little progress. Twenty years later, Africa had fallen further behind the industrialized world, clinging to a marginal existence in a world of globalization. It was a future few Africans in 1980 could bear to imagine.[17] As if to consciously reverse Kodjo's lament, African statesmen in the late 1990s spoke of an African Renaissance, imagining that the healing of Rwanda, the liberation of South Africa, and modest but encouraging signs of economic renewal in some African countries such as Botswana, Uganda, and Ghana foretold a bright new era for the entire continent. In a post–Cold War world weary of structural adjustment programs and heartlessness toward Africa, it was hoped, Africa— or at least its most stable countries—could finally move forward.

As Ferguson has pointed out, that moment lasted but a few years. It was, in fact, partially a product of the "Africa Talk" originating in the West that some African leaders had adapted. Like the Decade of Development, African Renaissance is too big, too abstract, too much an article of faith betraying missionary zeal and missionary naiveté. The most encouraging recent vision is of a different order, one that does not require a blithe dismissal of evidence of continued chaos or misery to sustain it. It is a vision of renewal born of tragedy. Hotel Rwanda brought African humanity and the perils of Western racism and indifference to genocide into American popular consciousness as nothing has since the horrifying news of the South African State of Emergency during the mid-eighties. The ample media attention devoted to the genocide in Darfur has heightened a sense of collective responsibility. This time, however, it is not simply Africa in Chaos, Africa prostrate, begging for Western salvation. The visibility of influential Africans has enabled Africa to regain a claim on the attention of America and the West. Admired African statesmen such as Desmond Tutu, Nelson Mandela, and UN Secretary-General Kofi Annan, along with African athletes, writers, and Nobel Peace Prize winner Wangari Maathai of Kenya have pushed Africa back from the margins of American consciousness. Rock stars (Bono, Bob Geldorf), development gurus (Jeffrey Sachs), philanthropists (Bill Gates), former presidents (Jimmy Carter), celebrities (George Clooney, Oprah Winfrey) and many others have vowed to "Make Poverty History," "Save Darfur," eliminate blood diamonds, and force wealthy nations to forgive African debts.

In some ways, despite the persistence of tragedy in Africa and Western "Africa Talk," the present is a moment of hope and bold optimism. Recalling the last such moment, as this book has attempted, will not simply disabuse optimists. It is necessary for a clear understanding of the obstacles facing those in the world community who wish to help, for it discloses the traps of Western hubris. Africans, Wangari Maathai has argued, must define and pursue development on their own terms and reconcile it with local cultures as they see fit, rather than taking their cues from Western experts. Her own environmentalism has been an expression of this African desire to move beyond development—eschewing top-down government schemes launched by academics or officials in the World Bank—and to replace abstractions with concrete problems and solutions. Today, what is most hopeful is not the arousal of American celebrities' conscience about Africa. It is that globalization and development, though flawed, have nonetheless created a world of fluid identities and possibilities that just might enable Africans to find their own path.

Notes

Introduction

1. "The New York Fair," *Time*, 17 July 1964; "The World of Already," *Time*, 5 June 1964.
2. Walter Carlson, "Fair, in Black, Predicts 'Substantial Surplus,'" *New York Times*, 5 June 1964, 36.
3. Overviews of the literature on U.S.–African relations since 1960 are Thomas J. Noer, "'Non-Benign Neglect': The United States and Black Africa in the Twentieth Century," in *American Foreign Relations: A Historiographical Review*, ed. Gerald K. Haines and J. Samuel Walker (Westport, Conn., 1981), 271–92; Peter Schraeder, "Sapphire Anniversary Reflections on the Study of United States Foreign Policy towards Africa," *Journal of Modern African Studies* 41:1 (2003), 139–52; and John Stoner, "The United States and Sub-Saharan Africa since 1961," in *American Foreign Relations since 1600: A Guide to the Literature*, ed. Robert L. Beisner (Santa Barbara, 2003), 1733–80.
4. The most relevant studies on policymaking toward Africa during the 1960s include Ibezim Chukwumerije, "The New Frontier and Africa, 1961–1963," diss., State University of New York at Stony Brook, 1976; Piero Gliejeses, *Conflicting Missions: Havana, Washington, and Africa, 1959–1976* (Chapel Hill, 2002); Andrew DeRoche, *Black, White, and Chrome: The United States and Zimbabwe, 1953–1998* (Trenton, N.J., 2001); idem, "Non-Alignment on the Racial Frontier: Zambia and the USA, 1964–68," *Cold War History* 7:2 (May 2007), 227–50; Larry Grubbs, "Bringing 'The Gospel of Modernization' to Nigeria: American Nation Builders and Development Planning in the 1960s," *Peace and Change* 31:3 (July 2006), 279–308; idem, "'Workshop of a Continent': American Representations of Whiteness and Modernity in 1960s South Africa," *Diplomatic History* 32:3 (June 2008), 405–39; David Gibbs, *The Political Economy of Third World Intervention: Mines, Money, and U.S. Policy in the Congo Crisis* (Chicago,

1991); Terrence Lyons, "Keeping Africa off the Agenda," in *Lyndon Johnson Confronts the World: American Foreign Policy, 1963–1968*, ed. Warren I. Cohen and Nancy Bernkopf Tucker (New York, 1994), 245–78; Richard D. Mahoney, *JFK: Ordeal in Africa* (New York, 1983); Mary E. Montgomery, "The Eyes of the World Were Watching: Ghana, Great Britain, and the United States, 1957–1966," diss., University of Maryland, 2004; Philip Emil Muehlenbeck, "Betting on the Dark Horses: John F. Kennedy's Courting of African Nationalist Leaders," diss., George Washington University, 2007; Thomas Noer, *Cold War and Black Liberation: The United States and White Rule in Africa, 1948–1968* (Columbia, Mo., 1985); idem, "New Frontiers and Old Priorities in Africa," in *Kennedy's Quest for Victory: American Foreign Policy, 1961–1963*, ed. Thomas G. Paterson (New York, 1989), 253–83; John Stoner, "Anti-Communism, Anti-Colonialism, and African Labor: The AFL-CIO in Africa, 1955–1975," diss., Columbia University, 2001; Peter Schraeder, *United States Foreign Policy Toward Africa: Incrementalism, Crisis, and Change* (Cambridge, U.K., 1994); Gerald E. Thomas, "The Black Revolt: The United States and Africa in the 1960s," in *The Diplomacy of the Crucial Decade: American Foreign Relations during the 1960s*, ed. Diane B. Kunz (New York, 1994), 320–60.

5. On African nationalism and decolonization, there is a vast literature. Particularly illuminating studies include those by the historian Frederick Cooper, *Decolonization and African Society: The Labor Question in French and British Africa* (Cambridge, U.K., 1996), and by the Ugandan political scientist Mahmood Mamdani, *Citizen and Subject: Contemporary Africa and the Legacy of Late Colonialism* (Princeton, 1996). The Nigerian doyen of African history, Toyin Falola, provides, among many other useful books, an overview of *Nationalism and African Intellectuals* (Rochester, N.Y., 2001). An excellent brief survey of late-colonial and postcolonial times with original insights is Cooper, *Africa since 1940: The Past of the Present* (Cambridge, U.K., 2002). The anthropologist James Ferguson provides perhaps the most provocative broad-ranging analysis of postcolonial Africa in *Global Shadows: Africa in the Neoliberal World Order* (Durham, N.C., 2006).

6. Major examples of the "new history of development" include early works by anthropologists James Ferguson, *The Anti-Politics Machine: "Development," Depoliticization, and Bureaucratic Power in Lesotho* (Cambridge, U.K., 1990), and Arturo Escobar, *Encountering Development: The Making and Unmaking of the Third World* (Princeton, 1995). Historians have made many recent contributions, including Frederick Cooper and Randall Packard, eds., *International Development and the Social Sciences: Essays on the History and Politics of Knowledge* (Berkeley, 1997); Nick Cullather, "Development? It's History," *Diplomatic History* 24:4 (Fall 2000), 641–53; idem, "Miracles of Modernization: The Green Revolution and the Apotheosis of Technology," *Diplomatic History* 28:2 (2004), 227–54; and David C. Engerman, Nils Gilman, Mark H. Haefele, and Michael E. Latham, eds., *Staging Growth: Modernization, Development, and the Global Cold War* (Amherst, Mass., 2003). A less critical work but an important, well-researched study is Amy L. S. Staples, *The Birth of Development: How the World Bank, Food and Agriculture Organization, and World Health Organization Changed the World, 1945–1965* (Kent, Ohio, 2006).

7. Africa receives relatively little attention in the recent work by historians specializing in American foreign relations. A major exception is Michael Mahoney, "*Estado*

Novo, Homen Novo (New State, New Man): Colonial and Anticolonial Development Ideologies in Mozambique, 1930–1977," in Engerman et al., *Staging Growth,* 165–97.

8. Brian T. Edwards, *Morocco Bound: Disorienting America's Maghreb, from Casablanca to the Marrakech Express* (Durham, N.C., 2005), 6–7.

9. On African American interest in Egypt, see Melani McAlister, *Epic Encounters: Culture, Media, and U.S. Interests in the Middle East since 1945,* updated ed. (Berkeley, 2005), 84–124.

10. William G. Martin and Michael O. West, "Introduction: The Rival Africas and Paradigms of Africanists and Africans at Home and Abroad," in *Out of One, Many Africas: Reconstructing the Study and Meaning of Africa,* ed. William G. Martin and Michael O. West (Urbana, Ill., 1999), 8, 10.

11. Dorothy Hammond and Alta Jablow, "'The African' in Western Literature," *Africa Today* 7:8 (December 1960), 8–9.

12. V. Y. Mudimbe, *The Invention of Africa: Gnosis, Philosophy, and the Order of Knowledge* (Indianapolis, Ind., 1988), 47; idem, *The Idea of Africa* (Bloomington, Ind., 1994).

13. Quoted in Edward H. McKinley, *The Lure of Africa: American Interests in Tropical Africa, 1919–1939* (Indianapolis, Ind., 1974), 170. A popular recent novel that evokes something of the American missionary mentality in the Congo in a later period is Barbara Kingsolver, *The Poisonwood Bible* (New York, 1998).

14. Jonathan Zimmerman, *Innocents Abroad: American Teachers in the American Century* (Cambridge, Mass., 2006), 201; Julius A. Amin, "The Perils of Missionary Diplomacy: The United States Peace Corps Volunteers in the Republic of Ghana," *The Western Journal of Black Studies* 23:1 (1999), 35–48. I discuss the Peace Corps experience in chapter 8. Studies of the missionary diplomacy of elites include Emily Rosenberg's *Financial Missionaries to the World: The Politics and Culture of Dollar Diplomacy, 1900–1930* (Cambridge, Mass., 1999), which demonstrates the intertwining of business, finance, and economics with cultural narratives and constructions of gender. Darlene Rivas, in an incisive study of Nelson Rockefeller's role as a "missionary capitalist" in the 1950s in Latin America, shows one man's effort to impart "respect for the dignity of individual workers and farmers, technical expertise (or 'knowhow'), capital, and values of efficiency and rationality" to poor countries. Darlene Rivas, *Missionary Capitalist: Nelson Rockefeller in Venezuela* (Chapel Hill, 2002), 5.

15. Immanuel Wallerstein, "The Evolving Role of the Africa Scholar in African Studies," *African Studies Review* 26:3/4 (September/December 1983), 155–59. Wallerstein's label and usage are adapted in Martin and West, "The Ascent, Triumph, and Disintegration of the Africanist Enterprise, USA," in *Out of One, Many Africas,* 106.

16. Bogumil Jewsiewicki, "African Historical Studies: Academic Knowledge as 'Usable Past' and Radical Scholarship," *African Studies Review* 32:3 (December 1989), 3.

17. On modernization's colonial and racial roots, see especially Michael Adas, "Modernization Theory and the American Revival of the Scientific and Technological Standards of Social Achievement and Human Worth," in Engerman et al., *Staging Growth,* 25–45, and Michael Latham, *Modernization as Ideology: American Social Science and "Nation Building" in the Kennedy Era* (Chapel Hill, 2000), 1–68. Nils Gilman, *Mandarins*

of the Future: Modernization Theory in Cold War America (Baltimore, 2003), 68–70. On Rostow, subject of many recent accounts, a fine summary is Mark H. Haefele, "Walt Rostow's Stages of Economic Growth: Ideas and Action," in Engerman et al., Staging Growth, 81–103.

18. Stephen J. Whitfield, "The American Century of Henry R. Luce," in Americanism: New Perspectives on the History of an Ideal, ed. Michael Kazin and Joseph A. McCartin (Chapel Hill, 2006), 94. On the invisibility of the colonies in Luce's magazine and essay, see Bruce Cummings, "The American Century and the Third World," Diplomatic History (1999).

19. Whitfield, "The American Century," quotations on 95, 92, and 98; Amy Kaplan, The Anarchy of Empire in the Making of U.S. Culture (Cambridge, Mass., 2002), 168.

20. William J. Lederer and Eugene Burdick, The Ugly American (New York, 1958). On The Ugly American as a key cultural text of the Cold War, see Jonathan Nashel, Edward Lansdale's Cold War (Amherst, Mass., 2005), and "The Road to Vietnam: Modernization Theory in Fact and Fiction," in Cold War Constructions: The Political Culture of United States Imperialism, 1945–1966, ed. Christian G. Appy (Amherst, 2000), 132–54; Latham, Modernization as Ideology, 135–39; and Robert D. Dean, Imperial Brotherhood: Gender and the Making of Cold War Foreign Policy (Amherst, Mass., 2001), 172–98.

21. A probing look at "sentimental" modernization and hegemony in American representations of Asia is Christina Klein, Cold War Orientalism: Asia in the Middlebrow Imagination, 1945–1961 (Berkeley, 2003).

22. See Firoze Manji and Carl O'Coill, "The Missionary Position: NGOs and Development in Africa," International Affairs 78:3 (July 2002), 567–83.

23. Quoted in Robert Massie, Loosing the Bonds: The United States and South Africa in the Apartheid Years (New York, 1997), 105. The definitive portrait, which devotes a chapter to his tenure in the State Department, is Thomas J. Noer, Soapy: A Biography of G. Mennen Williams (Ann Arbor, Mich., 2005).

24. Helen Kitchen, "Africa and the Kennedy Era," New Republic 143 (12 December 1960), 17–19.

25. Martin Staniland, American Intellectuals and African Nationalists, 1955–1970 (New Haven, 1991); Wofford quoted in Noer, Cold War and Black Liberation, 82.

26. On conservatives and Africa, see Staniland, American Intellectuals and African Nationalists, 214–64. See also Thomas J. Noer, "Segregationists and the World: The Foreign Policy of the White Resistance," and Michael Krenn, "The Unwelcome Mat: African Diplomats in Washington, D.C. during the Kennedy Years," in Window on Freedom: Race, Civil Rights, and Foreign Affairs, 1945–1988, ed. Brenda Gayle Plummer (Chapel Hill, 2003), 141–62 and 163–80.

27. On whiteness, and its international dimensions, most helpful are Richard Dyer, White (London, 1997); Alfred J. López, ed., Postcolonial Whiteness: A Critical Reader on Race and Empire (Albany, N.Y., 2005); Cynthia Levine-Rasky, ed., Working through Whiteness: International Perspectives (Albany, 2002); Alastair Bonnett, White Identities: Historical and International Perspectives (Harlow, U.K., 2000); Martin A. Berger, Sight Unseen: Whiteness and American Visual Culture (Berkeley, 2005); Gerald Horne, From the Barrel of a Gun: The United States and the War against Zimbabwe, 1965–1980 (Chapel Hill, 2001); Timothy L.

Schroer, *Recasting Race after World War II: Germans and African Americans in American-Occupied Germany* (Boulder, 2007); and George White Jr., *Holding the Line: Race, Racism, and American Foreign Policy toward Africa, 1953–1961* (Lanham, Md., 2005). See also Grubbs, "Workshop of a Continent."

28. Grubbs, "Workshop of a Continent," quotation on 407.

29. Among the most important recent works on African Americans and Cold War foreign policy are Thomas Borstlemann, *The Cold War and the Color Line: American Race Relations in the Global Arena* (Cambridge, Mass., 2001); Mary L. Dudziak, *Cold War Civil Rights: Race and the Image of American Democracy* (Princeton, 2000); Kevin Gaines, *American Africans in Ghana: Black Expatriates and the Civil Rights Era* (Chapel Hill, 2006); James H. Meriwether, *Proudly We Can Be Africans: Black Americans and Africa, 1935–1961* (Chapel Hill, 2002); Plummer, *Window on Freedom*; Brenda Gayle Plummer, *Rising Wind: Black Americans and U.S. Foreign Affairs, 1935–1960* (Chapel Hill, 1996); Penny M. Von Eschen, *Satchmo Blows up the World: Jazz Ambassadors Play the Cold War* (Cambridge, Mass., 2004); and idem, *Race against Empire: Black Americans and Anticolonialism, 1937–1957* (Ithaca, 1997). See also Staniland, *American Intellectuals and African Nationalists*, 178–213, on African Americans' response to African decolonization.

30. King quoted in Meriwether, *Proudly We Can Be Africans*, 202.

31. On radical interpretations of Africa, see Staniland, *American Intellectuals and African Nationalists*, 140–77. On conservatives and Africa, see Noer, "Segregationists and the World."

32. George B. N. Ayittey, *Africa in Chaos* (New York, 1998).

One. "The Most Innocent of Continents"

1. Memorandum of Discussion, 397th Meeting of the NSC, 26 February 1959; Memorandum of Conference with President Eisenhower, 1 November 1960, Department of State, *Foreign Relations of the United States, 1958–1960* (Washington, D.C.), 14:184, 238 (hereafter cited as FRUS). Recent overviews of Eisenhower's uncertain engagement with Africa include James H. Meriwether, "'A Torrent Overrunning Everything': Africa and the Eisenhower Administration," in *The Eisenhower Administration, the Third World, and the Globalization of the Cold War*, ed. Kathryn C. Statler and Andrew L. Johns (Lanham, Md., 2006), 175–96; Ebere Nwaubani, *The United States and Decolonization in West Africa, 1950–1960* (Rochester, N.Y., 2001); and George White Jr., *Holding the Line: Race, Racism, and American Foreign Policy toward Africa, 1953–1961* (Lanham, Md., 2005).

2. Note the acerbic capsule summary of him by historian John Fousek: "former isolationist and advertising mogul turned wartime price-control chief turned postwar liberal politician." Bowles was a part of the business elite that helped consolidate the early Cold War consensus. Fousek, *To Lead the Free World: American Nationalism and the Cultural Roots of the Cold War* (Chapel Hill, 2000), 129. See also Richard P. Dauer, *A North-South Mind in an East-West World: Chester Bowles and the Making of United States Cold War Foreign Policy* (Westport, Conn., 2005); Howard B. Schaffer, *Chester Bowles: New*

Dealer in the Cold War (Cambridge, Mass., 1993); and Chester Bowles, *Promises to Keep: My Years in Public Life, 1941–1969* (New York, 1971).

3. Chester Bowles, *Africa's Challenge to America* (Berkeley, 1956); James S. Coleman, "America and Africa," *World Politics* 9:4 (July 1957), 593–609. Coleman published one of the early classics of American scholarship on African politics, *Nigeria: Background to Nationalism* (Berkeley, 1958), and continued for many years as a leader in U.S.-based African Studies.

4. Bowles, *Africa's Challenge to America,* ix, 1–3, 51, 96–97; Coleman, "America and Africa," 593.

5. Bowles, *Africa's Challenge,* 50, 53, 5, 30. Bowles reiterated his optimism and interest in Africa in public and official writings. After serving as Kennedy's first Undersecretary of State until December 1961, he visited Africa as an at-large advisor on African, Asian, and Latin American affairs. Bowles, "Report of Mission to Africa, Oct.15–Nov. 9, 1962," 13 November 1962, box 3, National Security Files [hereafter NSF], John F. Kennedy Library, Boston [hereafter JFKL]. See also Bowles, "Myths about Africa—and the Reality," *New York Times,* 16 June 1963, 8, an essay praising Africans' postcolonial performance.

6. Coleman, "America and Africa," 606; Bowles, *Africa's Challenge,* 96; Policy Planning Council, "Selected Aspects of U.S. Economic Aid Policy for Africa," 24 July 1961, *FRUS, 1961–1963,* vol. 21, document 196 (available at http://www.state.gov/r/pa/ho/frus/); Henry L. Bretton, "Congo and Emergent Africa," *The Nation,* 15 October 1960, 243.

7. Immanuel Wallerstein, "Introduction to the Bison Books Edition," in Wallerstein, *Africa: The Politics of Independence and Unity* (Lincoln, Neb., 2005). Wallerstein refers here to the story he wrote in *Africa: The Politics of Independence* (New York, 1961); Guy Arnold, *A Guide to African Political and Economic Development* (Chicago, 2001), 120–21; Frederick Cooper, *Africa since 1940: The Past of the Present* (Cambridge, U.K., 2002), 91.

8. Mennen Williams, "The Challenge of Africa to the American Citizen," *Department of State Bulletin* (20 February 1961): 259; Edward R. Murrow, Address to the National Press Club, 24 May 1961, box 91, President's Office Files, JFKL; Elspeth Huxley, "Drums of Change Beat for Africa's Tribes," *New York Times Magazine,* 29 November 1959; William Attwood, *The Reds and the Blacks: A Personal Adventure* (New York, 1967), 85. Attwood, iv, dedicated his African memoirs to Bowles.

9. Melani McAlister, "A Cultural History of the War without End," in *History and September 11th,* ed. Joanne Meyerowitz (Philadelphia, 2003), 96–97; also McAlister, *Epic Encounters: Culture, Media, and U.S. Interests in the Middle East since 1945* (Berkeley, 2005), 303.

10. The amnesia is not, of course, intentionally produced—along with new narratives—by an individual or singular group. However, the kind of Africa discourse explored here is an aspect of American hegemony in the Gramscian sense. As will be seen below, the readiness of American academics, journalists, and philanthropists to adopt the perspective of the state in viewing Africa as a Cold War site, an opportunity (or "challenge," in the parlance of Bowles) for the nation dissolves

distinctions between disinterested research, journalism or charity, and self-interested foreign policy every bit as much as the colonial era collapsed religious, humanitarian, economic, and strategic concerns of Europeans in Africa.

11. Staniland, *American Intellectuals and African Nationalists*, 35–36.

12. Phillip W. Quigg, "The Changing American View of Africa," *Africa Report* (January 1969), 8. Quigg served as editor of *Foreign Affairs*, the chief organ of the foreign policy establishment.

13. On Tarzan and cultural constructions of Africa that persist, see Ruth Mayer, *Artificial Africas: Colonial Images in the Times of Globalization* (Hanover, N.H., 2002), 48–75. As she points out, the original novel, *Tarzan of the Apes* (1914), was itself a product of an imperialist early twentieth-century era in U.S. history, even if the story, set in European colonial Africa, threatens to disrupt the colonial roles of whites and blacks. Moreover, Burroughs's novel borrowed heavily for its "adventure formula" and exotic African setting from colonial fantasies by Rudyard Kipling and H. Rider Haggard (*King Solomon's Mines*), as well as the popular travel narratives of the American-backed explorer and colonial agent Henry Morton Stanley. Mayer, *Artificial Africas*, 49, 51.

14. Dennis Hickey and Kenneth Wylie, *An Enchanting Darkness: The American Vision of Africa in the Twentieth Century* (East Lansing, Mich., 1993), 19–20; "Partisanship at His Party Pleases President JFK," *Washington Post*, 29 July 1961, D4.

15. Melville J. Herskovits, *The Human Factor in Changing Africa* (New York, 1962), xi. Another book, co-edited with William R. Bascom, *Continuity and Change in African Cultures* (Chicago, 1959), exemplifies Herskovits's approach to research on social and cultural changes wrought by colonialism and the rise of African nationalism. On Herskovits, see Jerry Gershenhorn, *Melville J. Herskovits and the Racial Politics of Knowledge* (Lincoln, Neb., 2004).

16. Robert Theobald, "Preface," in *The New Nations of West Africa*, ed. Robert Theobald (New York, 1960), 3; John Scott, *Africa: World's Last Frontier*, quoted in ibid., 18; Curtis Prendergast, "Africa Joins the World," in ibid., 130; Congresswoman Frances P. Bolton, quoted in Staniland, *American Intellectuals and African Nationalists*, 39; Scott, *Africa*, quoted in *The New Nations of West Africa*, 22.

17. Smith Hempstone, *Africa—Angry Young Giant* (New York, 1961), 639–41.

18. Eugene R. Black, *Tales of Two Continents: Africa and South America* (Athens, Ga., 1961), 2.

19. Quotations in Staniland, *American Intellectuals and African Nationalists*, 63, 67, 68.

20. St. Clair Drake, review in "Books," *Africa Report* 8:1 (January 1963), 28; Harvey Glickman, "Seek Ye First the Political Kingdom . . . ," *Africa Report* 7:4 (April 1962), 19; Chester Bowles, "Myths About Africa—and the Reality," 8.

21. Waldemar Nielsen, "Africa Is Poised at the Razor's Edge," *New York Times Magazine* 9 February 1964, SM62; Staniland, *American Intellectuals and African Nationalists*, 58, 61–63.

22. Wolfgang Stolper, review of Arnold Rivkin, *Nation Building in Africa: Problems and Prospects*, in *Annals of the American Academy of Political and Social Science* 395 (May 1971), 207.

23. Bowles to Kennedy, 28 July 1961; Bowles to Rusk, 18 August 1961, FRUS, 1961–1963, vol. 25, documents 35, 40.

24. Charles F. Darlington, *African Betrayal* (New York: David McKay, 1968), 6, 74.

25. James Baldwin, "A Negro Assays the Negro Mood," *New York Times Magazine*, 12 March 1961.

26. Martin Luther King Jr. quoted in Meriwether, *Proudly We Can Be Africans*, 164–65; Nigerian quotation in Mary Dudziak, "Brown as a Cold War Case," *Journal of American History* (June 2004), 35.

27. Carl Rowan to Lyndon Johnson, 21 July 1964, FRUS, 1964–1968, vol. 24, document 187.

28. Rich examples are cited in Penny M. Von Eschen, "Who's the Real Ambassador? Exploding Cold War Racial Ideology," in *Cold War Constructions: The Political Culture of United States Imperialism, 1945–1966*, ed. Christian G. Appy (Amherst, Mass., 2000), especially 116–20.

29. Kirsten Walles, "J. F. Ade Ajayi," in *The Dark Webs: Perspectives on Colonialism in Africa*, ed. Toyin Falola (Durham, N.C., 2005).

30. Staniland, *American Intellectuals and African Nationalists*, 64–66.

31. James Ferguson, *Expectations of Modernity: Myths and Meanings of Urban Life on the Zambian Copperbelt* (Berkeley, 1999), 4–6.

32. Ibid., 2–6, quotations on 4 and 6. An impressive interdisciplinary literature on sensory experience and the history of the senses in social and cultural context has recently emerged. For an introduction, see Mark M. Smith, *Sensing the Past: Seeing, Hearing, Smelling, Tasting, and Touching in History* (Berkeley, 2007).

33. Curtis Prendergast, "Africa Joins the World," in *The New Nations of West Africa*, 130.

34. Harvey Glickman, "The Economists Look at Africa," *Africa Report* 6:5 (May 1961), 13.

35. Black, *Tales of Two Continents*, 5; Crawford Young, "Background to Independence," *Transition* 25 (1966), 34. On American interest in preserving the Belgian prosperity of the Congo, see also White, *Holding the Line*, 111–32.

36. "In the Congo's Jungles, a Boom and a Ferment," *U.S. News and World Report* 20 April 1959.

37. Albert P. Disdier, "The Congo's Economic Crisis," *Africa Special Report* 5:6 (June 1960), 6.

38. John Scott, *Africa: World's Last Frontier*, in *The New Nations of West Africa*, 36–37, 41.

39. Milton Bracker, "Times Sq. Echoes Ring in the Congo," *New York Times*, 15 February 1959, 12.

40. "In the Congo's Jungles, a Boom and a Ferment," *U.S. News and World Report* 20 April 1959; Homer Bigart, "The Belgian Congo—A Case History of Nationalism in Africa," *New York Times: News of the Week in Review*, 3 January 1960, E4.

41. Grubbs, "Workshop of a Continent," 409.

42. Ibid., 413–14.

43. Ibid., 414.

44. Ibid., 414–15.

45. Ibid., 415.

46. John Henrik Clarke, quoted in Staniland, *American Intellectuals and African Nationalists*,

205; Plummer, *Rising Wind*, 302–4. On African American views of Lumumba, see Meriwether, *Proudly We Can Be Africans*, 225–29, 232–38.

47. Edwin S. Munger, "Liberia's Economic and Human Progress," in *The New Nations of West Africa*, 89–90.

48. Holmes, Special Assistant to the Secretary of State, to John Foster Dulles, 6 February 1958; Memorandum of Discussion, 365th Meeting of the NSC, 8 May 1958, *FRUS, 1958–1960*, 14:1, 14:15–16; Memorandum of Conversation, 19 October 1961, *FRUS, 1961–1963*, Microfiche Supplement, document 549.

Two. *"Poised on the Razor's Edge"*

1. Harold Isaacs, *Emergent Americans: A Report on "Crossroads Africa"* (New York, 1961), reprinted in "The Emergent American: A Rebirth of Self-Esteem," *Current* 17 (September 1961), 23.

2. Ferguson, *Global Shadows*, 94–95, quotations on 95; on American scholars and nation building, see Latham, *Modernization as Ideology*; Gilman, *Mandarins of the Future*; and David Ekbladh, "From Consensus to Crisis: The Postwar Career of Nation-Building in U.S. Foreign Relations," in *Nation-Building: Beyond Afghanistan and Iraq*, ed. Francis Fukuyama (Baltimore, 2006), 19–41.

3. J. Isawa Elaigwu, in collaboration with Ali A. Mazrui, "Nation-Building and Changing Political Structures," in *Africa since 1935*, ed. Ali A. Mazrui (Berkeley, 1993), 438. A poignant and engrossing scholarly, philosophical, and personal account of the relationship between local, national, and transnational African identities is Kwame Anthony Appiah, *In My Father's House: Africa in the Philosophy of Culture* (New York, 1992).

4. Ferguson, *Global Shadows*, 184.

5. James S. Coleman, "American Political Science and Tropical Africa: Universalism vs. Relativism," *African Studies Review*, 26:3/4 (September–December 1983), 26, 38.

6. Deutsche quoted in Gilman, *Mandarins of the Future*, 6; Ferguson, *Global Shadows*, 177–78.

7. Quoted in Gilman, *Mandarins of the Future*, 6; Rupert Emerson, "African States and the Burdens They Bear," *African Studies Bulletin*, 10:1 (April 1967), 3. Emerson, after many years of specializing in Southeast Asian politics, wrote in the 1960s three books devoted exclusively to African politics, the most influential of which was *Africa and United States Policy* (1967). Staniland, *American Intellectuals and African Nationalists*, 119–20, n. 63; see also Gilman, *Mandarins of the Future*, 120–21.

8. Vera M. Dean, "Is Democracy Possible in Africa?" in *The New Nations of West Africa*, 122.

9. Tom Mboya, *New York Times Magazine*, 28 June 1959. Meriwether, *Proudly We Can Be Africans*, 146–47, attributes some of the Kenyan's popularity in the United States to the contrast between him and the more radical Mau Mau rebels. Some African Americans "regarded Mboya as the responsible alternative to Fanon" in Pan-African politics and compared him to Martin Luther King Jr. Gaines, *American Africans in Ghana*, 95.

10. Edward A. Jones, "Togo, West Africa—An Appraisal by an Afro-American," *Phylon* 22:3 (3rd Quarter 1961), 234, and Jones, "The Faces of Africa: Vignettes Showing the Contrasts in the Old and the New Africa," *Phylon* 23:3 (3rd Quarter 1962): 267. On Mabel Smythe, see Mary G. Rolinson, "Mabel Murphy Smythe: Black Atlantic Biography?" Paper delivered at the American Historical Association Annual Meeting, Atlanta, Ga., January 2007.

11. Staniland, *American Intellectuals and African Nationalists*, 182, 193. Quoted in George Houser, *No One Can Stop the Rain: Glimpses of Africa's Liberation Struggle* (New York, 1989), 81–90, quote on 86. On Mboya, see his *Freedom and After* (Boston, 1963) and *The Challenge of Nationhood: A Collection of Speeches and Writings* (New York, 1970); David Goldsmith, *Tom Mboya: The Man Kenya Wanted to Forget* (New York, 1982); Alan Rake, *Tom Mboya: Young Man of New Africa* (Garden City, N.Y., 1962).

12. David Goldsworthy, "Ethnicity and Leadership in Africa: The 'Untypical' Case of Tom Mboya," *Journal of Modern African Studies* 20:1 (March 1982), 114, 116.

13. On Drake's life and career, see Gaines, *American Africans in Ghana*, 44–50. The Virginia-born scholar developed a unique network of friendships, academic and political partnerships within the U.S., the diaspora, and West Africa, combining the zeal of an anti-racist activist with conventional anti-Communism and academic sociology. During the 1960s, Drake "remained a staunch supporter" of the increasingly authoritarian government of Kwame Nkrumah in Ghana. Ibid., 214–17.

14. St. Clair Drake, "Social Change and Social Problems in Contemporary Africa," in *United States and Africa*, ed. Walter Goldschmidt (New York, 1963), 239, 264–65.

15. Waldemar Nielsen, "Africa Is Poised on the Razor's Edge," *New York Times Magazine*, 9 February 1964, quotations on SM 11, 62.

16. Donald E. Pease, in *The Futures of American Studies*, ed. Pease and Robyn Wiegman (Durham, N.C., 2002), 157. "Ironically," write Ashley Dawson and Malini Johar Schueller, "at the very moment that radical anticolonial treatises questioning the universality of modernity were being written by Frantz Fanon, George Lamming, and Aimé Césaire, major texts of American studies were consolidating American exceptionalism." Thus, "imperial politics and culture are inextricably linked." Dawson and Schueller, "Introduction: Rethinking Imperialism Today," in *Exceptional State: Contemporary U.S. Culture and the New Imperialism*, ed. Dawson and Schueller (Durham, N.C., 2007), 5. See also Nils Gilman, "Modernization Theory, the Highest Stage of American Intellectual History," in Engerman et al., *Staging Growth*, 47–80, which explores the connections between 1950s American visions of global modernization, and the rise of "the end of ideology" and "consensus history" in the United States. On the Cold War proximity between Washington's interests and academics, see Bruce Cummings, "Boundary Displacements: Area Studies and International Studies during and after the Cold War," in *Universities and Empire: Money and Politics in the Social Sciences during the Cold War*, ed. Christopher Simpson (New York, 1998).

17. Staniland, *American Intellectuals and African Nationalists*, 29–31. On foundations and the Cold War, see Edward H. Berman, *The Influence of the Carnegie, Ford, and Rockefeller Foundations on American Foreign Policy* (Albany, N.Y., 1983).

18. The term "White Atlantic" is used in Victoria de Grazia, *Irresistible Empire: America's Advance through Twentieth-Century Europe* (Cambridge, Mass., 2005), 11.

19. Charles H. Wesley, quoted in Staniland, *American Intellectuals and African Nationalists*, 181, n. 8. Bunche, after fieldwork in West Africa and doctoral studies at Harvard, emerged as "the leading Africanist political scientist in the United States by 1940," though his close ties to foundations and universities led him into government service during World War II with the CIA's predecessor, the OSS, and the State Department, and then as a representative to the United Nations. Plummer, *Rising Wind*, 79.

20. Herskovits, *The Human Factor in Changing Africa*, ix, 18–20.

21. U Thant was Secretary-General of the United Nations; quotation in "Portrait: American Africanologist," *West Africa*, 27 October 1962, 1181; Martin and West, "The Ascent, Triumph, and Disintegration," in *Out of One, Many Africas*, 89.

22. Martin and West, "The Ascent, Triumph, and Disintegration," 88, 91–92. On Herskovits's opposition to funding that would have helped black scholars, see Gershenhorn, *Melville J. Herskovits*, 170, 179–82, 193–94, 197–99. Gershenhorn (170–71), however, argues that Herskovits was not "motivated by Cold War strategy" like foundation officials and policymakers, and that he in fact "criticized the Cold War assumptions on which" African Studies emerged. This is true, to a degree, when one is comparing Herskovits in the 1940s and '50s to the narrow Cold Warriors of the period. It is far less convincing when one views Herskovits in the late 1950s in the context of the Bowles-Kennedy-type optimism about African modernization as part of America's enlightened (Cold War) interest. Du Bois, in 1961, finding a different kind of patronage for his project, left the United States and its persistent harassment of him. See Gerald Horne, *Black and Red: W. E. B. Du Bois and the Afro-American Response to the Cold War* (Albany, N.Y., 1986).

23. "Portrait: American Africanologist"; Lyman Drake, "African Studies Association Meets," *Africa Special Report* 3:10 (October 1958), 2.

24. Immanuel Wallerstein, "Africa in the Shuffle," *Issue* 23:1 (Winter 1995), 22.

25. Martin and West, "The Ascent, Triumph, and Disintegration," 86. For a conciliatory response, see Wallerstein, "Afterword," *Out of One, Many Africas*, 213–16.

26. Quoted in Gershenhorn, *Melville J. Herskovits*, 196.

27. Martin and West, "The Ascent, Triumph, and Disintegration," 96.

28. "Herskovits Report Calls for Imaginative U.S. Africa Policy," *Africa Special Report* 4:11 (November 1959), 7, 12. On Herskovits' testimony before the committee in 1958 and 1960 and his report, see Gershenhorn, *Melville J. Herskovits*, 215–21.

29. Quoted in "Attitudes of Africans Toward East and West," in *The New Nations of West Africa*, 158.

30. Martin and West, "The Ascent, Triumph, and Disintegration," 89–91.

31. Immanuel Wallerstein, "Annual Meeting of the (American) African Studies Association," *Journal of Modern African Studies* 4:4 (December 1966): 535.

32. Martin and West, "The Ascent, Triumph, and Disintegration," 96.

33. Rupert Emerson, "African States and the Burdens They Bear," *African Studies Bulletin*, 10:1 (April 1967): 2.

34. Before joining the Kennedy administration, Bowles served on the Institute's Board of Directors.

35. "Waldemar Nielsen to Head AAI," *Africa Report* 6:10 (November 1961): 32; Julien Engel, "Three Major Foundations Contribute to AAI," *Africa Report* 8:2 (February 1963): 28. Nielsen in the 1960s published two volumes on U.S.–African relations: *African Battleline: American Policy Choices in Southern Africa* (New York, 1965), which staked out a moderate position on apartheid and colonialism, and *The Great Powers and Africa* (New York, 1969), a detailed overview of diplomacy and strategy in the postcolonial decade. In the 1970s he worked with Common Cause and published a book critiquing large foundations and their role in American society: *The Big Foundations* (New York, 1972). Waldemar A. Nielsen and Zoran S. Hodjera, "Sino-Soviet Bloc Technical Assistance—Another Bilateral Approach," *Annals of the American Academy of Political and Social Science* 323 (May 1959), 40–49.

36. Helen Kitchen, "Looking Ahead," *Africa Report* 10:8 (August 1965), 2. Kitchen served on the ASA Committee on Publications during the early sixties. "Committees of the African Studies Association, 1963–1964," *African Studies Bulletin*, 7:1 (March 1964), 25.

37. Lewis Nkosi, "Africa Report," *Journal of Modern African Studies*, 3:2 (August 1965), 320.

38. Africa Research Group, *Africa Retort: The Extended Family* (Cambridge, Mass., 1970), "Editor's Arsenal."

39. Quoted in Meriwether, *Proudly We Can Be Africans*, 202.

40. Quoted in David Hostetter, *Movement Matters: American Antiapartheid Activism and the Rise of Multicultural Politics* (New York, 2006), 22.

41. John A. Davis, "AMSAC Schedules Conference at Howard," *Africa Report* 8:3 (March 1963), 10; Meriwether, *Proudly We Can Be Africans*, 171–72; Plummer, *Rising Wind*, 254. AMSAC did stage a series of academic conferences devoted to political issues. Davis, chair of political science at City College, New York, co-edited a volume of essays after AMSAC's 1963 conference at Howard University: *Southern Africa in Transition*, ed. John A. Davis and James K. Baker (New York, 1966).

42. Plummer, *Rising Wind*, 307–8; Michael Krenn, *Black Diplomacy: African Americans and the State Department, 1945–1969* (Armonk, N.Y., 1999); Crockett to Palmer, 9 May 1966, *FRUS, 1964–68*, vol. 23, document 72.

43. Plummer, *Rising Wind*, 307–8, 310–12.

44. Lee C. White to Johnson, 28 December 1964, *FRUS, 1964–1968*, vol. 24, document 190.

45. Komer to Bundy, 6 January 1965, *FRUS, 1964–1968*, vol. 24, document 192.

46. Komer and Haynes to Bundy, 30 March 1965, *FRUS, 1964–1968*, vol. 24, document 194.

47. Gaines, *American Africans in Ghana*, 25.

48. "Telegraph of President Kennedy to the African Studies Association, October 12, 1962," *African Studies Bulletin* 5:4 (December 1962), 1.

49. Vernon McKay, "A Tribute to Governor Williams," *African Studies Bulletin* 5:4 (December 1962), 2–3, 5. On Wayne Fredericks, see Robert Kinloch Massie, *Loosing the Bonds: The United States and South Africa in the Apartheid Years* (New York, 1997), 112–14.

50. In 1962 Williams created the State Department Advisory Council on African Affairs, eventually chaired by McKay, that also included Herskovits, Wallerstein, Kitchen, George Houser of ACOA, and other scholars and activists. The council was used as a source of information and ideas on policy, and to promote the African Bureau's existing policies to other members of the administration and Congress. Massie, *Loosing the Bonds*, 132. McKay, in the words of an admirer, personified the policy-oriented Africanist as "a scholar, teacher, diplomat, and participant in State Department and United Nations activities." McKay had worked for several years in the State Department Office of Dependent Area Affairs before joining the faculty at the Johns Hopkins School of Advanced International Studies and becoming president of the ASA. Robert D. Baum, Review of McKay, *Africa in World Politics*, in *Africa Report* 8:7 (July 1963), 27. This book (New York, 1963) was McKay's most influential.

51. Massie, *Loosing the Bonds*, 113. When Fredericks left the State Department in 1967, he returned to the Ford Foundation as director of its Middle East and Africa program, which funded development projects; ibid., 319.

52. Coleman, "American Political Science and Tropical Africa," 49−50. Coleman, 52, credits Kenyan political scientist Ali Mazrui in 1969 with being "the first to blow the whistle" against modernization theory's implicit condescending to Africa.

53. *Transition* was later revealed to be among a number of cultural organs covertly funded by the Central Intelligence Agency as part of the cultural Cold War.

54. Nkrumah, *Ghana: The Autobiography of Kwame Nkrumah* (New York, 1957), 288.

55. "Constitution of the Convention People's Party (C.P.P.)," in ibid., 289.

56. Gilman, *Mandarins of the Future*, devotes a chapter to "Modernization Theory as a Foreign Policy Doctrine," 155−202.

Three. "The Gospel of Modernization"

1. G. Mennen Williams, *Africa for the Africans* (Grand Rapids, Mich., 1969).

2. Dean C. Tipps, "Modernization Theory and the Comparative Study of Societies: A Critical Perspective," *Comparative Studies in Society and History* 15:2 (March 1973), 199.

3. The major studies are Gilman, *Mandarins of the Future*, a masterful intellectual history with a focus on the academic network of modernization theorists; Michael E. Latham, *Modernization as Ideology: American Social Science and "Nation Building" in the Kennedy Era* (Chapel Hill, 2000), which traces modernization theory and its corresponding "ideology" of U.S. nation-building strategies to the Alliance for Progress, counter-insurgency in Vietnam, and the early Peace Corps; and Engerman et al., *Staging Growth*, which includes an array of stimulating essays. Two articles by Nick Cullather provide extremely helpful definitions of modernization theory and the development discourse that encompassed and outlasted it, along with many examples and insights: Cullather, "Development Doctrine and Modernization Theory," in *Encyclopedia of American Foreign Policy*, vol. 1, 2nd ed., ed. Alexander De Conde (2002), 477−91, and idem, "Development? It's History," *Diplomatic History*.

4. Frederick Cooper, *Colonialism in Question: Theory, Knowledge, History* (Berkeley, 2005), 39–40, 116–17.

5. Daniel Lerner, "Modernization—Social Aspects," in *International Encyclopedia of the Social Sciences*, ed. David L. Sills (New York, 1968), 10:386–87.

6. Economic historian Henry Rosovsky, quoted in Haefele, "Walt Rostow's Stages of Economic Growth," in Engerman et al., *Staging Growth*, 82.

7. Haefele, "Walt Rostow's Stages of Economic Growth," 85; Cullather, "Development Doctrine and Modernization Theory," 483.

8. Max F. Millikan and Donald L. M. Blackmer, eds., *The Emerging Nations: Their Growth and United States Policy* (Boston, 1961), vi–vii. This text, in addition to its influence on American policy, found an audience among South Korean academics, thanks to the U.S. Information Service, which made it, along with other key works on modernization theory, available as "a low-cost series of book translations for students" at South Korean universities. Sales proceeded briskly. Gregg Andrew Brazinsky, "Koreanizing Modernization: Modernization Theory and South Korean Intellectuals," in *Staging Growth*, 257–58.

9. Millikan and Blackmer, "Preface," in *The Emerging Nations*, ix.

10. Max F. Millikan and Walt W. Rostow, *A Proposal: Key to an Effective Foreign Policy* (New York, 1957), 48, 102.

11. Walt W. Rostow, *The Stages of Economic Growth: A Non-Communist Manifesto* (London, 1960), 44–45, 144.

12. *Africa Today* began in 1953 as a slender publication of the American Committee on Africa, a liberal group led by white activists like George Houser, a pacifist supporter of African liberation movements. See David Hostetter, *Movement Matters: American Anti-apartheid Activism and the Rise of Multicultural Politics* (New York, 2006); and George M. Houser, *No One Can Stop the Rain: Glimpses of Africa's Liberation Struggle* (New York, 1989).

13. Walt W. Rostow, "Lessons of History," *Africa Today* (November 1960), 5–7. Rostow had published in 1955 an essay in *Harper's* entitled, "Marx Was a City Boy, or Why Communism May Fail." See Engerman, "West Meets East," in Engerman et al., *Staging Growth*, 202.

14. Rostow, "Lessons of History, Part II," *Africa Today* (December 1960), 11–12.

15. "Plans for the Reorganization of Foreign Assistance," 4 March 1961; Memorandum, Rostow to Ted Sorensen, 16 March 1961, box 325, NSF, JFKL.

16. Memorandum, Rostow to National Security Advisor McGeorge Bundy, 13 May 1961, FRUS, 1961–1963, 21:291. See also Rostow's memos to Kennedy, 16 and 22 March 1961, box 325, NSF, JFKL.

17. John F. Kennedy, "Special Message to the Congress on Foreign Aid," 22 March 1961, *Public Papers of the President: John F. Kennedy, 1961* (Washington, 1962), 203, 205.

18. "Africa Task Force Report," 31 December 1960, box 1073, Pre-Presidential Papers, JFKL.

19. Walt Rostow, "Action Teams: Military and Foreign Policy," 17 November 1960, box 64a, President's Office Files (POF), JFKL; NIE 60/70–61: Probable Developments in Colonial Africa," 11 April 1961, FRUS, 1961–1963, 21:285; Memorandum, Henry J. Tasca to G. Mennen Williams, 9 March 1961, box 2, NSF, JFKL.

20. Lincoln Gordon, letter to Joseph E. Slater (Assistant Managing Director of the Development Loan Fund), 25 November 1960, Papers of James C. Thomson, JFKL.

21. Political scientists wrote many of the key texts on African modernization in the 1950s–60s, and some of these were major contributions to the overall literature on modernization. David Apter's *The Gold Coast in Transition*, published in 1955 with new editions in 1963 and 1972, became "the most famous, or notorious" effort to apply 1950s modernization theory to the politics of decolonization. Frederick Cooper, *Colonialism in Question*, 276, n. 15.

22. Harvey Glickman, "The Economists Look at Africa," *Africa Report* 6:5 (May 1961), 13; Henry L. Bretton, "Congo and Emergent Africa," *The Nation*, 15 October 1960, 241.

23. Edmond C. Hutchinson, "American Aid to Africa," *Annals of the American Academy* 354 (July 1964), 65, 69–70.

24. G. Mennen Williams, "Mobilizing Economic Resources for Africa," *Department of State Bulletin* 44 (24 April 1961), 584.

25. Mennen Williams, Report of trip, 26 October 1961, box 2, NSF, JFKL.

26. Williams quoted in "Notes on the Inter-Agency Meeting on African Education, 1 May 1963," box 381, NSF; Harris Wofford memorandum to Kennedy, 20 January 1962, box 67, POF, JFKL.

27. Quoted in Thomas J. Noer, "New Frontiers and Old Priorities in Africa," in *Kennedy's Quest for Victory*, 257–58.

28. Harris Wofford memorandum to Kennedy, 20 January 1962, box 67, POF, JFKL.

29. Melville J. Herskovits, "Editorial," *African Studies Bulletin* 1:1 (April 1958), 2.

30. Walter Goldschmidt, ed., *The United States and Africa* (New York, 1958); the volume was revised and updated in 1963.

31. Ibid., 146–49, 155. Berg would go on to direct a controversial World Bank report in 1980, *Accelerated Development in Sub-Saharan Africa*.

32. "Portrait: The Reasonable American," *West Africa*, 22 June 1963, 689.

33. Arnold Rivkin, *The African Presence in World Affairs* (New York, 1963), ix–x.

34. Ibid., x; John H. Morrow, Foreword to Morrow, ed., Arnold Rivkin, *Nation-Building in Africa: Problems and Prospects* (New Brunswick, N.J., 1969), vii.

35. "Rivkin to Head Africa Project at MIT," *Africa Special Report* 2:10 (November 1957), 14. Rivkin, *Africa and the West: Elements of Free World Policy* (New York, 1962).

36. Arnold Rivkin, *The New States of Africa* (New York, 1967), 2.

37. Arnold Rivkin, "Point Four in Africa," *Africa Special Report* 5:5 (May 1960), 11.

38. Ibid., 12.

39. Ibid., 11.

40. Rivkin, *Africa and the West*, vii–viii; "News and Notes," *Africa: Journal of the International African Institute*, 30:2 (April 1960), 184; Rivkin, *The African Presence in World Affairs*, xi; *Nations by Design: Institution-Building in Africa*, ed. Arnold Rivkin (Garden City, N.Y., 1968), ii.

41. Walt Rostow, "Action Teams: Military and Foreign Policy," November 17, 1960, box 64a, POF, JFKL; Rivkin, *The African Presence in World Affairs*, vii–xi, Millikan's quotation on viii.

42. Rivkin, *Africa and the West*, vii, 3–12, quotation on 142.

43. Ibid., 144–46.

44. Ibid., 158–60.

45. Ibid., 173–74; Rivkin, *The African Presence in World Affairs*, 22–23.

46. Rivkin, *Africa and the West*, 249–50, and *The African Presence in World Affairs*.

47. Rivkin, *Nation-Building in Africa*, 156, 161. Rivkin died in September 1968 at age forty-nine. Morrow, the first American ambassador to Guinea a decade earlier, had been a peer reviewer for the manuscript, and after Rivkin's death, he revised it for publication. Morrow, "Foreword," vii.

48. Vernon McKay, Review of Arnold Rivkin, *The African Presence in World Affairs*, in *Africa Report* 10:1 (January 1965), 36.

49. Harvey Glickman, "Africa and the West: An Incomplete View," *Africa Report* 7:5 (May 1962), 19.

50. Harry L. Bretton, review of Rivkin, *Africa and the West*, in *Annals of the American Academy of Political and Social Science* 343 (September 1962), 169; Herbert J. Shapiro, review of Rivkin, *The African Presence*, in *Journal of Politics* 26:4 (November 1964), 958–59; Ruth Schachter Morgenthau, review of Rivkin, *Africa and the West*, in *Political Science Quarterly* 77:3 (September 1962), 458–59.

51. Arnold Rivkin, "The World Bank in Africa," 13, 15.

52. "Portrait; A Fresh Look at West Africa," *West Africa*, 31 July 1965, 1281; quotations in Cooper, *Colonialism in Question*, 40. Lewis's opus was *The Theory of Economic Growth* (Homewood, Ill., 1955).

53. Michael Adas, *Dominance by Design: Technological Imperatives and America's Civilizing Mission* (Cambridge, Mass., 2006), 260–64.

54. Black, *Tales of Two Continents*, 17.

55. Williams, *Africa for the Africans*, 19; "Summary of Governor Williams' Trip to Africa," 25 September 1961, FRUS, 1961–63, vol. 21, document 200.

56. Mennen Williams's report on his third trip to Africa, 28 November 1961, NSF, JFKL.

Four. "The Moral Equivalent of Anti-Colonialism"

1. Telegram A-56 from Dakar, 10 April 1961; Telegram 281 from Dakar, 13 April 1961, box 1, Vice Presidential Security File, NSF, Lyndon Baines Johnson Library, Austin, Tex. (hereafter LBJL).

2. On political touch—the importance of handshaking in communicating political ideals or values, especially egalitarian ones—see Smith, *Sensing the Past*, 106. On the hapticity of LBJ's campaigns, see among other biographies, Robert Caro, *Means of Ascent* (New York, 1990).

3. "All the Way with LBJ," *Time*, 14 April 1961.

4. Ibid. Telegram 281 from Dakar, 13 April 1961; Telegram A-56 from Dakar, 10 April 1961. Mamadou Dia, a socialist theorist and the first prime minister of independent Senegal, expressed his vision of development in *The African Nations and World*

Solidarity (London, 1962). That year, after a failed coup against Senghor, he was imprisoned. Johnson, meanwhile, hosted Senghor in Washington as president in 1966, in the middle of an era of over a dozen years in which Senghor ruled a one-party state.

5. Oral History, Mennen Williams, LBJL. Williams used a haptic approach to winning hearts and minds in Africa, too, in an expression of informality and intimacy intended to negate *Ugly American* stereotypes.

6. Robert Komer to Lyndon Johnson, 27 March 1965, Papers of Ulric Haynes, NSF, LBJL.

7. Nicholas de B. Katzenbach to Lyndon Johnson, 12 March 1968, FRUS, 1964–1968, vol. 24, document 346.

8. Millikan and Blackmer, *The Emerging Nations*, 57.

9. David C. Engerman, "West Meets East," in Engerman et al., *Staging Growth*, 205. A major author on planning was W. Arthur Lewis, who wrote *Development Planning: The Essentials of Economic Policy* (London, 1966).

10. Tasca memorandum to Williams, March 9, 1961, box 2, NSF, JFKL. Many scholars have recently argued that "depoliticization" is an intended outcome of Western development programs; see, for example, Ferguson, *The Anti-Politics Machine*, and Arturo Escobar, *Encountering Development: The Making and Unmaking of the Third World* (Princeton, 1995). A unique study of the U.S. promotion of development planning during the Cold War is Dennis Merrill, "Negotiating Cold War Paradise: U.S. Tourism, Economic Planning, and Cultural Modernity in Twentieth-Century Puerto Rico," *Diplomatic History* 25:2 (Spring 2001), 179–214.

11. Minutes of Meeting of Advisory Committee on Economic Development, 8–9 November 1963, box 23, Papers of David E. Bell (AID Administrator beginning in December 1962), JFKL. On political development and modernization theory, see Gilman, *Mandarins of the Future*, esp. 138–53.

12. Policy Planning Council, "Selected Aspects of U.S. Economic Aid policy for Africa," 24 July 1961, FRUS, 1961–1963, 21:294–96.

13. Policy Planning Council, "Selected Aspects of U.S. Economic Aid Policy for Africa," 24 July 1961, FRUS, 1961–1963, vol. 21, document 196.

14. John Kenneth Galbraith memorandum to McGeorge Bundy (National Security Advisor), 1 February 1961, box 297, NSF, JFKL.

15. Vernon McKay, "The African Operations of the United States Government," in *The United States and Africa*, ed. Walter Goldschmidt, rev. ed. (New York, 1963), 281–84.

16. The Nigerian Six-Year Plan of 1962–68, and the extensive U.S. role in drafting and promoting it, a special case in American efforts in Africa, are discussed in chapter 5.

17. S. T. Parelman (Senior Planning Officer, State Department) memorandum to John O. Bell (Deputy Coordinator for Foreign Assistance, State Department), 1 March 1961, box 325, NSF, JFKL.

18. Adebayo Adedeji, "Comparative Strategies of Economic Decolonization in Africa," in *Africa since 1935*, 393.

19. See Wallerstein, *Africa: The Politics of Independence and Unity*, 130–51.

20. Michael Mahoney, "*Estado Novo, Homen Novo* (New State, New Man)," in Engerman et al., *Staging Growth*, 178–80.

21. Ironically, Cook—named U.S. Ambassador to Niger in 1961—would serve as ambassador to Senegal for almost two years in 1964–66, working closely with Senghor, whom he admired, while Mamadou Dia languished in prison. Senegal, while not repudiating socialism, adopted a far more cautious attitude toward unity and industrialization than that advanced in The African Nations and World Solidarity.

22. Cooper, *Africa since 1940*, 92.

23. NIE, 30 August 1960, FRUS, 1958–1960, 14:193.

24. NSC, "U.S. Policy Toward the Sudan," 10 January 1961, FRUS, 1961–1963, vol. 21, Microfiche Supplement, document 657.

25. Memorandum of Conversation, 4 October 1961, FRUS, 1961–1963, vol. 21, Microfiche Supplement, document 660.

26. Rusk to Kennedy, 10 April 1961; U.S. Embassy Khartoum telegram A-24 to State Department, 17 August 1961, box 160, NSF, JFKL.

27. Memorandum of Conversation, Kennedy and Abboud, 5 October 1961, box 160, NSF, JFKL.

28. L. D. Battle, Executive Secretary, State Department, to Rostow and George McGovern, 29 September 1961; Memorandum of Conversation, "Economic Discussion with President Abboud's Advisors," 6 October 1961, box 160, NSF, JFKL.

29. Memorandum of Conversation, "Economic Discussion with President Abboud's Advisors," 6 October 1961, box 160, NSF, JFKL.

30. Rostow to Kennedy, 6 October 1961, box 160, NSF, JFKL.

31. Telephone conversation transcript, Rostow and Ball, 6 October 1961, Papers of George Ball, JFKL.

32. Ibid.

33. Harold Saunders to Robert Komer and Walt Rostow, 9 October 1961, box 160, NSF, JFKL.

34. Bundy to Hamilton, 16 October 1961; Komer to Bundy, 16 October 1961, box 160, NSF, JFKL. In November, the White House noted that Bundy's memo had secured "a good deal of activity in AID," though the survey would not meet the 9 February deadline. Saunders to Rostow, 3 November 1961, box 160, NSF, JFKL.

35. Khartoum telegram to State Department, 19 October 1961, and 24 October 1961, box 160, NSF, JFKL; Richard J. H. Johnston, "Abboud Urges U.N. Seat Red China," New York Times, 13 October 1961, 3; "A Neutral from the Sudan," New York Times, 15 October 1961, E8.

36. Rostow to Foreign Minister Kheir, 25 November 1961, box 160, NSF, JFKL.

37. Memorandum, Robert W. Komer to Lyndon Johnson, 6 February 1965, box 99, NSF, Country Files, LBJL. The Sudan's Ten-Year Plan of 1961–70, like many others in Africa, started slowly, completed a few projects, and was abandoned by the late sixties.

38. Readers of *African Studies Bulletin* learned of the importance of the road, as the major U.S. project in the Sudan, in one of a number of items contributed during the

decade by U.S. officials: F. Dennis Conroy, "United States Economic Aid to Africa 2: Aid Program in the Sudan," *African Studies Bulletin* 7:1 (March 1964), 9.

39. Telegram, Khartoum Embassy to State Department, 1 December 1965, box 99, NSF, Country Files, LBJL.

40. Ulric Haynes to Robert Komer, 6 December 1965, Papers of Ulric Haynes, NSF, LBJL.

41. Statement of U.S. Policy on the Horn of Africa, Enclosure, NSC Report, 30 December 1960; NIE, 12 November 1958, *FRUS, 1958–1960*, 14:204, 175. On U.S. interests in Ethiopia, see Harold G. Marcus, *The Politics of Empire: Ethiopia, Great Britain, and the United States, 1941–1974* (Berkeley, 1983). On U.S. influence, see Baffour Agyeman-Duah, *The United States and Ethiopia: Military Assistance and the Quest for Security, 1953–1993* (Lanham, Md., 1994). For a general history of Ethiopia that places emphasis on the origins and consequences of the revolution that swept Haile Selassie from power, see Marcus, *A History of Ethiopia* (Berkeley, 1994).

42. Alphonse A. Castagno, "Ethiopia: Reshaping an Autocracy," *Africa Report* 8:9 (October 1963), 4.

43. "Lion of Judah," *Washington Post*, 3 October 1963, A20; "Competition Stiff for U.S. in Ethiopia," *Christian Science Monitor*, 13 May 1963, 10.

44. Marcus, *The Politics of Empire*, 98.

45. Telegram, U.S. Embassy, Addis Ababa, to Department of State, 19 December 1962; Robert Komer (National Security Council) to President Kennedy, 25 July 1963, box 69, NSF, JFKL.

46. Ulric Haynes to McGeorge Bundy, 5 June 1965, *FRUS, 1964–68*, vol. 24, document 197.

47. The Second Five-Year Plan of 1962–67 relied heavily on external funding for Ethiopian transport, industrial, and agricultural projects.

48. William A. Hance, *African Economic Development*, rev ed. (New York, 1967) 284–85; Lucius Battle to McGeorge Bundy, 30 September 1961; Battle to Bundy, 1 February 1962; Telegram, Ambassador John Kenneth Galbraith to Secretary of State Dean Rusk, 24 February 1962, all in box 69, NSF, JFKL; State Department to Embassy in Ethiopia, 19 May 1962, *FRUS, 1961–1963*, vol. 21, document 276. Haile Selassie I University, founded in 1962, was renamed Addis Ababa University after the revolution of 1974.

49. W. D. Fisher, quoted in Marcus, *The Politics of Empire*, 176; Memorandum of Conversation, "Assistance to Ethiopia," 2 October 1963, *FRUS, 1961–1963*, vol. 21, Microfiche Supplement, document 519.

50. Memorandum of Conversation, 25 July 1963, *FRUS, 1961–1963*, vol. 21, document 297.

51. Briefing Paper Prepared in Department of State, 29 September 1963, *FRUS, 1961–63*, vol. 21, document 300.

52. William Brubeck, National Security Council staff, to Kennedy, 30 September 1963, *FRUS, 1961–1963*, vol. 21, document 301.

53. W. D. Fisher, in Marcus, *The Politics of Empire*, 178; National Policy Paper, 19 December 1963, *FRUS, 1961–63*, vol. 21, document 309.

54. Rostow to Johnson, 11 February 1967, FRUS, 1964–1968, vol. 24, document 327.

55. Marcus, The Politics of Empire, x; Donald L. Donham, Marxist Modern: An Ethnographic History of the Ethiopian Revolution (Oxford, 1999).

56. Komer to Korry, 26 April 1965, document 304; Komer to Mennen Williams, 8 February 1966, document 309, FRUS, 1964–1968, vol. 24.

57. Report by Dr. Edward Mason of his Visit to the US Aid Mission in Ethiopia, August 1965, box 1, NSF, Agency File—AID, LBJL.

58. Edward S. Mason, Economic Planning in Underdeveloped Areas: Government and Business (New York, 1958), and Foreign Aid and Foreign Policy (New York, 1964).

59. Daniel Louchheim, "Development Plans Fail to Aid Ethiopia," Washington Post, 7 May 1967, K3.

60. Marcus, The Politics of Empire, 180–81.

61. Ibid., 169.

62. Ibid., 175; Rivkin, Nation-Building in Africa, 200–201.

63. On the Congo crisis, the most fully researched phase of American intervention in Africa, the most thorough recent study is Lise Namikas, "Battleground Africa: The Cold War and the Congo Crisis, 1960–1965," Ph.D. diss., University of Southern California, 2002. Still useful is Madeleine Kalb, The Congo Cables: The Cold War in Africa, from Eisenhower to Kennedy (New York, 1982).

64. Albert P. Disdier, "The Congo's Economic Crisis," Africa Special Report 5:6 (June 1960), 7, 15.

65. Ibid., 6.

66. Harlan Cleveland to Dean Rusk, 14 May 1962, box WH-29, Classified Subject File, Papers of Arthur M. Schlesinger, Jr., JFKL.

67. George C. McGhee, Under Secretary of State for Political Affairs to Kennedy, 22 January 1963, box 29, NSF, JFKL.

68. Rusk to Kennedy, 24 January 1963, FRUS, 1961–1963, 20:833.

69. Roger Hilsman to Dean Rusk, 1 February 1963, box WH-30, Classified Subject File, Papers of Arthur M. Schlesinger, Jr., JFKL. Cleveland, after participating in aid programs during the 1940s and '50s, directed studies on the growth of development organizations and networks for the Carnegie Corporation from 1956 to 1960 before becoming Kennedy's Assistant Secretary of State for International Organization. David Ekbladh, "From Consensus to Crisis," in Nation-Building, 26.

70. "Proposals for U.S. Policy in the Congo," Report of the Cleveland Mission, 20 February 1963, box WH-30, Classified Subject File, Papers of Arthur M. Schlesinger, Jr., JFKL. The Cleveland Report and Rusk's cover letter to Kennedy of 21 February 1963 are in box 30, NSF, JFKL. Rusk emphasized that the president need not commit to an exact amount of aid yet, as the main task revealed by the report was getting the UN to more effectively coordinate the multilateral aid.

71. Thomas L. Hughes to Rusk, 19 April 1963, box 29, NSF, JFKL.

72. CIA Special Report, "The Congo Economy," 14 June 1963, box 29, NSF, JFKL.

73. Rivkin, Nation-Building in Africa, 171–72.

74. Alvin M. Wolfe, "Capital and the Congo," in Davis and Baker, Southern Africa in Transition, 376–77.

75. Albert J. Meyers, "The Congo after 6 Years and a Billion in Aid," *U.S. News and World Report*, 18 April 1966, 65—67.

76. Memo entitled, "Why are we aiding so many African countries?" 20 November 1965, box 15, NSF, McGeorge Bundy Files, LBJL.

77. Haynes to Rostow, 8 June 1966, FRUS, 1964—1968, vol. 24, document 212.

78. Summary Notes of the 572nd Meeting of the National Security Council, 13 July 1967, Paper Prepared in the Department of State, undated, 1967, Document 226, FRUS, 1964—1968, vol. 24, documents 225, 226.

79. Roger Morris to Walt Rostow, 7 October 1968, box 1, Papers of Edward K. Hamilton, NSF, LBJL.

80. J. Anthony Lukas, "Smugglers in Leopoldville," *New York Times*, 28 May 1963, 1.

81. Stephen Weissman, *American Foreign Policy in the Congo, 1960—1964* (Ithaca, 1974), 208—9.

82. Quotation from Cooper, *Africa since 1940*, 166. On the U.S. military intervention, see Gleijeses, *Conflicting Missions*, 57—159.

83. Quoted in Rivkin, *Nation-Building in Africa*, 188.

84. Rivkin, *The New States of Africa*, 22—23.

85. Rivkin, *Nation-Building in Africa*, 156.

Five. *"A Significant Historical Demonstration"*

1. The diary is located in box 12 of the Wolfgang Stolper Papers at Rare Book, Manuscript, and Special Collections Library, Duke University, Durham, N.C. It was published as *Inside Independent Nigeria: Diaries of Wolfgang Stolper, 1960—1962*, ed. Clive S. Gray (Burlington, Vt., 2003). First quotation in Wolfgang Stolper, "Economic Development in Nigeria," *Journal of Economic History* 23:4 (December 1963), 391; on Stolper's appointment, Clive S. Gray, "Editor's Introduction," in *Inside Independent Nigeria*, ix—xx; Stolper, *Planning without Facts: Lessons in Resource Allocation from Nigeria's Development* (Cambridge, Mass., 1966), xv; Stolper quotations in *Inside Independent Nigeria*, 19.

2. Memorandum, Walt Rostow to John F. Kennedy, 7 July 1961, FRUS, 1961—1963, vol. 21, Microfiche Supplement, document 579.

3. Memorandum of Conversation, 7 July 1961, FRUS, 1961—1963, vol. 21, Microfiche Supplement, document 580. The comparison with Brazil proved ironic, given Kennedy's later difficulties with that nation. See Michael W. Weis, "The Twilight of Pan-Americanism: The Alliance for Progress, Neo-Colonialism, and Non-Alignment in Brazil, 1961—1964," *International History Review* 23:2 (June, 2001), 322—44.

4. Staniland, *American Intellectuals and African Nationalists*, 53.

5. Quoted in "Out of the Jungles—New Nations and Problems," *U.S. News and World Report*, 27 July 1959, 72—78, reprinted in *The New Nations of West Africa*, 78—79.

6. Major accounts of Nigeria's postcolonial history include Kenneth Post and Michael Vickers, *Structure and Conflict in Nigeria, 1960—1966* (Madison, 1973); Toyin Falola, *Economic Reforms and Modernization in Nigeria, 1945—1965* (Kent, Ohio, 2004), which

briefly treats the post-1960 period, and idem, The History of Nigeria (Westport, Conn., 1999); idem, ed., Nigeria in the Twentieth Century (Durham, N.C., 2002); idem and Julius O. Ihonvbere, eds., Nigeria and the International Capitalist System (Boulder, 1988); Julius O. Ihonvbere and Timothy M. Shaw, Illusions of Power: Nigeria in Transition (Trenton, N.J., 1998); Levi A. Nwachuku and G. N. Uzoigwe, Troubled Journey: Nigeria since the Civil War (Lanham, Md., 2004); Adebayo Oyebade, ed., The Transformation of Nigeria: Essays in Honor of Toyin Falola (Trenton, 2002);and William D. Graf, The Nigerian State: Political Economy, State, Class, and Political System in the Post-Colonial Era (London, 1988).

7. On U.S.–Nigerian relations during the 1950s, see Monica Lorine Belmonte, "Reining in Revolution: The United States Response to British Decolonization in Nigeria in an Era of Civil Rights, 1953–1960," Ph.D, diss., Georgetown University, 2003, which emphasizes the Eisenhower administration's preference for a conservative Nigerian state closely aligned to the outgoing British. On the 1960s, the two major studies are Bassey E. Ate, Decolonization and Dependence: The Development of Nigerian-U.S. Relations, 1960–1984 (Boulder, 1984), and R. Bruce Shepard, Nigeria, Africa, and the United States: From Kennedy to Reagan (Bloomington, Ind., 1991). Both discuss U.S. aid and the Nigerian plan, but focus heavily on conventional policymaking and diplomacy. A longer view is George Obiozor, Uneasy Friendship: Nigerian-American Relations (Enugu, Nigeria, 1992). On the United States and the Nigerian civil war, see Joseph E. Thompson, American Policy and African Famine: The Nigeria-Biafra War, 1966–1970 (Westport, Conn., 1990); Emmanuel N. Amadife, Pre-Theories and Theories of Foreign Policy-Making (Lanham, Md., 1999), which applies political science theories to U.S. decision-making during the Nigerian civil war; and E. Wayne Nafzinger, The Economics of Political Instability: The Nigerian-Biafran War (Boulder, 1983). Useful studies of Nigeria's place in world politics with some discussion of the United States include R. A. Akindele and Bassey E. Ate, eds., Nigeria's External Relations with the Major Developed Market-Economy Countries, 1960–1985 (Lagos, Nigeria, 1988); Maxim Matusevich, No Easy Row for a Russian Hoe: Ideology and Pragmatism in Nigerian-Soviet Relations, 1960–1991 (Trenton, 2003); and Hakeem Ibikunle Tijani, Britain, Leftist Nationalists, and the Transfer of Power in Nigeria, 1945–1965 (New York, 2006).

8. Reginald H. Green, "Four African Development Plans: Ghana, Kenya, Nigeria, and Tanzania," Journal of Modern African Studies 3:2 (1965), 259. On the plan and American influence, see Stolper, Planning without Facts; Falola, Economic Reforms and Modernization in Nigeria, 174–81; Ojetunji Aboyade, Foundations of an African Economy: A Study of Investment and Growth in Nigeria (New York, 1966); Gerald K. Helleiner, Peasant Agriculture, Government, and Economic Growth in Nigeria (Homewood, Ill., 1966); Edwin Dean, Plan Implementation in Nigeria: 1962–1966 (Ibadan, Nigeria, 1972); E. Wayne Nafzinger, "The Political Economy of Disintegration in Nigeria," Journal of Modern African Studies 11:4 (December 1973), 505–36; Okwudiba Nnoli, ed., Path to Nigerian Development (Dakar, Senegal, 1981); and P. N. C. Okigbo, National Development Planning in Nigeria, 1900–1992 (London, 1989); on the plan's colonial antecedents, see Toyin Falola, Development Planning and Decolonization in Nigeria (Gainesville, Fla., 1996).

9. Aboyade, Foundations of an African Economy, 166; Ate, Decolonization and Dependence, 51. On

Schumpeter's theoretical work on economic development as an antecedent to post–World War II concepts, see M. P. Cowan and R. W. Shenton, *Doctrines of Development* (London, 1996), 373–437.

10. Stolper, *Inside Independent Nigeria*, 5–6, 18, 10, 19, 194.

11. Ibid., 38, 202.

12. Ibid., 269, 88, 108, 246. Though Stolper evinced no interest in the historical origins of corruption in the colonial era, a good recent study that documents this is Toyin Falola and Akanmu Adebayo, *Culture, Politics and Money among the Yoruba* (New Brunswick, N.J., 2000).

13. Rostow's contact with MIT, Donald L. M. Blackmer, letter to Walt W. Rostow, 4 April 1961, box 144, NSF Country Files, Nigeria, JFKL. Rostow had asked for Rivkin's views on Nigerian development needs and, Blackmer noted, "we are also expecting word from Wolf Stolper, who has been in Nigeria for several months and who may well have more specific ideas and figures than Arnold could put together on short notice."

14. Rivkin to Rostow, 29 March 1961, box 144, NSF, JFKL.

15. Max Millikan to Stolper, 24 March 1961, box 6, accession, Stolper papers.

16. Stolper, *Inside Independent Nigeria*, 107–8, 120.

17. Minutes of an official meeting with the American mission, 5 June 1961, American Mission, box 1, Stolper papers.

18. Rivkin to Stolper, 22 June 1961, American Mission, box 1, Stolper papers.

19. "Report of the Special U.S. Economic Mission to Nigeria"; see also Ate, *Decolonization and Dependence*.

20. Tasca to Williams, 9 March 1961, box 2, NSF, JFKL.

21. Mennen Williams memorandum to John O. Bell (State Department), 23 March 1961, box 144; Henry Tasca memorandum to Mennen Williams, 9 March 1961, box 2; Fowler Hamilton memorandum to John F. Kennedy, 22 November 1961, box 144; David Bell (Budget Director) to Hamilton, 28 November 1961, box 144, NSF, JFKL. See also Shepard, *Nigeria, Africa, and the United States*, 20.

22. Rostow to Kennedy, 21 July 1961, FRUS, 1961–1963, vol. 21, Microfiche Supplement, document 582.

23. Memorandum of Conversation, 25 July 1961, box 144, NSF, JFKL.

24. Stolper, *Inside Independent Nigeria*, 160.

25. Rivkin to Stolper, 11 August 1961, box 20 accession, Stolper papers.

26. Wolfgang Stolper to Arnold Rivkin, 17 August 1961, American Mission, box 1, Stolper papers.

27. Rivkin to Stolper, 23 August 1961, box 20, accession, Stolper papers.

28. Stolper, *Inside Independent Nigeria*, 199, 201, 205.

29. Minutes of an official meeting with the American mission, 29 September 1961, American Mission, box 1, Stolper papers.

30. Palmer to State Department, 9 October 1961, box 144, NSF, JFKL.

31. Stolper, *Inside Independent Nigeria*, 152–53.

32. Stolper to Max Millikan, 14 November 1961, box 11, accession, Stolper papers.

33. Stolper, *Inside Independent Nigeria*, 220, 267. Ate, *Decolonization and Dependence*, has an

excellent analysis of Nigerian frustration with the American aid criteria and the problems of implementation that soured the relationship.

34. Stolper, *Inside Independent Nigeria*, 212, 220, 267, 287, 240, 288. In 1963 Stolper participated in an economic mission to Liberia, thereafter serving as chief of the USAID mission in Tunisia in 1963–64, and on a World Bank mission to Togo and Dahomey in 1967. During the early 1980s, he participated in UN and World Bank missions to Malawi and Benin. In his postscript and addendum to the published diaries, written in 1999 and 2001, respectively, Stolper expresses little nostalgia for Nigeria or concern for its fate, giving no evidence of any feeling of responsibility for the country's slide into debt and dependence. In his later years, Stolper concentrated on preserving the memory of his mentor, founding the International Schumpeter Society and publishing an appreciative biography. *Inside Independent Nigeria*, 288, "Postscript" by Wolfgang Stolper (written in 1999), 301, Gray, "Editor's Introduction," x. The biography is Stolper, *Joseph Alois Schumpeter: The Public Life of a Private Man* (Princeton, 1994).

35. Stolper to Donald Kingsley, 30 July 1962, box 11, accession, Stolper papers.

36. Stolper wrote the book while a visitor at Harvard, courtesy of economics professor Edward Mason. *Inside Independent Nigeria*, xxvii.

37. "Portrait: The Reasonable American," *West Africa*, 22 June 1963, 689.

38. Rivkin, *Africa and the West*, quote on 142; Rivkin, *The African Presence in World Affairs*; "Nigeria's National Development Plan," *Current History* 43 (December 1962), 321–28, and "Nigeria: A Unique Nation" *Current History* 45 (December 1963), 329–34.

39. Rivkin, *The African Presence*, 27, 44, 158; Rivkin, "Nigeria's National Development Plan," *Current History* 43 (December 1962), 322; the "unique nation" statement is quoted in Staniland, *American Intellectuals and African Nationalists*, 115, n. 50.

40. Rivkin, *The African Presence*, 247; "Nigeria: A Unique Nation," 330. A more nuanced and informed analysis of the politics of Nigerian diversity by an American scholar at the time is Richard L. Sklar, *Nigerian Political Parties: Power in an Emergent African Nation* (Princeton, 1963). The classic study that preceded independence is James S. Coleman, *Nigeria: Background to Nationalism* (Berkeley, 1958).

41. Rivkin, *The African Presence*, 249.

42. Rivkin, "Nigeria's National Development Plan," 323–34; *The African Presence*, 249.

43. Rivkin, "Nigeria's National Development Plan," 326, 368.

44. Ibid., 225, 250 on Awolowo; Aboyade, *Foundations of an African Economy*, 150–99, 367. Stolper described Aboyade as the man who "probably knows more than anyone else about capital formation in Nigeria." In 1962 the two men engaged in a public debate about the plan in northern Nigeria, and Stolper admitted in his diary that he shared many of Aboyade's concerns about it. Later, Stolper brought Aboyade to the University of Michigan as a visiting professor to teach a course on economic development. *Inside Independent Nigeria*, 72, 273–74, 301.

45. Eric Sevareid, "Nigeria Black Monolith . . . or Triptych?" *Washington Post*, 18 September 1960, E3.

46. David E. Lilienthal, "Why Nigeria Is 'Different,'" *New York Times*, 11 June 1961, SM40, 43, 46. Of many articles and books that compared and contrasted Nigeria's situa-

tion with the grim prospects of the Congo, mired in civil war and great-power intervention during the early 1960s, see, for example, Arch Parsons, "Nigeria: Contrast to the Congo," *New York Times*, 2 October 1960, SM10. Parsons, an officer of the Ford Foundation in Nigeria, offered a bland yet positive profile of the country accompanied by several photographs that conveyed an image of a stable, almost serene antithesis to the Congo.

47. Sevareid, "Nigeria."

48. Drew Pearson, "Nigerian Discourtesy," *Washington Post*, 3 October 1965, E7.

49. Telegram, State Department to Lagos Embassy, 23 January 1963; Telegram, State Department to Lagos Embassy, 31 January 1963, box 24, RG 59, Records of G. Mennen Williams, 1961–1966, Trips Files, National Archives Records Administration (NARA II), College Park, Md.

50. Telegram 1205, Ambassador Joseph Palmer to the State Department, 19 February 1963, box 144, NSF, JFKL.

51. Telegram, Mennen Williams to Wayne Fredericks, 13 February 1963, box 24, Trips Files, Williams Records.

52. Memorandum of Conversation, Mennen Williams and Nigerian Ambassador Julius Udochi, 8 March 1963, FRUS, 1961–63, vol. 21, Microfiche Supplement, document 587.

53. Memorandum, Robert W. Akers (Deputy Director, United States Information Agency) to McGeorge Bundy (National Security Advisor), 20 November 1965, box 15, NSF McGeorge Bundy Files, LBJL.

54. Williams memorandum to Dean Rusk, 25 February 1963, box 381; Telegram 1205, Joseph Palmer to Secretary of State, 19 February 1963, box 144, NSF Country Files, Nigeria, JFKL.

55. CIA, Special Report, "Regional Strains Threaten Nigerian Federation," 3 April 1964, box 96, Country Files, NSF, LBJL.

56. William Trimble memorandum to Henry Tasca, Deputy Assistant Secretary of State for African Affairs, 27 December 1962, box 5, Trimble Papers, Seeley G. Mudd Library, Princeton University.

57. Memorandum of Conversation, "US AID Program: Arthur D. Little Contract," 21 October 1963; Memorandum of Conversation, George Johnson and Dean Rusk, "University of Nigeria," 17 August 1962, box 144, NSF, Nigeria, JFKL.

58. Memorandum of Conversation, Dean Rusk, Dr. George M. Johnson, Vice-Chancellor of the University of Nigeria, and Ras O. Johnson, Chief of the Education Division of the Africa-Europe Bureau of AID, 17 August 1962, box 144; Harold Saunders memorandum to Robert Komer, 5 November 1962, box 407, NSF, JFKL.

59. Memorandum of Conversation, "Call on the President by the Nigerian Parliamentary Delegation," 14 June 1962, box 144, NSF Country Files, Nigeria, JFKL.

60. On Nigerian leaders' interest in the Soviet model of industrialization, and the reasons why Nigerian-Soviet relations remained strained, see Matusevich, *No Easy Row for a Russian Hoe*.

61. Telegram, SecState 60, Ambassador Elbert G. Matthews to the State Department, 10 July 1964, box 96, NSF Country Files—Nigeria, LBJL.

62. Rowan to Johnson, 21 July 1964, *FRUS, 1964–68*, 24:284.

63. Telegram 1148, Lagos Embassy to State Department, 22 May 1962; Memorandum, McGeorge Bundy to Mennen Williams, 24 May 1962, box 144, NSF, Country Files, Nigeria, JFKL. Palmer, 46 years old when appointed ambassador in October 1960, had been educated at Harvard before beginning a career in the Foreign Service. See biographical sketch attached to Brubeck to Bundy, 12 July 1963, box 144, NSF, JFKL.

64. Telegram 1410, State Department to Lagos Embassy, 24 May 1962; Telegram 1193, Ambassador Palmer to the State Department, 1 June 1962, box 144, NSF, Country Files, Nigeria, JFKL.

65. Memorandum, State Department to Pedro Sanjuan and David K. Edminster, "Chukwuma Azikiwe," 8 June 1962; Telegram, Ambassador Palmer to State Department, 21 June 1962, box 144, NSF Country Files, Nigeria, JFKL.

66. Arnold Beichman, "Outlook in Nigeria for Profitable Investment," *Christian Science Monitor*, 5 August 1960, 12.

67. "Nation on Trial," *Time*, 1 March 1963.

68. Arnold Beichman, "Outlook in Nigeria for Profitable Investment," *Christian Science Monitor*, 5 August 1960, 12.

69. Stolper, *Inside Independent Nigeria*, 202.

70. Ibid., 108, 246; NIE, 26 August 1965, *FRUS, 1964–1968*, vol. 24, document 360. On corruption's roots, an excellent study of one region of Nigeria is Falola and Adebayo, *Culture, Politics, and Money among the Yoruba*, which traces the issue from pre-colonial times to the contemporary era, emphasizing the British role.

71. Ate, *Decolonization and Dependence*, 60–61, 81–84.

72. Immanuel Wallerstein, "Nigeria: Slow Road to Trouble," quoted in Staniland, *American Intellectuals and African Nationalists*, 116, n. 54; on the "new class," Staniland, 107–8; Ate, *Decolonization and Dependence*, 55–56. See also Falola, *History of Nigeria*, 108–9.

73. Donald H. Louchheim, "Planners Pin Hopes on Nigeria as 'Perfect Test Case,'" *Washington Post*, 27 June 1965, A18. In Nigeria Stolper had enjoyed rapport with the USAID official Clive Gray, editor of *Inside Independent Nigeria*.

74. "Presentation on Nigeria," 6 November 1965, box 96, NSF Country Files, LBJL.

75. Koren to Hughes, 18 January 1966, *FRUS, 1964–1968*, vol. 24, document 362. Major works on the Nigerian civil war include the citations above on Nigerian history, as well as John de St. Jorre, *The Nigerian Civil War* (London, 1972); John Stremlau, *The International Politics of the Nigerian Civil War* (Princeton, 1977); Olusegun Obasanjo, *My Command: An Account of the Nigerian Civil War* (Ibadan, Nigeria, 1980); and A. M. H. Kirk-Greene, *Crisis and Conflict: A Documentary Sourcebook*, 2 vols. (London, 1971).

76. Rusk to State Department from Manila, 27 October 1966, *FRUS, 1964–1968*, vol. 24, document 368.

77. Memorandum, "Nigeria," Edward Hamilton to National Security Advisor Walt W. Rostow, 25 May 1967; Memorandum, Hamilton to Rostow, 20 July 1967; Memorandum, Hamilton to George Christian, 14 August 1968, box 96, NSF, Country Files—Nigeria, LBJL.

78. Summary Notes of 572d Meeting of the NSC, 13 July 1967, FRUS, 1964–1968, vol. 24, document 225.

79. Stolper returned to Nigeria after the war. At Aboyade's invitation, he accepted a visiting position at Ibadan, sponsored by the Rockefeller Foundation. However, the American encountered a tense atmosphere of distrust. When Nigerian junior faculty "openly accused" Stolper of being a spy, Aboyade did not defend him. When his sojourn ended, Stolper ran a gauntlet of indignities at the airport, and "was glad finally to settle in my first class seat on Swissair." Inside Independent Nigeria, 302.

80. Staniland, American Intellectuals and African Nationalists, 206.

81. Collin Gonze, "Introduction," in Stanley Diamond, Nigeria: Model of a Colonial Failure (New York: ACOA, 1967), v.

82. George Jenkins, "The Scholars' Paper Nigeria," Africa Report 12:5 (May 1967), 48–51.

83. Ate, Decolonization and Dependence, 81, 83; Shepard, Nigeria, 28–29.

84. The continued belief, in Nigeria and the West, that Nigeria is destined to emerge as a stable democracy and developed regional power in Africa is evident in articles such as O. Carl Unegbu, "Nigeria: Bellwether of African Democracy," World Policy Journal 20:1 (2003), 41–47.

Six. "Decade of Disillusionment"

1. Telegram from Conakry Embassy to State Department, 21 April 1962, FRUS, 1961–1963, vol. 21, Microfiche Supplement, document 491.

2. Bundy quoted in Lyons, "Keeping Africa Off the Agenda," in Lyndon Johnson Confronts the World, 249; Memorandum, Ulric Haynes to Lyndon Johnson, 1 November 1965, Papers of Ulric Haynes, NSF, LBJL.

3. Bowles telegram to State Department, 30 October 1962, box 144, NSF, JFKL.

4. Ekbladh, "From Consensus to Crisis," in Nation-Building, 29–30.

5. Wallerstein, Africa: The Politics of Unity, 130.

6. Memorandum, Mennen Williams to Chester Bowles 29 September 1961, FRUS, 1961–1963, vol. 21, document 201.

7. Williams to Fowler Hamilton, USAID Administrator, 23 February, 1962, box 10, Mennen Williams Papers, RG 59, National Archives II.

8. Report on Mennen Williams Third Trip to Africa, 29 September–26 October 1961, box 23, Williams Papers, RG 59, NA.

9. Williams to Rusk, "Major Conclusions of Williams African Trip," 25 February 1963, box 24, Williams Papers, RG 59.

10. Haynes to Komer, 20 October 1965, Papers of Ulric Haynes, NSF, LBJL.

11. Memorandum, Walt Rostow to Dean Rusk, 23 April 1966, box 15, NSF, Walt Rostow Files, LBJL.

12. NIE, 22 April 1965, FRUS, 1964–1968, vol. 24, document 195.

13. Paper Prepared in the Department of State, undated, 1967, FRUS, 1964–1968, vol. 24, document 226.

14. Komer to Johnson, 19 June 1965, Document 199, FRUS, 1964–1968, vol. 24, document 199.

15. Lyons, "Keeping Africa Off the Agenda," in *Lyndon Johnson Confronts the World*, 265–66.

16. Telephone Conversation transcript, Ball and McGeorge Bundy, 13 July 1963, Papers of George Ball, JFKL.

17. Memorandum of Discussion, 397th Meeting of the NSC, 26 February 1959; Memorandum of Conference with President Eisenhower, 1 November 1960, FRUS, 1958–1960, 14:183, 237.

18. Paper Prepared in Policy Planning Council, 20 November 1968, FRUS, 1964–1968, vol. 24, document 409.

19. Memorandum, Mennen Williams to Dean Rusk, 1 February 1963, Williams Papers.

20. "Portrait: A Fresh Look at West Africa," *West Africa*, 31 July 1965, 851.

21. Haynes to Johnson, 8 November 1965; Haynes to Komer, 17 November 1965, Papers of Ulric Haynes, NSF, LBJL.

22. Hendrik van Ossoo, African Bureau, to Haynes, 5 November 1965; Haynes to Komer, 6 November 1965, box 1, Papers of Edward K. Hamilton, NSF, LBJL.

23. On the American role, especially that of the CIA, see Mary Montgomery, "The Eyes of the World Were Watching: Ghana, Great Britain, and the United States, 1957–1966," diss., University of Maryland, 2005, 216–26; and John Prados, *Safe for Democracy: The Secret Wars of the CIA* (Chicago, 2006), 328–30.

24. Komer to Johnson, 10 March 1966, FRUS, 1964–1968, vol. 24, document 208.

25. NIE, 7 July 1966, FRUS, 1964–1968, vol. 24, document 213.

26. On the diplomacy of the U.S.–Ghanaian agreement to build a massive dam on the Volta River, which featured an astonishing amount of internal debate in Washington and mounting tension with Nkrumah, see Montgomery, "The Eyes of the World Were Watching," 133–77; Noer, "The New Frontier and African Neutralism;" and Mahoney, JFK, 157–86. The Volta project yielded a disappointment economically. The Akosombo Dam failed to kick-start industrialization, though its construction did add significantly to Ghana's external debt.

27. Memorandum of conversation between Milton Obote and Mennen Williams, 17 June 1963, box 167A, NSF, JFKL.

28. Komer to Kennedy, 26 November 1962, 28 November 1962, FRUS, 1961–1963, vol. 21, documents 284, 286. Five months later, according to a White House aide, the U.S. had forty Peace Corps volunteers in Somalia and an aid program of "$4.6 million in development grants, $4.4 million in loan funds, and $1.7 million in PL-480 aid." William Brubeck to Bundy, 18 March 1963, document 291.

29. Memorandum of Conversation, 27 November 1962, FRUS, 1961–1963, vol. 21, Microfiche Supplement, document 513.

30. Briefing Memorandum for the Vice President Concerning the Republic of Senegal, 1961, box 1, Vice Presidential Security File, NSF, LBJL.

31. Williams to Hollis Chenery, USAID, 13 February 1962, box 10, Williams Papers.

32. Embassy Dakar telegram to State Department, 30 April 1963, box 158, NSF, JFKL.

Kaiser served as ambassador in 1961–64, the second American to hold the post. His reminiscences are in *Journeying Far and Wide* (New York, 1992).

33. Memorandum, Walt Rostow to Lyndon Johnson, 27 September 1966, box 98, NSF, Country Files—Senegal, LBJL.

34. Memorandum, Edward Hamilton to Walt Rostow, 31 August 1966, box 98, NSF, Country Files—Senegal, LBJL.

35. Attwood, *The Reds and The Blacks*, 92.

36. Robert W. Akers, Deputy Director of USIA, to McGeorge Bundy, 20 November 1965, box 15, McGeorge Bundy Files, NSF, LBJL.

37. Nielsen, *The Great Powers and Africa*, 396.

38. "Portrait: U.N. Congo Man," *West Africa* 30 December 1961, 1437; Robert K. Gardiner, "The Decade of Discouragement," *Africa Report* 12:9 (December 1967), 17–18; on the ECA and OAU's differences, Edmond Kwam Kouassi, "Africa and the United Nations since 1945," in *Africa since 1935*, 893–94.

39. Okot p'Bitek, "Indigenous Ills," *Transition* 32 (1967).

40. Memorandum of Conversation, 14 July 1961, Memorandum of Conversation, 17 July 1961, FRUS, 1961–1963, vol. 21, Microfiche Supplement, documents 679, 680. On his economic and political philosophy, see Julius K. Nyerere, *Freedom and Unity: A Selection from Writings and Speeches, 1952–65* (London, 1967).

41. Walter Rodney, *How Europe Underdeveloped Africa* (London, 1972).

42. Memorandum of Conversation, 28 September 1966, box 98, NSF, Country Files—Senegal, LBJL.

43. Mennen Williams to Johnson (E), 28 March, 1963, box 11, Williams Papers.

44. Policy Planning Council, "Selected aspects of U.S. economic aid policy for Africa," 24 July 1961, FRUS, 1961–1963, 21:296; Harold Saunders memorandum to Robert Komer, 5 November 1962; Saunders to Komer, 7 November 1962, box 407; Henry J. Tasca memorandum to Mennen Williams, 9 March 1961, box 2; George Ball memorandum to Walt Rostow, 18 March 1961, box 325, NSF, JFKL.

45. G. Griffith Johnson (Assistant Secretary of State for Economic Affairs) memorandum to Thomas C. Mann (Undersecretary of State for Economic Affairs), 12 March 1965, document 258; Benjamin H. Read (Executive Secretary, Department of State) memorandum to Walt Rostow (National Security Advisor), 25 June 1966, FRUS, 1964–1968, vol. 9, document 322.

46. G. Griffith Johnson to Thomas C. Mann, 12 March 1965, FRUS, 1964–1968, vol. 9, document 258.

47. Ball to Kennedy, 12 November 1963, FRUS, 1961–1963, vol. 9, document 290.

48. Quoted in Nielsen, *The Great Powers and Africa*, 341.

49. Report of Vice President Humphrey to President Johnson, 12 January 1968, FRUS, 1964–1968, vol. 24, document 231.

50. Ruth Schachter Morgenthau, "African Socialism: Declaration of Ideological Independence," *Africa Report* 8:5 (May 1963), 3. In 1962, Senghor had invited Rostow to attend the conference in Dakar on "Development and African Roads to Socialism." Brubeck to Bundy, 16 August 1962, box 158, NSF, JFKL.

51. "Resolution on Neo-Colonialism," in Wallerstein, *Africa: The Politics of Independence and Unity*, 266–69.

52. Kwame Nkrumah, *Neo-Colonialism: The Last Stage of Imperialism* (New York, 1966), xi.

53. Wallerstein, *Africa: The Politics of Independence and Unity*, 132, 140, 146.

54. Engerman, "West Meets East," 216.

55. Adedeji, "Comparative Strategies of Economic Decolonization in Africa," in *Africa since 1935*, 393.

56. Martin and West, "The Ascent," in *Out of One, Many Africas*, 97–104, quotations on 97, 99, 104; Africa Research Group, *Africa Retort*, "Editor's Arsenal," 2–7.

Seven. "Just Not a Rational Being"

1. Ambassador George A, Morgan to Walt Rostow, 10 August 1966; Morgan, "A Qualitative Concept of African Aid," 10 August 1966, box 15, NSF, Walt Rostow Files, LBJL.

2. Quotations about the Peace Corps in Latham, *Modernization as Ideology*, 118, 123.

3. Alan McPherson, *Yankee No! Anti-Americanism in U.S.–Latin American Relations* (Cambridge, Mass., 2003), 168.

4. Paul Hofmann, "Africa Changes, Red-Tape Doesn't," *New York Times*, 9 October 1960, 4.

5. Staniland, *American Intellectuals and African Nationalists*; Ruth Mayer, *Artificial Africas: Colonial Images in the Times of Globalization* (Hanover, N.H., 2002).

6. Brian Crozier, *The Morning After: A Study of Independence* (New York, 1963), 114–15.

7. "Out of the Jungles—New Nations and Problems," *U.S. News and World Report*, 27 July 1959, reprinted in *The New Nations of West Africa*, 78–79.

8. On the frequent use of "the African," see Staniland, *American Intellectuals and African Nationalists*, 42 and n. 76; Darlington, *African Betrayal*, 8.

9. Mahoney, *JFK*, 39.

10. Quoted in Kalb, *The Congo Cables*, 37. The record of the conversation is in FRUS, 1958–1960, 14:359–66.

11. Quoted in Kalb, *Congo Cables*, 377.

12. Stolper, *Inside Independent Nigeria*, 208–9; Chester Bowles, "Report of Mission," 13 November 1962, box 3, NSF, JFKL; Robert H. Johnson memorandum to Walt Rostow, 6 March 1961, box 2, NSF; "Report of G. Mennen Williams on his third trip to Africa, Sept 29 to Oct 26, 1961," 28 November 1961, box 2, NSF, JFKL.

13. Komer to Korry, 26 April 1965, FRUS, 1964–1968, vol. 24, document 304.

14. Quoted in Westad, *The Global Cold War*, 142.

15. Gleijeses, *Conflicting Missions*, 57–76.

16. Quoted in Westad, *Global Cold War*, 142.

17. Quoted in Staniland, *American Intellectuals and African Nationalists*, 33.

18. Ibid.; Smith, *Sensing the Past*, 130.

19. Quoted in "Out of the Jungles—New Nations and Problems."

20. C. C. Miniclier, "Markets Are Super," *Washington Post*, 6 June 1968, D4.

21. Memorandum of Conversation, Bowles and W. C. Naude, 29 November 1962, *FRUS, 1961–1963*, vol. 21, Microfiche Supplement, document 650.

22. Daniel Lerner, "Modernization," in *International Encyclopedia of the Social Sciences*, 390.

23. J. Douglas Porteous, "Smellscape," in *The Smell Culture Reader*, ed. Jim Drobnick (Oxford, 2006), 94–95.

24. Elspeth Huxley, *The Flame Trees of Thika*, quoted in Chinua Achebe, *Home and Exile* (New York, 2000), 57.

25. William A. Payne, "American Press Coverage of Africa," *Africa Report* 11:1 (January 1966), 45–46.

26. Ibid., 46–48.

27. Mildred Adams, "Key Pieces in the African Puzzle," *New York Times Magazine*, quoted in Staniland, *American Intellectuals and African Nationalists*, 38–39.

28. "Two African Views of the U.S. Press . . . ," *Africa Report* 6:5 (May 1961), 16.

29. Emmanuel Adagogo Jaja, "Problems of an African Editor," *Africa Report* 11: 1 (January 1966), 40.

30. "The Western Press—an African View," *Africa Report* 7:10 (November 1962), 26.

31. Katie Louchheim, "Katie Likes to Shatter Their Visions of America," *Washington Post*, 5 August 1962, F3.

32. Lawrence C. Vambe, "Report on America," *Africa Special Report* 3:2 (February 1958), 9–11.

33. Alioune Diop, "America: A French African's View," *Africa Special Report* 3:2 (February 1958), 13.

34. Nkrumah, *Neo-Colonialism*, 246.

35. Quoted in Zimmerman, *Innocents Abroad*, 206.

36. Lloyd Garrison, "Nigeria Doing Home-Grown Television Shows," *New York Times*, 8 September 1963, X15.

37. Quoted in Staniland, *American Intellectuals and African Nationalists*, 39.

38. Frances P. Bolton, "Africa—A Giant Stretches," *Africa Special Report* 2:7 (30 July 1957), 3.

39. Charles F. Darlington, in Darlington and Alice B. Darlington, *African Betrayal* (New York, 1968), 54.

40. Jennifer Lynn Walton, "Moral Masculinity: The Culture of Foreign Relations during the Kennedy Administration," Ph.D. diss., Ohio State University, 2004, 137, 142.

41. Mahoney, *JFK*, 38–39.

42. Telephone Conversation transcript, Ball and Fowler Hamilton, 22 December 1961, Papers of George Ball, JFKL.

43. Vera M. Dean, "Is Democracy Possible in Africa?" in *The New Nations of West Africa*, 122.

44. Attwood, *The Reds and the Blacks*, 74.

45. Ibid., 59; Cleveland to Rusk, 2 May 1961, *FRUS, 1961–1963*, vol. 25, document 169.

46. Rostow to Kennedy, 4 March 1961, *FRUS, 1961–1963*, vol. 21, Microfiche Supplement, document 470.

47. Telegram from Nairobi embassy to State Department, 14 December 1963, *FRUS, 1961–1963*, vol. 21, Microfiche Supplement, document 544.

48. Memorandum on the Substance of Discussion at the Department of State–Joint Chiefs of Staff Meeting, 5 January 1962, FRUS, 1961–1963, vol. 21, document 204; Williams, *Africa for the Africans*, 13.

49. Walton, "Moral Masculinity," 148–50.

50. "Report of G. Mennen Williams on his Third Trip to Africa," 28 November 1961, box 2; Adlai Stevenson telegram to Rusk, 23 January 1963, NSF, JFKL; Stevenson quotations in Noer, *ColdWar and Black Liberation*, 84, and Mahoney, *JFK*, 230–31; on Chester Bowles, see Noer, *ColdWar and Black Liberation*, 131; Chester Bowles, "Report of Mission to Africa," 13 November 1962, box 3, NSF, JFKL.

51. Harold K. Schneider, Review of Melville Herskovits, *The Human Factor in Changing Africa*, in *Africa Report* 8:3 (March 1963), 27.

52. NIE, "The Probable Interrelationships of the Independent African States," 31 August 1961, FRUS, 1961–1963, vol. 21, document 198.

53. Fredericks to Rusk, 11 October 1961, FRUS, 1961–1963, vol. 21, Microfiche Supplement, document 440.

54. Memorandum of Conversation, 19 November 1963, FRUS, 1961–1963, vol. 21, document 253.

55. Memorandum of Conversation, 3 November 1961, FRUS, 1961–1963, vol. 21, Microfiche Supplement, document 630.

56. Central Intelligence Agency memorandum, "Bloc Aid to Guinea," 20 May 1963, box 385, NSF, JFKL, V. Y. Mudimbe, *The Invention of Africa*, 91.

57. Samuel E. Belk, NSC Staff, to Kaysen, 17 May 1963, FRUS, 1961–1963, vol. 21, document 267.

58. Brubeck to Kennedy, 12 November 1963, FRUS, 1961–1963, vol. 21, document 269.

59. Thomas R. Byrne letter to Ralph Dungan, 22 May 1962, box 388, NSF, JFKL.

60. Central Intelligence Agency Special Memorandum, "A Reassessment of Julius Nyerere," 10 June 1965, NSF, Country Files, box 100, LBJL.

61. Ambassador quoted in Westad, *Global ColdWar*, 143; Haynes to Rostow, 8 June 1966, FRUS, 1964–1968, vol. 24, document 212.

62. Quoted in Staniland, *American Intellectuals and African Nationalists*, 89.

63. Deputy Assistant Secretary of State for African Affairs Wayne Fredericks to Rusk, 5 March 1966, FRUS, 1964–1968, vol. 24, document 207.

64. Komer to Johnson, 10 March 1966, FRUS, 1964–1968, vol. 24, document 208.

65. Draft Paper Prepared in the Department of State, undated, FRUS, 1964–1968, vol. 24, document 191.

66. Samuel Huntington, *Political Order in Changing Societies* (New Haven, 1968), 192. On Huntington's place in relation to modernization theory, see Gilman, *Mandarins of the Future*.

67. Immanuel Wallerstein, Review of *African Diplomacy: Studies in the Determinants of Foreign Policy*, ed. Vernon McKay (New York, 1966), in *Political Science Quarterly* 83:3 (September 1968), 491–92.

Eight. "Fetish Nation"

1. Eric Sevareid, "Nigeria: Black Monolith . . . or Triptych?" *Washington Post*, 18 September 1960, E3.

2. The tropes of "tribe" in academic and popular discourse during the early years of independence, and how subsequent scholarship has exploded them—at least in academe—are discussed in a vast literature on African ethnicity and identity. A good overview is Ronald R. Atkinson, "The (Re)Construction of Ethnicity in Africa: Extending the Chronology, Conceptualization, and Discourse," in *Ethnicity and Nationalism in Africa: Constructivist Reflections and Contemporary Politics*, ed. P. Yeros (London, 1999), 15–44.

3. Statement of U.S. Policy Toward Africa South of the Sahara Prior to Calendar Year 1960, Enclosure, NSC Report, 26 August 1958, FRUS, 1958–1960, 14:36.

4. Memorandum of Discussion, 456th Meeting of the NSC, 18 August 1960, FRUS, 1958–1960, 14:155, 157.

5. Colin Legum, quoted in Staniland, *American Intellectuals and African Nationalists*, 40.

6. Advertisement, *New York Times Magazine*, 11 June 1959, 68.

7. Robert Coughlan, "Black Magic: Vital Force," *Life*, 26 January 1959; Elspeth Huxley, "Drums of Change Beat for Africa's Tribes," *New York Times Magazine*, 29 November 1959.

8. Wright, *Black Power*, quoted in Meriwether, *Proudly We Can Be Africans*, 156; Drake, "Social Change and Social Problems in Contemporary Africa," 264–65.

9. Report of the President's Task Force on Foreign Economic Policy, undated but sent to Johnson in November 1964, FRUS, 1964–1968, vol. 9, document 20.

10. Waldemar A. Nielsen, "Africa Is Poised on the Razor's Edge," *New York Times Magazine*, 9 February 1964, 2, quoted in Edmond C. Hutchinson, "American Aid to Africa," *Annals of the American Academy of Political and Social Science* 354, *Africa in Motion* (July 1964): 67.

11. Hutchinson, "American Aid to Africa," 69.

12. Ray Vicker, "Back to Tribalism," *Wall Street Journal*, 19 January 1961, 16; Aaron Segal, "Rwanda—The Underlying Causes," *Africa Report* 9:4 (April 1964), 3.

13. Although the literature on the Rwandan genocide (and Western inaction) is vast, a particularly useful account is Mahmood Mamdani, *When Victims Become Killers: Colonialism, Nativism, and the Genocide in Rwanda* (Princeton, 2001), a powerful antidote to conventional American assumptions about tribalism.

14. "African Explosions," *New York Times*, 21 January 1960, 30.

15. On religion and foreign affairs, see Andrew J. Rotter, "Christians, Muslims, and Hindus: Religion and U.S.–South Asian Relations, 1947–1954," *Diplomatic History* 24 (Fall 2000), 593–613; Seth Jacobs, *America's Miracle Man in Vietnam: Ngo Dinh Diem, Religion, Race, and U.S. Intervention in Southeast Asia* (Durham, N.C., 2004); David Zietsma, "'Sin Has No History': Religion, National Identity, and U.S. Intervention, 1937–1941," *Diplomatic History* 31:3 (June 2007), 531–65. Dorothy Hammond and Alta Jablow, "'The African' in Western Literature," *Africa Today* 7:8 (December 1960), 9; Curtin, *The Image of Africa*, 23, 406–7.

16. Memorandum of Discussion, 365th NSC Meeting, 8 May 1958; Memorandum of Discussion, 375th Meeting, 7 August 1958, FRUS, 1958–1960, 14:14, 20.

17. Adas, *Dominance by Design*, 266.

18. Africa Research Group, *Africa Retort*, 7, 31–32.

19. Ed Cray, "South African Witchcraft," *Western Folklore* 23:1 (January 1964), 51; "Out of the Jungles—New Nations and Problems," *U.S. News and World Report*, 27 July 1959.

20. Ray Vicker, "Jungle Jumble," *Wall Street Journal*, 23 January 1959, 8.

21. Stolper, *Inside Independent Nigeria*, 21, 27, 85.

22. Paul Hofmann, "Nigeria in a Storm over Juju Rain Bill," *New York Times*, 3 October 1960, 1.

23. Stolper, *Inside Independent Nigeria*, 54.

24. Donald H. Louchheim, "U.S. Astronaut and African Oba: Space and Adagbon Aderinwin," *Washington Post*, 29 September 1965, A1; Lloyd Garrison, "Astronauts' Tour: Another Endurance Feat," *New York Times*, 1 October 1965, 4.

25. Darlington, *African Betrayal*, 57.

26. Joseph E. Evans, "Toward a Policy for Africa," *Wall Street Journal*, 20 March 1961, 14.

27. Latham, *Modernization as Ideology*, 118, 128. On the Peace Corps in Africa, see Elizabeth Cobbs Hoffman, *All You Need Is Love: The Peace Corps and the Spirit of the 1960s* (Cambridge, Mass., 1998), 148–82, on Ghana, and Julius A. Amin, *The Peace Corps in Cameroon* (Kent, Ohio, 1992), a study by an African pupil of Peace Corps teachers that focuses on the 1960s; idem, "The Perils of Missionary Diplomacy: The United States Peace Corps Volunteers in the Republic of Ghana," *The Western Journal of Black Studies* 23:1 (1999); idem, "United States Peace Corps Volunteers in Guinea: A Case Study of US-African Relations during the Cold War," *Journal of Contemporary African Studies* 16:2 (1998); see also Jonathan Zimmerman, "Beyond Double Consciousness: Black Peace Corps Volunteers in Africa, 1961–1971," *Journal of American History* 82:3 (December 1995), 999–1028; Fritz Fischer, *Making Them Like Us: Peace Corps Volunteers in the 1960s* (Washington, 1998); and Gary May, "Passing the Torch and Lighting Fires: The Peace Corps," in *Kennedy's Quest for Victory*, 284–316.

28. Vernon McKay, "The African Operations of United States Government Agencies," in *The United States and Africa*, 288; Harold Saunders memorandum to National Security Advisor McGeorge Bundy, 18 January 1963, box 284; Chester Bowles, "Report of Mission to Africa, October 15–November 9, 1962," November 13, 1962, box 3; Mennen Williams memorandum to Dean Rusk, February 25, 1963, box 381, NSF, JFKL.

29. Nkrumah, *Neo-Colonialism*, 247–49; on Nkrumah's growing suspicions about the CIA–Peace Corps connection, see Cobbs Hoffman, *All You Need Is Love*, 160–62. In Accra in 1964, Malcolm X noted that the United States "sends peace-corps teams to Africa but pays South African mercenaries to kill Congolese citizens fighting for the liberation of their country." Cobbs Hoffman, 164.

30. Walt Rostow memorandum to President Kennedy, 28 February 1961, FRUS, 1961–1963, vol. 9, document 94; Shriver letter to Kennedy, 15 March 1963, box 69;

Harold Saunders memorandum to McGeorge Bundy, 18 January 1963, box 284, NSF, JFKL. On the Peace Corps in Ethiopia, see May, "Passing the Torch and Lighting Fires," 288–316.

31. Harris Wofford memorandum to President Kennedy, 7 March 1962; Wofford letter to Kennedy, 23 January 1962, box 67, President's Office Files, JFKL.

32. May, "Passing the Torch and Lighting Fires," 286.

33. Ibid., 288–92.

34. Ibid., 288–92, 299.

35. Ibid., 310–11.

36. Zimmerman, Innocents Abroad, quotations on 203, 207, 209.

37. May, "Passing the Torch and Lighting Fires," 313–15.

38. Rivkin described in Stolper, Inside Independent Nigeria, 119; Peace Corps report, "Program Proposals for Nigeria," 23 March 1961, box 144, NSF, JFKL. William Trimble telegram to Joseph Palmer, 18 January 1963, box 5, Trimble Papers, Seeley Mudd Library; Robert Dean, Imperial Brotherhood: Gender and the Making of Cold War Foreign Policy (Amherst, Mass., 2001), 193; Ate, Decolonization and Dependence, 105.

39. Lagos embassy to State Department, 15 October 1961; Rusk telegram to Palmer, 17 October 1961; Palmer telegram to Rusk, 17 October 1961, box 144, NSF, JFKL. Michelmore's sensory perception of Nigeria was fairly common among volunteers. One described arrival in Ghana: "I was put off at first by the heat, humidity, food, and what seemed dirtiness of the streets in Accra." Quoted in Amin, "The Perils of Missionary Diplomacy," 42.

40. Palmer to State Department, 16 October 1961; Palmer to State Department, 17 October 1961; Palmer to State Department, 27 October 1961, box 144, NSF, JFKL. Wolfgang Stolper told Palmer that Michelmore—whom he refers to as "the Peace Corps girl" in his diary—had done nothing wrong, and that Nigerians' emotional response had been "absurd." His own diary, reflected Stolper, "would really send shivers down Palmer's spine." Inside Independent Nigeria, 208, 223.

41. Harvey Glickman, "When Africans and Americans Meet . . . ," Africa Report 7:7 (July 1962), 17.

42. Memorandum of Conversation, 3 November 1961, FRUS, 1961–1963, vol. 21, Microfiche Supplement, document 630.

43. State Department, Background Paper, "Visit of Prime Minister Egal of the Somali Republic," 11 March 1968, box 99, NSF, Country Files, LBJL.

44. Peter Schwab, Review of Fletcher Knebel, The Zinzin Road, in Journal of Modern African Studies 4:3 (November 1966), 398.

45. Brian E. Schwimmer and D. Michael Warren, Anthropology and the Peace Corps: Case Studies in Career Preparation (Ames, Iowa, 1993).

46. May, "Passing the Torch and Lighting Fires," 298.

47. Leonard Levitt, "How Do You Like Africa, White Man, Is It Like New York?" Harper's, January 1967, 88. Levitt published a book about his Peace Corps adventure, An African Season (New York, 1967).

48. Drake, "Social Change and Social Problems in Contemporary Africa," 268.

49. Plummer, Rising Wind, 309; Zimmerman, "Beyond Double Consciousness: Black

Peace Corps Volunteers in Africa, 1961–1971," *Journal of American History* 82:3 (December 1995).

50. Amin, "United States Peace Corps Volunteers in Guinea," 218; Ian Sclanders, "The Peace Corps: Nursery for Diplomats," *Nation* 199:2 (27 July 1964), 33. Cobbs Hoffman, *All You Need Is Love*, argues the Peace Corps was quite effective, especially in Ghana. It "had not changed the world," she admits, but had helped Ghanaian education, improved America's image, and taught Americans something about Ghanaians (181). Certainly, individual Ghanaians and Americans benefited from the encounter. But to declare the mission in Ghana a success—"it had triumphed," claims Cobbs Hoffman—is to evaluate it quite generously by using a low threshold. Since the mission was a by-product of the Cold War missionary liberalism of *The Ugly American*, mediated by Kennedy's African diplomacy, the more meaningful standard by which to evaluate its performance is the zeal to impart "can do" values to a people in the "preconditions stage" of development.

51. Vernon McKay, "A United States Policy for the New Africa," in *The New Nations of West Africa*, 167.

52. NIE, "The Probable Interrelationships of the Independent African States," 31 August 1961, FRUS, 1961–1963, vol. 21, document 198.

53. Memorandum of Conversation, 3 November 1961, FRUS, 1961–1963, vol. 21, Microfiche Supplement, document 630.

54. Haynes to Komer, 18 May 1965, FRUS, 1964–1968, vol. 24, document 196.

55. On Cook, see Gaines, *American Africans in Ghana*, 95–97, 252.

56. Plummer, *Rising Wind*, 256; Von Eschen, *Satchmo Blows Up the World*, 151–61, quotations on 153 and 151, respectively. See also Gaines, *American Africans in Ghana*, 251–54. By 1977, Nigeria would host a black world's fair that celebrated "a distinctive black and African modernity from the collective wellsprings of traditional culture, a culture that it would recuperate and reinforce as the foundation of industrial development." Andrew Apter, *The Pan-African Nation: Oil and the Spectacle of Culture in Nigeria* (Chicago, 2005), 5.

Conclusion

1. Ulric Haynes to McGeorge Bundy, 15 June 1965, FRUS, 1964–1968, vol. 24, document 198.

2. Edward Hamilton to Rostow, 11 June 1968; State Department telegram to Accra embassy, 22 June 1968; Embassy Accra telegram to State Department, 25 June 1968; Katzenbach to Lyndon Johnson, n.d.; State Department circular telegram to African embassies, 6 August 1968, box 25, International Travel and Meetings File, NSF, LBJL.

3. Nielsen, *The Great Powers and Africa*, 402. The profound success of African American lobbying on sanctions against South Africa is evident in Massie, *Loosing the Bonds*, Hostetter, *Movement Matters*, and Francis Njubi Nesbitt, *Race for Sanctions: African Americans against Apartheid, 1946–1994* (Bloomington, Ind., 2004).

4. Carol Lancaster, *Aid to Africa: So Much to Do, So Little Done* (Chicago, 1999), 86, and Katherine A. S. Sibley, "Foreign Aid," in *Encyclopedia of American Foreign Policy*, vol. I, 2nd ed. (2002), 93.

5. Report of the Task Force on the Review of African Development Policies and Programs, "Policy for Development in Africa," 22 July 1966, FRUS, 1964–1968, vol. 24, document 215.

6. Harilaos Stecopoulos, "Putting an Old Africa on Our Map: British Imperial Legacies and Contemporary US Culture," in *Exceptional State*, 221–23.

7. Michael Maren, *The Road to Hell: The Ravaging Effects of Foreign Aid and International Charity* (New York, 1997), 1.

8. Bill Berkeley, *The Graves Are Not Yet Full: Race, Tribe, and Power in the Heart of Africa* (New York, 2002); Mahmood Mamdani, *Good Muslim, Bad Muslim: America, the Cold War, and the Roots of Terror* (New York, 2004), 19. Other major examples of this depressing genre include Howard French, *A Continent for the Taking: The Tragedy and Hope of Africa* (New York, 2004); Robert Guest, *The Shackled Continent: Power, Corruption, and African Lives* (Washington, 2004); and Martin Meredith, *The Fate of Africa: From the Hopes of Freedom to the Heart of Despair* (New York, 2005).

9. Ferguson, *Global Shadows*, 2.

10. Carol Lancaster and Ann Van Dusen, *Organizing U.S. Foreign Aid: Confronting the Challenges of the Twenty-First Century* (Washington, 2005), quotation on 1.

11. William G. Martin, "The World Economy and the African State," in *Borders, Nationalism, and the African State*, 307–8.

12. Lancaster and Van Dusen, *Organizing U.S. Foreign Aid*, 16–17.

13. Jeffrey Herbst, "Africa Trades Down," *Foreign Policy* (November/December 2007), 84.

14. Robert L. West, abstract, "Particular Problems of Aid Coordination for the Republic of the Congo-Leopoldville," *African Studies Bulletin* 7:4 (December 1964), 22.

15. Bush quoted in Sheryl Gay Stolberg, "Bush, in Africa, Emphasizes Success," *New York Times*, 17 February 2008.

16. "Bush Touts His Gains in Africa before Trip," *Wall Street Journal*, 15 February 2008, A4.

17. Quoted in Catherine Coquery-Vidrovitch, "Economic Changes in Africa in the World Context," in *Africa since 1935*, 305.

LARRY GRUBBS earned his PhD from the University of South Carolina and is a lecturer in the History Department at Georgia State University. He lives in Atlanta.